Trade Policy Review

United Arab Emirates 2012

World Trade Organization
Geneva, May 2012

WTO/GATT TRADE POLICY REVIEWS CURRENTLY AVAILABLE

Albania 2010
Antigua and Barbuda 2001
Angola 2006
Argentina 1999, 2007
Armania 2010
Australia 1989, 1994, 1998, 2002, 2007, 2011
Austria 1992
Bahrain 2000, 2007
Bangladesh 1992, 2000, 2006
Barbados 2002, 2008
Belize 2010
Belize and Suriname 2004
Benin 1997
Benin, Burkina Faso and Mali 2004, 2010
Bolivia 1993, 1999, 2005
Brazil 1992, 1995, 2000, 2004, 2009
Brunei Darussalam 2001, 2008
Bulgaria 2003
Burundi 2003
Cambodia 2011
Cameroon 1995, 2001
Cameroon and Gabon 2007
Canada 1990, 1992, 1994, 1996, 1998, 2000, 2003, 2007, 2011
Central African Republic 2007
Chad 2007
Chile 1991, 1997, 2003, 2009
China 2006, 2008, 2010
Colombia 1990, 1996, 2006
Congo 2006, 2010
Costa Rica 1995, 2001, 2007
Côte d'Ivoire 1995
Croatia 2010
Cyprus 1997
Czech Republic 1996, 2001
Djibouti 2006
Dominica 2001
Dominican Republic 1996, 2002, 2008
East African Community 2006
Ecuador 2005
Egypt 1992, 1999, 2005
El Salvador 1996, 2003, 2010
European Communities (European Union) 1991, 1993, 1995, 1997, 2000, 2002, 2004, 2007, 2009, 2011
Fiji 1997, 2009
Finland 1997
Gabon 2001
Gambia 2004, 2010
Georgia 2009
Ghana 1992, 2001, 2008
Grenada 2001
Guatemala 2002, 2009
Guinea 1999, 2005, 2011
Guyana 2003, 2009
Haiti 2003
Honduras 2003, 2010
Hong Kong, China 1990, 1994, 1998, 2002, 2006, 2010
Hungary 1991, 1998
Iceland 1994, 2000, 2006
India 1993, 1998, 2002, 2007, 2011
Indonesia 1995, 1998, 2003, 2007
Israel 1995, 1999, 2006
Jamaica 1998, 2005, 2011
Japan 1992, 1995, 1998, 2000, 2002, 2005, 2007, 2009, 2011
Jordan 2008
Kenya 1993, 2000
Kyrgyz Republic 2006
Liechtenstein 2000, 2004
Macao, China 1994, 2001, 2007
Madagascar 2001, 2008
Malawi 2002, 2010
Malaysia 1993, 1997, 2001, 2006, 2010
Maldives 2003, 2009
Mauritania 2002, 2011
Mauritius 1995, 2001, 2008
Mexico 1993, 1997, 2002, 2008
Mongolia 2005
Morocco 1990, 1996, 2003, 2009
Mozambique 2001, 2009
Nepal 2012
New Zealand 1990, 1996, 2003, 2009
Nicaragua 1999, 2006
Niger/Senegal 2003, 2009
Nigeria 1991, 1998, 2005, 2011
Norway 1991, 1996, 2000, 2004, 2008
Oman 2008
Pakistan 1995, 2002, 2008
Panama 2007
Papua New Guinea 1999, 2010
Paraguay 1997, 2005, 2011
Peru 1994, 2000, 2007
Philippines 1993, 1999, 2005
Poland 1992, 2000
Qatar 2005
Republic of Korea 1992, 1996, 2000, 2004, 2008
Romania 1992, 1999, 2005
Rwanda 2004
Saint Kitts and Nevis 2001
Saint Lucia 2001
Saint Vincent and the Grenadines 2001
Separate Customs Territory of Taiwan, Penghu, Kinmen, and Matsu 2006, 2010
Sierra Leone 2005
Singapore 1992, 1996, 2000, 2004, 2008
Slovak Republic 1995, 2001
Slovenia 2002
Solomon Islands 1998, 2009
Southern African Customs Union 1998, 2003, 2009
Sri Lanka 1995, 2004, 2010
Sweden 1995
Switzerland and Liechtenstein 1991, 1996, 2000, 2004, 2008
Tanzania 2000
Thailand 1991, 1995, 1999, 2003, 2007, 2011
The Kingdom of Saudi Arabia 2012
The State of Kuwait 2012
Togo 1999, 2006
Trinidad & Tobago 1998, 2005, 2012
Tunisia 1994, 2005
Turkey 1994, 1998, 2003, 2007
Uganda 1995, 2001
United Arab Emirates 2006, 2012
United States 1990, 1992, 1994, 1996, 1999, 2001, 2004, 2006, 2008, 2010
Uruguay 1992, 1998, 2006
Venezuela 1996, 2002
Zambia 1996, 2002, 2009
Zimbabwe 1995, 2011

Co-Published by the World Trade Organization and Bernan Press. Printed in the U.S.A.

ISBN 13: 978-1-59888-586-6
ISSN: 1556-2050

All reports are available in English, French, and Spanish.

For more information, please contact:

WTO PUBLICATIONS
Centre William Rappard
Rue de Lausanne 154
1211 Geneva 21, Switzerland
Telephone: (41 22) 739 5208, 5308
Fax: (41 22) 739 5792
Email: publications@wto.org
www.wto.org

BERNAN PRESS, a wholly owned subsidiary of
The Rowman & Littlefield Publishing Group, Inc.
4501 Forbes Boulevard, Suite 200
Lanham, MD 20706, U.S.A.
Telephone: (301) 459-7666 (Washington, D.C. area)
(800) 865-3457 (toll-free)
Email:customercare@bernan.com
www.bernan.com

PREFACE

The Trade Policy Review Mechanism (TPRM) was first established on a trial basis by the GATT CONTRACTING PARTIES in April 1989. The Mechanism became a permanent feature of the World Trade Organization under the Marrakesh Agreement which established the WTO in January 1995.

The objectives of the TPRM are to contribute to improved adherence by all WTO Members to rules, disciplines and commitments made under the Multilateral Trade Agreements and, where applicable, the Plurilateral Trade Agreements, and hence to the smoother functioning of the multilateral trading system, by achieving greater transparency in, and understanding of, the trade policies and practices of Members. Accordingly, the review mechanism enables the regular collective appreciation and evaluation of the full range of individual Members' trade policies and practices and their impact on the functioning of the multilateral trading system. It is not intended to serve as a basis for the enforcement of specific obligations under the Agreements or for dispute settlement procedures, or to impose new policy commitments on Members.

The assessment carried out under the TPRM takes place, to the extent relevant, against the background of the wider economic and developmental needs, policies and objectives of the Member concerned, as well as its external environment. However, the function of the review mechanism is to examine the impact of a Member's trade policies and practices on the multilateral trading system.

Under the TPRM, the trade policies of all Members are subject to periodic review. The four largest trading entities in terms of world market share, counting the European Union as one, are reviewed every two years, the 16 next largest trading entities every four years, and other Members every six years; a longer period may be fixed for least-developed countries.

The reviews are conducted by the Trade Policy Review Body (TPRB) on the basis of two documents: a policy statement by the Member under review and a comprehensive report drawn up by the WTO Secretariat on its own responsibility.

TABLE OF CONTENTS

Note: The documents that comprise this publication are available online at: http://www.wto.org/english/tratop_e/tpr_e/tp_rep_e.htm.

PART A

CONCLUDING REMARKS BY THE CHAIRPERSON

OF THE TRADE POLICY REVIEW BODY,

H.E. MR. EDUARDO MUÑOZ GÓMEZ

AT THE TRADE POLICY REVIEW

OF THE UNITED ARAB EMIRATES

27 AND 29 MARCH 2012

CONCLUDING REMARKS BY THE CHAIRPERSON

1. This second Trade Policy Review of the United Arab Emirates has given us a much better understanding of the recent developments in its trade and trade-related policies and practices together with the future challenges that it faces. We are grateful for the active participation of the Emirati delegation headed by H.E. Sheikha Lubna Bint Khalid Al Qasimi, Minister of Foreign Trade. I would also like to thank the discussant, Mrs. Reenat Sandhu, Deputy Permanent Representative of India and Members of the TPRB for contributing to our fruitful exchange of views.

2. Members commended the UAE for the bold steps taken to diversify the economy away from oil and gas. The UAE's high export earnings and open trade regime, with a simple average MFN applied tariff of 4.9% in 2011, have enabled it to successfully weather the global crisis without backsliding on trade liberalization. Members encouraged the UAE to continue its reforms in order to achieve its goal, based on the *UAE Vision 2021,* to transform the economy into one that is knowledge-based, highly productive, and competitive. A key challenge for the UAE is to expand foreign participation in investment projects outside free trade zones, for which the current 49% foreign participation limit constitutes an obstacle. Members also invited the UAE to improve its competition regime by adopting full-fledged competition legislation.

3. Members welcomed the UAE's commitment to the multilateral trading system and encouraged it to further foster its participation given that it benefits from the open trading system and is relying on trade for its own goals of economic diversification. The UAE participates in two regional trade agreements, the Gulf Cooperation Council (GCC) and the Greater-Arab Free Trade Area (GAFTA). Members requested the UAE to work with its GCC partners to fully consolidate the GCC's customs union and to ensure that the customs union is reviewed as soon as possible under the WTO Transparency Mechanism.

4. The numerous statements, questions and replies voiced in the course of this Review have highlighted some key areas for further action or improvements. I note from the UAE's statements that action is already being taken or is being considered in several of these areas:

- **Tariffs, customs and trade facilitation:** While recognizing the UAE's relatively low level of tariff protection, Members encouraged further action, including bringing its bound rates close to its applied tariff rates, and requested more information regarding the list of "special goods". Members also encouraged the UAE to facilitate the process to obtain a trade licence and to remove requirements for the legalization and consularization of trade documents.

- **Investment and business environment:** Acknowledging that the UAE's investment regime was currently more restrictive than its trade regime, Members welcomed current efforts to further promote foreign investment. They encouraged the UAE to speed-up the promulgation of its new law on the liberalization of foreign investment and modernize the business environment. Members also encouraged the UAE to eliminate local services/agent requirements, and to increase the transparency, accountability, and effectiveness of government administration.

- **SPS and TBT:** The UAE was encouraged to improve transparency through prompt WTO notifications and by allowing interested parties more time to review and comment on TBT and SPS measures, while eliminating certain technical requirements to further reduce the cost for traders. Members also invited the UAE to adopt international standards as national or GCC standards, wherever possible. We've noted the UAE's stated need for technical assistance in this area and hope that adequate and timely cooperation will be forthcoming.

- **Government procurement:** Members invited the UAE to consider amending its government procurement regime by removing the requirement to employ a UAE national in order to submit tenders and to review its transparency procedures for all bidders as well as its offset programme. The UAE was also invited to join the Government Procurement Agreement as soon as possible.

- **Competition:** Acknowledging the current absence of full-fledged competition legislation, Members commended the UAE for preparing a draft competition policy law and urged to bring it into effect as soon as possible. Questions were raised about the procedures and criteria for fixing prices and the exemptions of state-owned enterprises and small and medium-sized enterprises from competition regulations.

- **Intellectual property:** Members welcomed the passage of new legislation on protection of undisclosed information, and requested more information on compulsory licensing and on the programmes to increase awareness of IP protection. They encouraged the UAE to further strengthen its implementation and enforcement actions.

- **Energy:** The UAE was encouraged to take further steps towards easing current foreign direct investment restrictions in the oil and gas sectors.

- **Services:** Noting the progress made by the UAE in the liberalization of trade in services, Members expressed their concern about certain restrictions such as the need to use local agents and limiting foreign participation especially in the transport and telecommunications sectors. They encouraged the UAE to introduce more competition into these key sectors and to remove restrictions on foreign participation.

- **Financial Services:** Some Members requested the UAE to relax restrictions on new licences for foreign banks and branches of foreign banks. In the area of insurance services, Members called for the lifting of the moratorium for new licences and to increase foreign equity in domestic insurance companies.

5. In conclusion, this Review has confirmed the important role played by the UAE in the multilateral trading system and the benefits of maintaining an open economy. We wish the UAE all the success as it continues to move along the path of a more open and competitive trade and investment regime. Once again, I thank the delegation of the UAE led by Minister H.E. Sheikha Lubna Al Qasimi, the discussant and Members for contributing to an informative and interesting review. I also wish to express my appreciation to the delegation of the UAE for its oral and written responses during the meeting. We look forward to receiving any outstanding responses within the coming month.

PART B

REPORT BY THE WTO SECRETARIAT

This report was drafted by Mr. Angelo Silvy, Mrs. Eugenia Lizano, and Mrs. Mena Hassan.

CONTENTS

CHARTS

TABLES

APPENDIX TABLES

SUMMARY

1. The UAE's trade regime is open, with low tariffs and few non-tariff barriers to trade. The UAE's openness was instrumental in achieving the solid growth registered prior to the global crisis and has facilitated the diversification of economic activity. The investment regime remains considerably more restrictive than the trade regime, as foreign participation in any domestic company or activity is limited to 49% of the capital; however, 100% foreign ownership is allowed in any of the UAE's free zones.

2. The global financial crisis brought an end to a period of rapid growth. The economy contracted in 2009, and grew by just 1.4% (total real GDP) in 2010. In the aftermath of the crisis, GDP growth was affected by lower oil prices, turmoil in the financial markets, particularly in Dubai's financial sector, and a price correction in the Dubai property market. As a response to the crisis, the authorities supported banks by providing liquidity and deposit guarantees, and through recapitalization.

(1) Economic Environment

3. The UAE's economic performance was very strong over the period 2005-08, achieving an annual average growth rate of 5.5%. Growth was based to a large extent on a successful strategy of diversification, into services, real estate, and manufacturing. Non-hydrocarbon GDP growth was particularly high and made possible by a policy to promote investment. The global financial crisis combined with lower oil prices and the price correction in the Dubai real estate market brought an end to this period of high growth, and the economy of the UAE contracted by 1.6% in 2009. The crisis led to an increase in debt, particularly of Dubai's government-related enterprises (GREs).

4. Reacting to the crisis, the Federal Government applied strong countercyclical monetary and fiscal policies and adopted rescue packages for GREs, including an important debt restructuring. The UAE economy started to emerge from the crisis in 2010, with real GDP growing by 1.4%. The global crisis had the effect of cooling off the economy, stopping the acceleration in price increases observed in the 2005-08 period. However, as growth resumes, inflation is forecast to accelerate somewhat, although to below the pre-crisis levels.

5. Departing from a situation of traditional surplus, as a result of the crisis and of the expansionary fiscal policy adopted, the Federal Government ran fiscal deficits in 2009 and 2010. The authorities have been taking steps to reduce this deficit by containing the growth of spending, and reducing producer subsidies and transfers. However, stronger efforts might be needed to achieve fiscal consolidation.

6. Exports of goods increased rapidly throughout 2006-08, but declined by some 17% in 2009, reflecting lower oil prices and the global economic crisis. Imports followed a similar pattern, but both exports and imports started to recover in 2010 as growth picked up. The UAE runs a structural trade balance surplus, which peaked at US$62.9 billion in 2008, declined in 2009 as a consequence of a considerable drop in oil exports and despite a reduction in imports, and increased again in 2010 and 2011, mainly due to higher non-hydrocarbon exports and re-exports. The surplus in the current account balance reached 3.8% of GDP in 2010.

(2) Trade Policy Regime: Framework and Objectives

7. The UAE has a liberal trade regime, although a number of limitations and conditions are set on foreign investment. Improved market access for its products through multilateral trade liberalization and bilateral and regional trade agreements is a main trade policy objective. Policy formulation and implementation in the UAE takes place both at the federal and the emirate level; the emirates have a relatively high degree of independence.

8. The UAE has been an active player in the Doha Development Agenda, presenting proposals to eliminate tariffs and non-tariff barriers (NTBs) on raw materials and submitting an initial offer in trade in services. The UAE has not been involved in any dispute settlement case during the period under review.

9. The UAE attaches great importance to regional trade agreements as a valuable complement to, though not a substitute for, a rule-based and non-discriminatory multilateral trade system. The UAE is a founding member of the Gulf Cooperation Council (GCC). During the period under review, the UAE has advanced in the process of regional integration, through its participation in the GCC. However, the full consolidation of the GCC's customs union was still pending in mid-2011, and was expected for the end of the year. Free-trade agreements between the GCC and EFTA, and the GCC and Singapore have been signed, but in late 2011, were still awaiting implementation. The UAE is also a member of the Pan Arab Free Trade Agreement (PAFTA).

10. The UAE's open trade regime contrasts with its relatively more closed investment regime. An important development during the period under review, has been the initiation of drafting of a new Investment Law to expand foreign participation and foster foreign investment and transfer of know-how. However, foreign investment continues to be subject to limitations, and all investment projects must have 51% domestic capital. In addition, the use of local agents to conduct business continues to be mandatory, and although legislation to enforce agency contracts was amended during the review period, it is still skewed in favour of the agent, as the termination of a contract by the investor is difficult.

(3) Trade Policies and Practices by Measure

11. Since its previous Review in 2006, the United Arab Emirates has streamlined procedures to process documents and reduced the time required to clear Customs, mainly by introducing totally electronic clearance procedures and a risk assessment system. Nevertheless, the UAE still requires that imports be processed by a designated trade agent, and nationality restrictions are applied in this respect. A trade agent requires a trading licence, granted only to UAE nationals and to companies that are at least 51% owned by UAE nationals.

12. The UAE has applied the Gulf Cooperation Council's (GCC) Common External Tariff since 2003. The tariff structure comprises four *ad valorem* tariff rates: zero, 5%, which is the general tariff rate, and 50% and 100%, applied on alcohol and tobacco, respectively. Some 97% of all tariff lines are *ad valorem*; duties are levied on the c.i.f. value of imports. Alternate or specific duties apply to 0.3% of all tariff lines. Since the last Review of the UAE, the average tariff rate has fallen slightly, from 5.1%, to 4.9%. The UAE has bound all tariff lines. Bound rates are in general considerably higher than applied rates, ranging from zero to 200%, giving scope for reduction. The UAE does not apply other duties and charges on imports.

13. Import prohibitions are in place on some 30 HS tariff lines, and another 244 lines at the HS 8-digit level are considered restricted goods. Restrictions and prohibitions are mostly applied on safety, religious or moral grounds. No import licensing regime is in place, and the transaction value of goods is generally used for valuation purposes.

14. In 2005 the UAE issued national legislation to adopt and implement the provisions on anti-dumping, countervailing, and safeguards measures contained in the GCC Treaty. No anti-dumping or countervailing measures were taken during the period under review; no investigations were initiated.

15. The Emirates Standardization and Metrology Authority (ESMA) develops and adopts standards, which are prepared by its technical committees at the request of the Government, industry, or consumers. In general, standards are developed according to existing international and regional standards. Drafts are circulated to the relevant bodies for comments. There is no central body in charge of preparing technical regulations in the UAE. These may be developed by the ESMA, initially in the form of a standard and then made mandatory, or may be devised directly by a Ministry; all technical regulations are approved by Cabinet decision for legal implementation. The ESMA monitors the application of standards and technical regulations. During the period under review, the UAE made over 90 notifications to the TBT Committee.

16. The UAE has an extensive body of national legislation to regulate SPS measures; most of the laws are based on GCC standards. SPS measures are enforced at the federal and the emirate level. All plants and plant products entering the UAE are subject to quarantine, and require a phytosanitary certificate. Similarly all animals and animal products are subject to quarantine and require a sanitary certificate. All shipments of food are inspected to ensure compliance with labelling and shelf-life regulations.

17. The UAE does not apply export taxes, charges, and levies, other than a tax on steel scrap exports. Exports of dual-use goods require a licence. The UAE applies a number of programmes to promote exports, including a Free Trade Zones (FTZ) programme. Foreign ownership in firms established in FTZs may be up to 100% and investors are exempt from paying personal income taxes and corporate taxes for 15 years, renewable for an additional 15 years. Additionally, goods may be imported into an FTZ duty free. Companies located in the FTZs are exempted from agency/distributorship, sponsorship, and national ownership requirements. FTZs produce both goods and provide services.

18. There is no competition policy legislation in the UAE, but a draft competition law, including restrictive agreements, abuse of a dominant position, and mergers and acquisitions, is under consideration by the Ministerial Cabinet. The economy would benefit from the adoption of a competition law given the relative concentration of producers/suppliers in some sectors.

19. The UAE is not a party or an observer to the WTO Plurilateral Agreement on Government Procurement. Government procurement continues to give preference to local companies and suppliers, as foreign participation is limited by nationality requirements. However, there is a strong reliance on foreign companies, particularly for major projects for which local expertise is not always available. An offset programme is in place for defence contracts. Given the federal nature of the UAE, the majority of procurement (by value) is at the emirate level.

20. All main intellectual property laws provide for measures aimed at preventing violation of intellectual property rights, including preventive seizure, confiscation, removal or destruction of products and equipment, as well as elimination of the effects of the illegal acts, and compensation, and imprisonment in certain instances. In recent years, the UAE has implemented programmes to increase awareness regarding intellectual property protection. The goal is to establish an environment that promotes innovation, to attract investment in intellectual-property-related areas in the UAE.

(4) TRADE POLICIES BY SECTOR

21. The oil sector and connected industries continue to play a major role in the UAE economy. However, attempts are under way to diversify the economy, particularly into services and manufacturing. The petroleum sector accounted for 29% of GDP, 69% of government income, and 85% of export revenues in 2009. The UAE's estimates of proven crude oil reserves are 97.8 billion barrels, equivalent to almost 8.5% of the world's reserves, while production reached 2.32 million barrels/per day in 2010. Some 95% of all petroleum production is in the emirate of Abu Dhabi.

22. In accordance with the Constitution, management of natural resources in the UAE is vested in each individual emirate and not with the Federal Government. Foreign equity in projects is determined by the competent authorities of the local government of the emirate where the natural resource is located.

23. Agriculture represents a small share of the UAE's economy, accounting for just 1% of GDP. Total cultivated land has decreased in recent years, and the UAE remains a major net food importer. Foreigners, other than GCC nationals, are not allowed to own agricultural land in the UAE, but may own up to a 49% stake in agri-business companies. Fishing is restricted to UAE and GCC nationals. Notifications to the WTO on agriculture remained pending in December 2011.

24. In its quest to diversify the economy away from oil, during the period under review, the UAE has continued to develop its manufacturing sector. However, some of the main manufacturing industries, such as petrochemicals, remain linked to the oil industry. Nevertheless, there have been important developments in aluminium production and pharmaceutical products. Most manufactured imports face a 5% tariff. However, all materials that are used in the production of a licensed industrial project enter the UAE duty free.

25. The services sector is growing rapidly, particularly in air and maritime transport, telecommunications, and tourism. However, developments in the sector would benefit in general from some flexibility of the foreign investment ownership limitations currently in place.

26. In financial services, the emirate of Dubai was particularly affected by the global financial and economic crisis. There was a sharp contraction in equity markets in 2008 and 2009; market capitalization, and the general share price index continued falling in 2010. The authorities responded to the crisis by stepping up regulation, including raising minimum capital adequacy ratios for banks, which were raised from 10% to 12% in 2010, and by pumping liquidity into the system and recapitalizing banks. Other measures adopted to counter the financial crisis included a moratorium on new licences for commercial banks and placing a limit on the number of branches permitted to licensed foreign banks. Currently, locally incorporated banks in the UAE are well capitalized, with a minimum capital-adequacy ratio well above the legal requirement, at an average of 21.2% at end-September 2011.

27. Foreign banks must open branches in the UAE to provide services there; since 2010, the number of branches they may open has been limited to a maximum of eight branches in the UAE. Subsidiaries of foreign banks are prohibited. Foreign banks are granted national treatment for paid-up capital requirements, but not with respect to the taxation of profits: foreign banks are subject to a 20% tax on profits, but this is not applied to national banks.

28. National and foreign insurance companies wishing to establish in an emirate must apply to the Insurance Authority for an establishment procedure, then for licensing. Conditions for the granting of licences include economic needs criteria and the appointment of a minimum number of UAE nationals as staff. Eligible foreign insurance companies may open a branch, appoint a local insurance agent and/or enter into an agency contract with a local insurance agent representing them.

29. A major development in the telecommunications sector during the review period was the termination of the monopoly in telephony services. However, competition in the sector remains low; there is a duopoly in mobile telephony, which result in relatively high prices. The market could benefit from increased competition in the sector.

30. The UAE has one of the largest air transport industries in the world. It has five airlines, two of which are major international carriers, and two major airports, one of which is one of the busiest in the world (Dubai). The airline industry in the UAE benefits from the country's "open skies" policy, good civil aviation infrastructure, and competition between the different emirates. The authorities are expecting the sector to continue to grow rapidly in the near future. For this expansion, both main airports and airlines need to exploit their roles as hubs and transfer carriers, due to the UAE's relatively small domestic market.

31. There are plans to increase the capacity and activities of ports. However, despite the policy of granting concessions to private service providers in some areas, port management remains a prerogative of the different emirates. Like in other service areas, despite coordination to some extent at the federal level, the fact that each emirate has policies in the same area could lead to overcapacity. Further coordination among emirates could ensure that investment projects are complementary and lead to a more integrated development policy approach.

32. Prior to the 2008-09 global financial crisis, the UAE underwent a construction boom, which helped sustain the emergence of conglomerates in this sector. However, in the aftermath of the crisis, the construction sector suffered a major downturn, with prices falling by 50% in Dubai and 40% in Abu Dhabi. The impact of the crisis was exacerbated by the large number of new units on the market resulting from the boom.

33. Tourism is of growing importance in the UAE, in particular considering efforts displayed to build infrastructure and the various developments in the area. In 2008, the National Council for Tourism and Antiquities (NCTA) was established to help align UAE tourism-related policies at the federal level. However, each emirate issues tourism licences. The creation of the NCTA is expected to give further impetus to the promotion of tourism.

I. ECONOMIC ENVIRONMENT

(1) OVERVIEW

1. The economy of the UAE has developed a strong services sector due to the strategy of diversification implemented during the last decade, but the oil industry continues to be of prime importance. Abu Dhabi produces 95% of the country's oil and gas, and owns one of the largest sovereign wealth funds in the world. Dubai, the second largest emirate, has a more diversified economy, driven by re-export trade, services, and real estate.

2. After a period of fast growth, boosted by investment and construction, the economy of the UAE was strongly affected by the global financial crisis, which led to a sharp contraction of GDP in 2009. The crisis also led to an increase in debt, particularly of Dubai's government-related enterprises (GREs).

3. The Federal Government reacted to the crisis by applying strong countercyclical monetary and fiscal policies and by adopting rescue packages for GREs, including an important debt restructuring. All in all, there was a strong transfer of resources from the oil-producing emirate of Abu Dhabi, to the more service-oriented emirate of Dubai, which was the hardest affected by the crisis. Departing from a situation of traditional surplus, as a result of the crisis, the federal Government ran fiscal deficits in 2009 and 2010; however, due to acceleration in oil revenues, the fiscal accounts are expected to have shown a surplus again in 2011.

4. As a result of the measures applied and to an increase in oil prices, the UAE economy started to emerge from the crisis in 2010, with real GDP growing by 1.4%. The global crisis had the effect of cooling off the economy, stopping the acceleration in price increases observed in the 2005-08 period. However, as growth resumes, inflation is forecast to accelerate somewhat, although to below the pre-crisis levels.

5. Exports of goods increased rapidly throughout 2006-08, but declined by some 17% in 2009, reflecting lower oil prices and the global economic crisis. Imports followed a similar pattern, but both exports and imports started to recover in 2010 as growth picked up. The UAE runs a structural trade balance surplus, which peaked at US$62.9 billion in 2008, declined in 2009 as a consequence of a considerable drop in oil exports and despite a reduction in imports, and increased again in 2010 in 2011, mainly due to higher non-hydrocarbon exports and re-exports.

(2) STRUCTURE OF THE ECONOMY

6. The United Arab Emirates (UAE) is a federation of seven emirates: Abu Dhabi, Ajman, Dubai, Fujairah, Ras al-Khaimah, Sharjah, and Umm al-Quwain; Abu Dhabi City is the federal capital. The UAE has 85% of world oil reserves and the fifth largest gas reserves (Chapter IV(4)). The authorities estimate that these reserves will last more than 100 years at current production rates. The UAE has a federal structure and there are many common policies at the federal level, including monetary policy, but each emirate manages its own budget independently.

7. The three major emirates, in terms of participation in GDP, are Abu Dhabi, Dubai, and Sharjah. Abu Dhabi accounts for over 50% of the UAE's total GDP, some 40% of the population, and 95% of crude oil and gas production. Mainly resulting from the proceeds of its oil and gas industries, Abu Dhabi owns one of world's largest sovereign wealth funds, and is estimated to have more than US$300 billion assets under management.[1] Dubai, the second largest emirate in terms of economic

[1] IMF (2011a).

size, accounts for about a third of the UAE's total GDP. Dubai has a more diversified economy, with a large financial sector, as well as a developed air transport industry and tourism sector (Chapter IV). Dubai also plays the role of regional commercial hub and is an important transhipment and re-export centre.

8. In 2010, total GDP reached US$297.65 billion (Table I.1); with a population of some 8.26 million, GDP per capita was some US$36,017. In 2010, the UAE ranked 32nd out of 179 countries in terms of the UNDP Human Development Indicators.

Table I.1
Economic indicators, 2005-10

	2005	2006	2007	2008	2009[a]	2010
National accounts[b]						
GDP (AED billion)	663.3	815.7	948.1	1,156.3	992.8	1,093.1
GDP (US$ billion)	180.6	222.1	258.2	314.8	270.3	297.6
Real GDP, annual percentage change	4.8	9.9	3.2	3.3	-1.6	1.4
Real hydrocarbon GDP	2.3	11.2	-7.1	-2.3	3.9	-5.6
Real non-hydrocarbon GDP	6.4	9.1	9.4	6.2	-4.2	5.0
GDP by economic activity (share of GDP (%))[b]						
Agriculture, livestock and fishing	1.4	1.1	1.0	0.8	1.0	0.9
Mining and quarrying	34.4	37.5	33.9	37.1	29.1	31.6
Crude oil and natural gas	34.3	37.4	33.8	37.0	28.9	31.5
Quarrying	0.1	0.2	0.2	0.1	0.1	0.1
Manufacturing industries	10.6	9.7	9.0	8.6	10.1	9.7
Electricity, gas and water	1.9	1.9	1.8	1.8	2.4	2.6
Construction	8.7	8.9	10.0	10.6	11.8	11.6
Services	46.3	44.0	47.9	45.0	50.4	48.0
Wholesale retail trade and repairing services	13.6	13.1	13.9	12.8	13.5	12.8
Restaurants and hotels	2.0	1.9	1.9	1.8	2.1	2.1
Transports, storage and communication	7.9	7.6	8.0	7.7	9.3	9.1
Real estate and business services	10.7	10.0	11.7	10.9	10.7	9.9
Financial sector	6.4	6.3	7.2	6.3	7.2	6.8
Government	3.5	3.0	3.0	3.3	4.8	4.6
Other services	2.2	2.1	2.1	2.2	2.7	2.8
Social and personal services	1.8	1.7	1.8	1.8	2.3	2.4
Domestic services of households	0.4	0.4	0.4	0.4	0.4	0.4
(Less: imputed bank services)	3.3	3.0	3.6	3.9	4.7	4.4
			(% of GDP)			
Final consumption expenditure	65.1	64.0	68.3	68.3	70.6	67.7
Government expenditure	6.9	6.2	5.9	5.8	9.0	8.2
Private expenditure	58.3	57.8	62.3	62.5	61.7	59.4
Gross fixed capital formation	18.4	17.4	23.0	21.2	22.3	23.8
Change in stocks	0.9	0.8	0.8	1.3	1.6	1.5
XGS / GDP (%)	67.6	68.6	72.3	79.0	74.7	75.3
MGS/ GDP (%)	52.0	50.8	64.4	69.8	69.2	68.2

Table I.1 (cont'd)

	2005	2006	2007	2008	2009[a]	2010
Consolidated government finances		(US$ billion, unless otherwise indicated)				
Total revenue	53.6	74.9	85.3	121.7	68.3	85.8
Hydrocarbon[c]	41.0	59.0	63.6	98.4	47.4	65.1
Non-hydrocarbon	12.5	15.9	21.7	23.2	20.9	20.6
Customs	1.0	1.3	2.2	2.4	2.2	2.3
Profit transfers	1.3	1.5	3.5	1.4	1.1	1.1
Income tax[d]	0.1	0.3	0.2	0.3	0.4	0.4
Fees and charges	4.1	3.7	2.6	6.5	6.6	6.9
Investment income[e]	3.7	6.3	8.4	6.3	4.5	3.6
Other	2.4	2.8	4.8	6.3	6.1	6.4
Total expenditure and grants	28.4	34.7	45.7	70.7	103.9	92.1
Current expenditure	22.9	29.0	34.7	47.0	58.9	67.7
Wages and salaries[f]	4.3	4.9	5.7	7.9	8.9	9.1
Goods and services	6.9	6.9	9.9	13.4	18.4	23.1
Abu Dhabi "federal services"[g]	6.2	6.9	8.5	12.4	15.2	19.7
Subsidies and transfers[h]	5.3	10.1	9.9	11.2	12.4	10.3
Interest payments	0.0	0.0	0.1	0.8	1.6	2.6
Other	0.2	0.2	0.5	1.3	2.4	2.9
Development expenditure	3.8	3.2	4.7	8.6	12.3	10.5
Loans and equity (net)[i]	1.4	2.4	5.7	14.1	31.8	13.6
Foreign grants[j]	0.3	0.1	0.6	1.0	0.9	0.3
Overall balance (consolidated)[k]	25.1	40.2	39.8	51.8	-33.9	-3.8
Overall balance (consolidated), % of GDP	13.9	18.1	15.4	16.5	-12.6	-1.3
Non-hydrocarbon balance (excl. investment income)	-16.5	-13.7	-18.9	-26.7	-44.7	-36.5
Non-hydrocarbon primary balance (excl. investment income)	..	..	-18.8	-26.3	-43.9	-35.2
Abu Dhabi Overall balance (% of Abu Dhabi's GDP)	..	..	15.2	16.0	-19.7	-8.1
Abu Dhabi Non-hydrocarbon balance (excl. investment income)	..	..	-48.8	-61.4	-79.3	-69.8
Abu Dhabi Non-hydrocarbon primary balance (excl. investment income)	..	..	-48.8	-61.5	-79.5	-70.0
Dubai's Overall balance (% of Dubai's and northern emirates GDP)	..	..	-0.3	-1.8	-13.9	-4.9
External sector		(US$ billion, unless otherwise indicated)				
Trade balance (goods)	42.8	57.5	46.5	63.8	42.5	63.5
Exports	117.3	145.6	178.6	240.1	192.2	221.9
Exports of oil and products	49.3	62.9	65.7	91.4	59.6	66.8
Imports	-74.5	-88.1	-132.1	-176.3	-149.7	-158.3
Services, net	-14.6	-18	-26	-33.8	-27.4	-28.1
Current account balance	20.9	33.9	15.4	23.3	8.2	23.3
Current account balance (% GDP)	11.6	15.3	6	7.4	3	7.7
Capital and financial account	0.1	0.7	27.9	-19.9	9.3	2
Overall balance	2.5	6.6	49.9	-46.8	-6	7.3
Gross reserves of Central Bank	21.3	28	77.9	30.9	24.7	32
Local currency per U.S. dollar (period average)	3.7	3.7	3.7	3.7	3.7	3.7
Nominal effective exchange rate (2000=100)	..	..	86.1	84.2	88.3	87.5
Real effective exchange rate (2000=100)	..	..	99.8	102.8	107.9	103.7
Monetary sector						
Money and quasi money (M2) (AED billion)	324,064	399,293	565,702	674,310	740,618	786,388
Money and quasi money (M2) (annual % change)	33.8	23.2	41.7	19.2	9.8	6.2
Money and quasi money (M2) as % of GDP	48.9	49.0	59.7	58.3	74.6	71.9

Table I.1 (cont'd)

	2005	2006	2007	2008	2009[a]	2010
Memorandum						
Inward FDI stock (% of GDP)	15.2	18.2	21.1	21.7	26.7	25.6
Outward FDI stock (% of GDP)	5.3	9.2	13.6	16.1	19.8	18.7
CPI inflation (%)	6.2	9.3	11.1	12.3	1.6	1.7
External debt (US$ billion)	41.0	80.6	130.1	135.8	132	138
External debt as a % of GDP	30.6	49.2	50.4	43.1	48.1	46.2

.. Not available.

a Preliminary.
b Statistical information in 2010 is from IMF (2011b), Country Report No. 11/112, May.
c Includes IMF estimates of revenues from other government entities operating in the oil and gas sector.
d Taxes on profit of foreign banks. Income taxes on gas companies are included under hydrocarbon revenues.
e IMF staff estimates.
f Excludes military wages and salaries.
g Largely military and internal security expenditures paid by Abu Dhabi but not in the federal accounts.
h Includes Government's contribution to the pension fund in 2005 of AED 6,207 million.
i Includes Government's share in the 2005 privatization of the telecom company, Etisalat
j Intra-governmental grants are netted out in the consolidated fiscal accounts.
k Consolidated accounts of the Federal Government, Abu Dhabi, Dubai and Sharjah.

Source: UAE National Bureau of Statistics; UAE Central Bank; and IMF (2011b), Country Report No. 11/112, May.

9. Despite the diversification strategy implemented during the last decade, the UAE economy is still dominated to a considerable extent by the oil sector. The production of crude oil and natural gas accounted for some 31.6% of GDP in 2010; this share increases to over one third of GDP if oil-related manufactured production is included. Manufacturing represented some 9.7% of GDP in 2010. Of this share, some 50% is accounted for by metal products, machinery and equipment, and mining non-metal products; the rest is evenly distributed among chemical products, foodstuffs and beverages, textiles and garments, and wood and furniture. There are smaller contributions from the paper and basic metal industries. Despite being affected by the global crisis, construction continued to account for 11.6% of GDP in 2010. The agriculture sector (including livestock and fishing, but not processed food production) is of small economic importance in the UAE, accounting for less than 1% of total GDP.

10. Services as a whole accounted for 48% of GDP in 2010; the most important subsectors were: wholesale retail trade and repairing services (concentrated mainly in Dubai), which accounted for 12.8% of GDP in 2010; real estate and business services (9.9%); transport, storage and communication (9.1%); financial services (6.8%); and Government (4.6%) (Table I.1).

11. Although the economic regime is in general open and business-friendly, important competition and investment restrictions remain in place, with the exception of business conducted in free zones (Chapter II(6) and Chapter III(3)(iv)). Some of these restrictions include exclusive dealership arrangements, the general prohibition on foreign majority ownership of local companies and substantial state involvement in selected activities. Also, state involvement in the economy is large; a considerable number of UAE companies, in all sectors, are totally or partly government-owned (GREs).

12. GREs account for an important part of the UAE's economy and have historically been a source of growth. GREs are mainly commercial corporations, financial institutions, and investment bodies owned directly by the Governments of Abu Dhabi and Dubai, or by the emirates' rulers. They are organized under the umbrella of major holding companies with activities in various sectors and have the implicit guarantee of the government that owns them. GREs receive government transfers and had easy access to capital markets due to the implicit government guarantee. The development of

GREs has been particularly strong in Dubai, and more recently, in Abu Dhabi.[2] GREs in both emirates engage extensively in real estate and infrastructure projects and were considerably affected by the global financial crisis and the price correction in the local property market, which, despite government support, forced some Dubai GREs to reschedule their debts (Chapter IV(5)(i)).

13. An important development during the period under review, which resulted in an improvement in the information provided by the UAE, was the establishment in 2009 of the National Bureau of Statistics (NBS) of the United Arab Emirates, by Federal Law No. 9 of 2009, to satisfy the needs of the national development of the country and to organize the work of the national statistical system. The NBS has an independent budget and reports directly to the Cabinet. The NBS is now the sole official statistical source for the State.[3]

(3) OUTPUT, PRICES, AND EMPLOYMENT

14. The UAE's economic performance was very strong over the period 2005-08, achieving an annual average growth rate of 5.5%. Growth was based to a large extent on a successful strategy of diversification, into services, real estate, and manufacture. Growth of non-hydrocarbon GDP, at an annual average rate of 8.2% during the period, was considerably faster than that of hydrocarbon GDP (annual average rate of 0.6%). The high non-hydrocarbon GDP growth was made possible by a policy of strong investment, which resulted in massive capital formation and by the large inflow of foreign labour, which allowed the policy of diversification to succeed.[4] This influx was partly behind the rapid development of the non-oil sector, both in manufacturing production and in services, including real estate.

15. The global financial crisis combined with lower oil prices and the price correction in the Dubai real estate market brought an end to this period of high growth, and the economy of the UAE contracted by 1.6% in 2009. In the wake of the financial crisis, the authorities adopted countercyclical measures to boost output and prop-up the banking industry (see below). In particular, the authorities supported the banking sector through liquidity injection, the recapitalization of institutions, and deposit guarantees. The money supply expanded rapidly, as did government expenditure, with the fiscal deficit rising quickly (see below).

16. The position of many highly-leveraged government-related entities (GREs) deteriorated rapidly (see Chapter IV(5)(i)) as they found themselves with substantial short-term obligations amidst lower revenues and declining prices of the assets they held, particularly real estate. This forced Dubai World (DW), a major Dubai GRE, to seek a debt standstill in November 2009 (Box IV.2). The Government of the Emirate of Abu Dhabi provided financial support to the Emirate of Dubai, through its participation in the Dubai Financial Support Fund (DFSF), established in July 2009 to provide financial assistance to GREs of strategic importance and by injecting AED 16 billion of capital into five large banks based in Abu Dhabi. The restructuring of some US$24.9 billion of DW debt was agreed by all creditors in late October 2010. Other Dubai GREs (Dubai Holding Commercial Operations Group (DHCOG), Dubai Group (DG) and Dubai International Capital (DIC)), also engaged in debt restructuring negotiations with banks.

---

[2] For an extensive discussion on GREs, see IMF (2011b), Chapter I.

[3] NBS online information. Viewed at: www.uaestatistics.gov.ae.

[4] In its May 2011 Article IV Consultation Staff Report, the IMF states that the growth of labour and capital, rather than total factor productivity, accounts for most non-oil output expansion over the 1981-2000 period. It also noted that, in turn, this expansion was possible because of the UAE's open foreign labour policy, which enabled the private sector to recruit expatriate workers at competitive wages. See IMF (2011a).

17. The UAE economy started to emerge from the crisis in 2010, when GDP is estimated to have grown by 1.4%, triggered in particular by a recovery of the non-hydrocarbon sector, which expanded by 5%. The IMF estimates that non-hydrocarbon GDP will grow by some 3.3% in 2011, led by strong tourism, logistics, and trade in Dubai; and by large public investment spending in Abu Dhabi. GDP as a whole is projected to expand at the same rate. However, there are downside risks for future growth particularly due to the still-ailing real estate sector and the short-term refinancing needs of GREs.

18. At the beginning of the period under review (2006-08), inflationary pressures continued to mount, reflecting strong domestic demand. Annual average Consumer Price Index (CPI) inflation reached a peak of 12.3% in 2008, before declining sharply in 2009 to 1.6% and 1.7% in 2010, reflecting falling domestic demand. However, due to stronger domestic demand, inflation picked up some in 2011, and is estimated by the IMF to have averaged 2.5%.

19. The employment situation in the UAE is particular to the country, with low unemployment among the foreign population and higher rates among nationals. Over the past two decades, the UAE applied a policy of attaining growth through a massive utilization of labour and capital factors. As a result, immigration was encouraged and the population grew rapidly, to some 8.26 million in 2009, of whom only about one million are UAE nationals. The workforce totalled 5.28 million in 2009; the private sector employed 58.4% of the workforce and the rest was employed mostly by Government at the federal or emirate level, or by GREs.[5] While unemployment is low among the foreign community, at some 3%, unemployment among nationals reached 14% in 2009, with a general unemployment rate of 4.2%. To boost employment, especially among nationals, the UAE Government has been conducting an "emiratization" policy to increase the number of nationals employed in private sector activities, particularly banking, insurance, and trading.

(4) MONETARY POLICY AND EXCHANGE RATE REGIME

20. Monetary policy is formulated and conducted by the Central Bank of the UAE (CBUAE). The Central Bank is also responsible for the formulation and implementation of banking and credit policies, so as to ensure the stability of the currency and the growth of the national economy of the UAE in a balanced manner.[6] The CBUAE has authority over the banking and financial sectors, except for the financial institutions operating in the Dubai International Financial Centre (DIFC). The UAE adopts a fixed exchange rate of the dirham against the U.S. dollar policy, and by law the CBUAE must ensure the free convertibility of the national currency into foreign currencies. Hence, the CBUAE has to keep enough reserves to maintain the currency's peg to the dollar. As a result, there is no autonomous monetary policy. The CBUAE also acts as banker of last resort to the Government and the financial sector, and as the Government's financial advisor.

21. Under Law No. (10) of 1980, the CBUAE may use a number of instruments to attain its monetary objectives. The fixed peg of the dirham to the U.S. dollar, however, means that local interest rates must be aligned to those of the dollar across the maturity curve. As a result, and as mentioned above, the effectiveness of monetary policy instruments at the Central Bank's disposal has been reduced. The main instruments used by the CBUAE to regulate domestic liquidity are: (1) the

[5] Almost 85% of UAE nationals worked for the federal or emirate governments in 2009. During the financial crisis, jobs were created at the government level to help nationals face the crisis, raising the percentage of nationals working for the Government from 80.3% to 84.9%. Ministry of Economy (2010).

[6] CBU online information. Viewed at: http://www.centralbank.ae/en/index.php?option=com_content&view=article&id=68&Itemid=107.

minimum reserve requirement; (2) US$/AED swaps for dirham liquidity[7]; (3) advances and overdraft facility for banks[8]; (4) prudential regulation; (5) issuance by the CBUAE of certificates of deposit and repo facilities on certificates of deposit (CDs); and (6) liquidity support facilities made available to commercial banks since the advent of the international crisis.

22. In October 2011, the minimum reserve requirement was 14% on current, savings, and call accounts, and 1% only on time deposits. These ratios apply to both deposits in dirhams and in foreign currencies. In addition, banks are required to keep at the Central Bank 30% of their dirham deposits abroad with non-resident banks (including their Head Office and branches in the case of foreign banks). The US$/AED swap facility is available to all banks operating in the UAE under the jurisdiction of the CBUAE. Certificates of deposit (CDs) are issued by the Central Bank, as a tool for liquidity management; issuance is mainly demand-driven as banks with excess liquidity can invest their surplus funds in CDs of varying maturities. The CDs programme, launched in 1985, was amended in 1994 and in 2007: the New Expanded Central Bank CDs Issuance System became effective 28 November 2007.[9] A liquidity support facility was set up in September 2008, when banks were facing a shortfall in liquidity due to the global financial crisis.[10]

23. The CBUAE places a number of prudential requirements on banks. Its capital adequacy ratio requirement is 12% compared with an 8% Basel requirement. Banks are also required to maintain a ratio of loans and advances to stable resources equal to one.[11]

24. Reflecting high nominal GDP growth in 2006-08, the money supply expanded considerably during the period. This was due to the increase in bank credit to the private sector and to state-owned enterprises. The trend continued in 2009 due to the liquidity injected into the system by the CBUAE and the recapitalizing of banks in the middle of the global financial crisis, although at a lower rate than before (less than 10% in 2009 down from 19% in 2008). This slowdown in broad money growth amid increased liquidity available was due to weak demand for credit by firms and households in addition to the cautious attitude of banks towards lending. Any excess liquidity by the banks was invested in certificates of deposit with the Central Bank. The three-month inter-bank rate for the AED (EIBOR) declined from a peak of 4.7% in October 2008 to 2.1% in January 2011 and to 1.5% in mid-October 2011.

---

[7] US$/AED swaps are a way of injecting dirham liquidity. Swap arrangements involve a simultaneous sale and forward purchase of U.S. dollars against the purchase/forward sale of equivalent dirham amounts for a fixed term at specified forward rates. Swap terms may be of one week, one month, 3 months, 6 months, 9 months, or 12 months.

[8] Under this mechanism, the Central Bank can provide banks with loans and advances for up to 7 days without collateral, and for up to 6 months against collateral. The CBU provides an overdraft facility to commercial banks that allows them to utilize their required reserves free of charge for up to seven days.

[9] The system is an auction-based issuance for CDs denominated in UAE dirhams, U.S. dollars, and euros. CDs of maturities ranging from 1 week to 12 months are issued daily, while CDs of maturities ranging between 2 and 5 years are issued monthly. Under the new issuance system, banks may repurchase (repo) their CDs from the CBUAE or from other banks to access liquidity. The repo term offered by the Central Bank is of up to 3 months as long as the balance life of the CD used as collateral goes beyond the repo term. Banks may also seek U.S. dollar funding by using their holdings of CDs as collateral. Banks may redeem CDs with the CBUAE at any point during the life of the CD as long as the CD is free from any encumbrance.

[10] Under this facility, a bank may submit its portfolio of securities to the CBUAE for evaluation. The CBUAE will accept as eligible the securities that comply with its guidelines, and assign a credit line to the bank based on the adjusted value of the eligible securities. The bank may then access CBUAE funds on a weekly rollover basis for as long as it needs the facility.

[11] The numerator of this ratio comprises loans and advances (including interbank placements with a remaining maturity of more than three months), while the denominator comprises free capital and reserves, interbank deposits received with a remaining maturity of more than six months, and 85% of customer deposits.

25. The UAE has a fixed exchange rate regime, whereby the domestic currency, the UAE dirham (AED) is pegged (since November 1997) to the U.S. dollar at an exchange rate of AED 3.6725/US$1. The UAE's exchange system is free of restrictions on payments and transfers for international transactions, except for certain restrictions under terrorist financing provisions, taken in accordance with UN resolutions. The UAE accepted the obligations under Article VIII of the IMF Statutes on 13 February 1974.

26. According to IMF estimates, the AED exchange rate is broadly in line with fundamentals, being overvalued by just 1% at the end of 2010. Also according to IMF calculations, following a period of strong real appreciation between 2005 and 2008, the trade-weighted real effective exchange rate (REER) depreciated by 10.2% from its peak in March 2009 until end 2010.[12] The UAE withdrew in May 2009 from plans to create a monetary union at Gulf Cooperation Council (GCC) level.

(5) Fiscal Policy

27. Despite large revenues from the oil industry, fiscal accounts in the UAE have deteriorated in the aftermath of the global financial crisis. From a surplus equivalent to 16.5% of GDP in 2008, the fiscal accounts deteriorated to post a deficit equivalent to 12.6% of GDP in 2009, with the non-hydrocarbon deficit reaching 44.7% of GDP. The deficit shrank to 1.3% of GDP in 2010 as a consequence of higher hydrocarbon revenues and a return to a more pro-cyclical policy stance. The non-hydrocarbon primary fiscal deficit (excluding investment income) contracted sharply, largely due to slower project implementation in Abu Dhabi, and to lower transfers to Dubai GREs.

28. The UAE posts a structural non-hydrocarbon fiscal deficit varies between a fifth and a third of GDP (Table I.1). The deficit is particularly large in the case of Abu Dhabi, where it reached almost 80% of GDP in 2009. The authorities indicated that steps have been taken to reduce this deficit by containing the growth of spending, and reducing producer subsidies and transfers. However, stronger efforts might be needed to achieve fiscal consolidation (see below).

29. In the context of this Review, the authorities highlighted that volatile oil prices make it difficult for the UAE to maintain stable fiscal indicators. They also indicated that the general policy to achieve fiscal consolidation is to reduce general expenditure and improve tax collection, while promoting economic growth. Among the elements being considered is the introduction of a value-added tax and income tax on companies, as well as the reduction/cancellation of some duty exemptions granted to companies and government agencies.

30. As the IMF notes, the active use of countercyclical fiscal policy could mitigate boom-bust cycles in the UAE economy, but the authorities have resorted to this type of policy stance only in extreme cases, like the strong 2009 recession. The IMF's assessment is that this contributed to the overheating of the economy prior to the crisis, while in 2010, the contractionary fiscal stance slowed the recovery.[13] The IMF recommends delinking government and GRE spending from the volatility of oil prices and aiming fiscal policy, particularly Abu Dhabi's where most hydrocarbon production takes place, at ensuring long-term sustainability and intergenerational equity.[14] It also recommends that Dubai undertake fiscal consolidation to lower its debt-to-GDP ratio.

---

[12] See IMF (2011a).

[13] In a fixed exchange rate regime like the UAE's, fiscal policy is the main effective macroeconomic policy since monetary policy, as discussed above, is not effective in affecting output.

[14] IMF (2011b), Chapter III.

31. The IMF also considers that, given the federal structure, closer fiscal coordination among the emirates is key to promoting both short-term demand management and medium-term sustainability. This coordination should seek to avoid procyclicality and reduce fiscal risks. A Fiscal Coordination Council was created to this end.

32. The authorities are aware of the importance of achieving fiscal consolidation and are preparing to introduce a VAT in the context of the GCC, which is expected to enhance revenue and facilitate such consolidation.

33. The UAE's total debt increased substantially during the financial crisis, mainly due to a substantially higher fiscal deficit and to the refinancing needs of Dubai World and other GREs. Total UAE gross public debt is estimated to have reached US$236 billion, or 78% of GDP at end 2010. Of this total, Abu Dhabi's debt is US$104 billion (54.2% of Abu Dhabi's GDP), Dubai's US$113 billion (102.6% of Dubai's and the Northern Emirates GDP), US$5.2 is debt of other emirates, and US$19.1 billion is federal government debt (6.3% of GDP). In December 2010, the debt of Dubai's GREs was US$76 billion, while that of Abu Dhabi was US$92.4 billion. Debt accounting for almost 20% of GDP matures in 2011 and 2012 and is likely to be refinanced, pushing the concentration of maturities to the 2014-15 period.

(6) BALANCE OF PAYMENTS

34. The UAE runs a structural trade balance surplus, which peaked in 2008, at US$62.9 billion, declined in 2009 as a consequence of a considerable drop in oil exports, despite a reduction in imports, and increased again in 2010, to US$50.9 billion, mainly due to an increase in non-hydrocarbon exports and in re-exports (Table I.2). The services balance showed a deficit throughout the period under review; posting a deficit of US$29.9 billion in 2010. The transfers balance was negative by US$11.3 billion. However, due to the strong trade surplus, the current account balance has traditionally showed a surplus in recent years. This surplus peaked at US$35.2 billion or 15.3% of GDP in 2006, before starting to decline, to reach a low of US$7.8 billion (2.9% of GDP) in 2009, in the middle of the financial crisis. The surplus grew again in 2010, to reach US$11.2 billion, (3.8% of GDP).

Table I.2
Balance of payments, 2005-10
(US$ billion)

	2005	2006	2007	2008	2009	2010
Current account balance	24.4	35.2	31.6	21.6	7.8	11.2
(% of GDP)	13.5	15.8	12.2	6.9	2.9	3.8
Trade balance (f.o.b.)	42.8	56.4	58.9	62.9	42.1	50.9
Trade balance (c.i.f.)	32.6	44.6	43.0	38.9	21.7	28.9
Exports and re-exports	117.3	142.5	175.5	239.2	191.8	212.3
Total exports of hydrocarbons	55.1	70.1	24.5	102.1	67.9	75.1
Crude oil exports	43.5	58.1	4.9	85.4	54.1	60.1
Petroleum products exports	5.8	4.9	8.1	6.0	5.4	6.1
Gas exports	5.8	7.1	11.5	10.6	8.3	8.8
Non-hydrocarbon exports	22.4	26.4	88.8	43.0	44.0	51.0
Free zone exports	17.4	20.5	62.3	26.5	26.2	26.8
Exports from Customs territory	5.0	5.9	26.5	16.4	17.8	24.2
Re-exports[a]	39.8	46.0	62.3	94.2	80.0	86.2
Imports	-74.5	-86.1	-116.6	-176.3	-149.7	-161.4
Imports to customs territory	-67.4	-77.1	-107.8	-140.0	-121.8	-129.4
Imports to free zones	-17.2	-20.8	-24.7	-60.4	-48.3	-54.0

Table I.2 (cont'd)

	2005	2006	2007	2008	2009	2010
Investment income, net	2.9	4.7	5.9	3.1	3.2	1.6
Services, net	-14.6	-17.8	-23.9	-33.8	-27.3	-29.9
Credits	4.8	6.8	8.0	9.6	10.2	11.7
Debits	-19.4	-24.9	-34.0	-43.4	-37.6	-39.9
Transfers, net	-6.7	-8.2	-9.3	-10.6	-10.2	-11.3
Private	-6.2	-7.6	-8.7	-10.0	-9.5	-10.6
Official[b]	-0.5	-0.6	-0.6	-0.6	-0.7	-0.7
Financial account balance	-14.7	-16.1	11.3	-55.3	-9.7	2.0
Private capital	15.0	23.9	59.2	-25.8	-4.2	6.3
Direct investment, net	7.1	1.9	-0.4	-2.1	1.3	1.9
Portfolio securities, net	6.1	1.2	1.4	2.2	2.5	1.0
Commercial banks	-3.4	9.7	48.6	-12.2	-9.9	-1.3
Private non-banks and other	5.1	11.1	9.6	-13.7	1.9	4.6
Official capital	-29.7	-39.9	-47.9	-29.5	-5.4	-4.2
Errors and omissions	-7.1	-12.6	7.0	-13.1	-4.3	-5.9
Overall balance	2.6	6.5	49.9	-46.8	-6.1	7.3
Change in Central Bank net foreign assets[c]	-2.6	-6.5	-49.9	46.9	6.1	-7.3
Memorandum items:						
Overall balance (% of GDP)	1.4	3.0	19.3	-14.9	-2.2	2.4
Central Bank gross reserves (IMF information)	21.3	28.0	77.9	30.9	24.7	32.0

a Not formally compiled; estimated at 40% to 70% of UAE emirates imports.
b Includes changes in government external assets.
c A minus sign equals increase.

Source: Central Bank of the United Arab Emirates.

35. Flows of private capital, which had been increasing rapidly until 2007, declined considerably in 2008 and were negative in 2009, reflecting the extent of the global financial crisis and its effects on the UAE market. There was a sizeable reduction of foreign exchange reserves between 2007 and 2009, from US$77.9 billion to US$24.7 billion, before recovering in 2010 (to US$32 billion), when there was a net inflow of private capital again. The level of reserves continued to rise in 2011, due to the improvement in the current account of the balance of payments.

36. The UAE's external debt increased sharply during the period under review, partly as a consequence of the increased leverage of GREs; the situation was exacerbated by the effects of the financial crisis. The external debt increased from US$41 billion (30.6% of GDP) in 2005 to an estimated US$138 billion (46.2% of GDP) in 2010.

(7) Developments in Trade[15]

37. The UAE is an open economy, as witnessed by its high ratio of imports plus exports of goods and services to GDP, which was almost 143% in 2010.

(i) Composition of trade in goods

38. Exports of goods increased rapidly between 2006 and 2008, when they peaked at US$210 billion, according to COMTRADE data; in 2009, exports declined by some 17% reflecting lower oil prices and the global economic crisis (Table AI.1). Imports also peaked in 2008 (US$175.5 billion) and declined in 2009; however they started to recover in 2010 as growth picked up.

[15] The information in this section is based on the United Nations' COMTRADE database, and may differ from the figures provided in the balance-of-payments section.

39. The main export product continues to be crude oil, which accounted for about a third of total exports and re-exports in 2010, while fuels as a whole accounted for over 37% of the total. If re-exports are excluded, fuels accounted for half of total exports, while crude oil represented 44.3% of the total. Including re-exports, exports of manufactured goods represented some 26.6% of the total, the main products being machinery and equipment, diamonds, automotive products, and jewellery. However, if re-exports are excluded, manufactured products accounted for just 4.7% of total UAE exports in 2010.[16]

40. It is estimated that nearly two thirds of non-hydrocarbon exports originate in free zones, mainly the Dubai Jebel Ali Free Zone Authority (Jafza); the main products exported from free zones consist of machinery and appliances, including computers and other consumer electronics. Non-hydrocarbon exports from outside the free zones include clothing, tobacco products, and aluminium. Re-exports are an important source of revenue, representing around one third of total merchandise exports (Table AI.1). This reflects the importance of the UAE as a centre for re-exports, mainly to India, Iran, and Iraq.

41. Imports of manufactures account for over half of total imports; the main single item is machinery and equipment, with imports representing almost a third of the total (Table AI.2). Imports of gold, automotive products, diamonds and clothing are next in importance.[17]

(ii) Direction of trade

42. Data presented by COMTRADE do not allow easy identification of the main trading partners, as the category "other" is very large, accounting for about one third of the total. According to the Ministry of Foreign Trade, the ten top major non-oil export destinations in 2010 were: India (33.7% of the total); Switzerland (16.2%); Saudi Arabia (4.5%); Brazil (3.5%); Iran (3.3%); Norway (3.2%); Pakistan (2.5%); Oman (2.2%); Qatar (2.2%); and Kuwait (2.0%). Including re-exports, the main destinations were: India; Iran; Iraq; Switzerland; Saudi Arabia; Afghanistan; Bahrain; Kuwait; Qatar; Hong Kong, China; and Belgium.

43. The main import sources in 2010 according to the UAE Ministry of Foreign Trade statistics (includes only non-oil imports) were: India (17.1%); China (10.3%); the United States (8.5%); Germany (6.1%); Japan (5.9%); the United Kingdom (3.6%); Italy (3.1%); France (2.6%); South Korea (2.5%); and Saudi Arabia (2.5%).

(iii) Trade in services

44. The services trade deficit doubled between 2005 and 2010, when it reached US$29.9 billion. The UAE is an important exporter of tourism, and air and maritime transport services. It is a net importer of financial (including insurance), construction, and professional services.

---

[16] According to information provided by the UAE authorities, the ten main export categories by HS Code in 2010 were: gold (HS 71.08); light vessels (HS 89.05); waste and scrap of precious metals (HS 71.12); cane or beet sugar in solid form (HS 17.01); polymers of ethylene (HS 39.01); petroleum oils an oils obtained from other bituminous metals (HS 27.10); other plates, film, sheets, foil and strip of plastics (HS 72.04); polyacetals (HS 39.07); and articles of jewellery (HS 71.13).

[17] According to information provided by the UAE authorities, the ten main import categories by HS code in 2010 were: gold (HS 71.08); diamonds (HS 71.02); motor cars (HS 87.03); articles of jewellery (HS 71.13); telephone sets (HS 85.17); parts of aircraft (HS 88.03); aircraft (HS 88.02); turbo jets and gas turbines (HS 84.11); parts and accessories of tractors (HS 87.08); and petroleum oils and oils obtained from bituminous metals (HS 27.10).

(8) DEVELOPMENTS IN FOREIGN INVESTMENT

45. Foreign direct investment (FDI) inflows increased rapidly during the period under review; the stock of FDI more than tripled between 2005 and 2009, when it reached US$52.9 billion, representing some 21% of GDP (Table I.3). FDI inflows slowed down somewhat due to the global crisis, particularly in 2008, but accelerated again in 2009.

46. The Government has launched efforts to improve the collection of statistics on FDI, particularly by source. The leading sectors attracting FDI are financial services, construction and building, real estate, and wholesale and retail trade.

Table I.3
Foreign direct investment stock by economic sector, 2005-09
(AED billion and %)

	2005	2006	2007	2008	2009	% of total 2009
Total (AED billion)	**61.9**	**74.6**	**128.1**	**154.6**	**195.7**	**100.0**
Total (US$ million)	**16.7**	**20.2**	**34.6**	**41.8**	**52.9**	
Agriculture and fisheries	0.2	0.1	0.2	0.3	0.3	0.2
Extraction industries	1.6	1.9	4.0	4.8	5.1	2.6
Manufacturing industries	6.2	7.2	10.5	12.7	18.9	9.7
Electricity and water	1.3	1.6	6.2	7.4	4.1	2.1
Construction and building	15.0	16.4	24.7	29.8	42.9	21.9
Wholesale and retail trade	8.9	10.3	13.2	16.0	26.9	13.7
Hotels and restaurants	1.3	1.3	1.3	1.6	3.5	1.8
Transportation and communications	2.8	5.4	5.3	6.4	14.3	7.3
Financial institutions	16.0	17.1	26.5	32.0	44.9	22.9
Real estate	8.2	12.8	35.7	43.1	33.6	17.2
Other	0.4	0.5	0.4	0.5	1.3	0.7

Source: Ministry of Economy (2010), *Annual Economic and Social Report 2009.*

47. The UAE is also an important investor abroad, mainly the emirate of Abu Dhabi through the Abu Dhabi Investment Authority (ADIA), one of the world's largest government financial investment vehicles. ADIA is responsible for investing all of the Abu Dhabi Government's oil revenues and assets worldwide. The total amount of its investments is undisclosed. Since 2005, ADIA has been investing in equities, and investment-grade credit within fixed income. In 2007, ADIA started investing in infrastructure

(9) OUTLOOK

48. In 2011, the UAE economy was continuing to recover from the effects of the global financial crisis. The IMF is forecasting GDP growth of 3.3% in 2011, with similar rates for both the hydrocarbon and non-hydrocarbon sectors. Inflation is expected to accelerate to 4.5% as domestic demand recovers. The increase in hydrocarbons revenue and expenditure moderation are expected to result in an improvement in the fiscal accounts, leading to an overall surplus of 6.5%, more in line with what was common before the global crisis. Both exports and imports of goods are expected to increase, and the surplus in the current account of the balance of payments is estimated to be in the 10% range.

49. The outlook for the UAE economy hinges strongly on the evolution of hydrocarbons markets and on the capacity to refinance GRE's debt. Also, it will be important for the Government to continue diversifying the economy away from oil, and to apply countercyclical policies when required. The real estate overhang is expected to continue to be a factor depressing growth perspectives.

II. TRADE POLICY REGIME: FRAMEWORK AND OBJECTIVES

(1) INTRODUCTION

1. The UAE conducts an open trade policy and has a relatively liberal trade regime, although a number of limitations and conditions are set on foreign investment. In broad terms, its foreign trade strategy aims at promoting trade relations, increasing the contribution of foreign trade to GDP, and fostering foreign investment flows. Improved market access for its products through multilateral trade liberalization and bilateral and regional trade agreements is a main trade policy objective.

2. The UAE has been an active participant in the DDA, presenting proposals to eliminate tariffs and non-tariff barriers (NTBs) on raw materials, and submitting an initial offer in the area of trade in services. During the period under review, the UAE advanced in the process of regional integration, through its participation in the GCC. However, the full consolidation of the GCC's customs union was still pending in mid-2011, and was expected for the end of the year. Free-trade agreements have been signed between the GCC and EFTA, and the GCC and Singapore, but in late 2011, were still awaiting implementation.

3. The UAE's open trade regime contrasts with its relatively more closed investment regime. An important change during the period under review was the initiation of the drafting of a new Investment Law to expand foreign participation and foster foreign investment and transfer of know-how. However, foreign investment continues to be subject to limitations, and all investment projects must have 51% domestic capital. Also, the use of local agents to conduct business continues to be mandatory, and although legislation to enforce agency contracts was amended during the review period, it is still skewed in favour of the agent, making the termination of a contract by the investor rather difficult.

(2) GENERAL CONSTITUTIONAL AND LEGAL FRAMEWORK

4. The United Arab Emirates (UAE) was established in 1971 as a federal state comprising seven emirates: Abu Dhabi, Dubai, Sharjah, Fujairah, Umm al Qaiwian, Ajman, and Ra's al Khaimah.[1] According to the Federal Constitution, which was provisional until 1996, each emirate has its own jurisdiction and local government, but the federal authority has overall responsibility for, *inter alia*, foreign affairs, foreign trade, security and defence, nationality and immigration issues, education, public health, currency issues, banking, Customs, postal services, telephone and other communications services, air-traffic control and licensing of aircraft, and labour issues. All responsibilities not granted to the federal government are reserved to the local governments.[2]

5. The federal system comprises five separate authorities represented in: the Federal Supreme Council, the President and the Vice President, the Council of Ministers, the National Council, and the Federal Judiciary. These authorities may fall under the Executive, the Legislative, and the Judiciary.

(a) Executive

6. The Executive branch consists of the Prime Minister, and a Council of Ministers (the Cabinet). The Federal Supreme Council is composed of the rulers or emirs of the seven emirates. The Supreme Council elects and appoints the President, the Vice President and the judges of the Federal Supreme Court. The Supreme Council also formulates government policy at the federal level,

[1] Ra's al Khaimah formally acceded to the federation in 1972.

[2] Articles 120 and 121 of the Federal Constitution stipulate the responsibilities of the federal authority. Articles 116 and 122 state the responsibilities at emirate level.

proposes and ratifies federal laws, and ratifies international treaties. The President, elected by the Board of Rulers, exercises a range of powers, and has the right to convene and preside over meetings of the Supreme Council. The President is also responsible for signing laws, decrees and decisions sanctioned by the Supreme Council. The Cabinet is the Executive authority for the Government, overseeing the enforcement of legislation and regulations. Currently, the Ruler of Abu Dhabi holds the presidency, and the Ruler of Dubai is the Vice President and Prime Minister.[3]

(b) Legislative

7. The Federal National Council (FNC) is entrusted with legislative powers. The FNC consists of 40 members drawn from the 7 emirates.[4] While traditionally directly appointed, a process of electing FNC members was established in 2006, with the aim of eventually having a wholly-elected Council. As a result, half of the FNC members are elected to serve four-year terms and the other half are appointed by the rulers of the constituent emirates.[5] The FNC plays the role of a consultative assembly and has both legislative and supervisory responsibility, as provided by the Constitution. The FNC functions more as a review body of national legislation than as a legislative body. Laws are prepared by ministries and approved by the Supreme Council. The main tasks of the FNC are to, *inter alia*: (i) discuss constitutional amendments and draft laws, which may be approved, amended or rejected; (ii) review the annual draft budget of the Federation; (iii) debate international treaties and conventions; and (iv) influence the Government's work through discussion, question and answer sessions, recommendations and follow-up on complaints.

8. Each Ministry negotiates international agreements within its own jurisdiction, as per Federal Law No. 1 of 1972. However, only the Ministry of Foreign Affairs is authorized to sign such agreements; and it may delegate its authority to other ministries.[6] The Supreme Council is responsible for ratifying and endorsing international agreements.[7] The Government is obliged, under the Constitution, to notify the FNC of international agreements as decided by the President, and to present them to the FNC for discussions prior to ratification. International treaties and agreements, once ratified, prevail over domestic legal instruments. In descending legal order, the Constitution is followed by laws, decree-laws, ordinary decrees, and regulations.

9. Policies, including trade policy are formulated and implemented by means of legislation. Bills are proposed by the relevant ministries; they are presented first to the Cabinet, then to the FNC, and finally to the President for approval.[8] Upon ratification by the Federal Supreme Council, the bills are signed by the President and proclaimed as federal laws through publication in the *Official Gazette*.

---

[3] Sheikh Zayed bin Sultan Al Nahyan was the first President of the UAE and Ruler of Abu Dhabi until his death in November 2004. His son, Sheikh Khalifa bin Zayed Al Nahyan was elected by Members of the Supreme Council as the new President on 3 November 2004. Sheikh Mohamed bin Rashid Al Maktoum, has been the Ruler of Dubai, Vice President, and Prime Minister of the UAE since January 2006.

[4] Article 68 of the Constitution. Article 71 prohibits any member of the FNC from holding any other post in the Federal Government, including ministerial positions.

[5] The number of seats assigned to each emirate is based on its population; Abu Dhabi and Dubai hold the largest number, with eight seats each.

[6] Articles 47/4, 60/7, and 91 of the Constitution treat the same issue.

[7] Article 47 of the Constitution. Under Article 49 of the Constitution, substantive decisions by the Supreme Council must be taken by a majority of five of the seven members, and include the votes of Abu Dhabi and Dubai. Decisions relating to procedural matters are taken by simple majority.

[8] Chapter 1, part 5 of the UAE Constitution (Articles 100-115), regulates the legislative procedures at the federal level.

(c) Judiciary

10. The judiciary in the UAE comprises a federal and a local judiciary.[9] The Federal Judiciary, which is accorded independence under the Constitution, includes the courts of first instance, courts of appeal and the Federal Supreme Court. Traditional Sharia courts are separate from this hierarchy. Cases are first taken to the courts of first instance, which comprise a body of judges. Criminal, civil, and commercial cases are heard by a single judge and a decision is taken unless the law stipulates otherwise.[10] The Court of Appeal comprises a panel of three judges whose decisions become final. The Federal Supreme Court comprises five judges appointed by the Supreme Council. The judges decide on the constitutionality of federal laws, and arbitrate on inter-emirate disputes between the Federal Government and the emirates. They may also enquire into the role of public officials in governance in cases of corruption and fraud.[11]

11. There are no specialized courts in economic/commercial matters at the federal level. However, Law No. 338 of 2009, issued by the Minister of Justice, established a specialized department at the courts of first instance to deal with consumer protection cases. Abu Dhabi is the only emirate to have a commercial court. Established in May 2008, the court is specialized in trade and investment-related cases. Commercial disputes are increasingly being handled in traditional Sharia courts based on Islamic law.[12]

12. Each of the seven emirates has its own local executive council that functions in parallel and in coordination with the federal government. The emirate of Abu Dhabi has an Executive Council, which oversees separate departments that function like ministries. It also has several autonomous agencies and a 60-member National Consultative Council with a role similar to that of the FNC. Dubai and Sharjah also have an Executive Council. In other emirates, the Ruler has a *diwan* (office) through which the concerns of citizens may be directed to the Government.

(3) DEVELOPMENT AND ADMINISTRATION OF TRADE POLICY

(i) Agencies involved in trade policy implementation

13. Since 2008, the development and administration of trade policy has been under the responsibility of the Ministry of Foreign Trade (previously the Ministry of Economy and Planning), in coordination with other ministries at the federal level and trade-related bodies and local departments. These include, *inter alia*, the Ministry of Economy, Ministry of Finance, Federal Customs Authority, Ministry of Environment and Water, Emirates Authority for Standardization and Metrology (ESMA), Ministry of Labour and Social Affairs, Ministry of Justice and Islamic Affairs, Ministry of Public Health, Ministry of Energy, and the municipalities of Abu Dhabi and Dubai.

14. Private-sector participation in trade policy formulation is through the Federation of UAE Chambers of Commerce and Industry (FCCI). A draft law is sent to the FCCI, and is forwarded to the

[9] At the time of unification under the Federation, the emirates were accorded the constitutional right of joining the federal judicial system or retaining their independent systems. Four of the emirates opted to join the federal system; Abu Dhabi, Dubai, and Ras-al Khaimah maintained their local judiciary.

[10] Article 116 of the Constitution states that all matters not specifically stipulated as falling within federal jurisdiction may be considered within the emirate concerned.

[11] Litigation in Ras-al Khaimah remains at the two levels: Court of First Instance and Court of Appeal. Abu Dhabi and Dubai both have three levels of litigation: Court of First Instance, Court of Appeal, and Court of Cassation (highest court of appeal).

[12] For further information see emirate of Abu Dhabi – Judicial Department online information. Viewed at: www.adjd.ae.

chambers in each emirate for comments. Prior to trade negotiations, the private sector is consulted and its interests are taken on board by the Ministry of Foreign Trade.

15. After the launch of the Doha Development Agenda, a National Committee (NC) was set up (in 2002) to deal with WTO matters. Under the supervision of the Ministry of Foreign Trade, the NC acts as an advisory body to the UAE negotiating team. The NC is supported by five sub-committees, covering market access for non-agricultural products, intellectual property rights, protection of domestic production, trade in services, and trade facilitation.

(ii) Main trade laws

16. The main trade-related laws are the GCC Common External Customs Tariff (2007) and GCC Common Customs Law (2007); Federal Commercial Companies Law No. 8 of 1984 and amendments; and Federal Commercial Agencies Law No. 18 of 1981 and amendments. The main trade-related laws and regulations of the UAE are presented in Table II.1.

Table II.1
Main federal trade-related laws, 2011

Area	Legislation
Tariff	GCC Common External Customs Tariff
Customs regulations; import and export procedures; rules of origin	GCC Common Customs Law of 1 January 2007 (Decision of the Supreme Council of the GCC regulating the customs procedures for the establishment of the customs union; 21-22 December 2002)
Commercial companies law	Federal Company Law No. 8 of 1984 concerning commercial companies and the amending laws and decrees thereof
Regulation of commercial agencies (exclusive distribution rights)	Federal Law No. 18 of 1981 concerning the organization of commercial agencies, as amended by Federal Act No. 14 of 1988; No.13 of 2006 and No. 2 of 2010
Commercial register	Federal Law No. 5 of 1975
Trade	Federal Law No. 13 of 2007 on Commodities subject to Import and Export Control Procedures
Civil transactions (Civil Code)	Federal Law No. 5 of 1985
Commercial transactions	Federal Law No. 18 of 1993
Contingency trade measures	Federal Law No.7 of 2005 promulgating the GCC Common Law on Anti-Dumping, Countervailing Measures and Safeguards
Government procurement	UAE Federal Order No. 16 of 1975 (the public tenders law)
	Ministerial Decision No. 20 of 2000 on Administration of Contracts System
	Federal Law No. 7 of 1976 establishing the State Audit Institution
Regulation of industrial affairs	Federal Law No. 1 of 1979 organizing industrial affairs
Intellectual property rights	Federal Law No. 7 of 2002 concerning copyrights and neighbouring rights as amended by Law no. 32 of 2006
	Federal Law No 37 of 1992 on trade marks as amended by Law No. 8 of 2002
	Federal Law No. 17 of 2002 on the industrial regulation and protection of patents, industrial drawings and designs as amended by Law No. 31 of 2006
Pharmaceutical profession and pharmaceutical companies	Federal Law No. 4 of 1983 on the Pharmaceutical Profession and Pharmaceutical companies
Financial services	Federal Law No.8 of 2004 regarding Financial Free Zones
	Federal Law No. 10 of 1980 concerning the Central Bank, the monetary system and organization of banking
	Federal Law No. 4 of 2000 (Stocks and Commodities Authority)
	Federal law No. 6 of 2010 regarding the Credit Information

Table II.1 (cont'd)

Area	Legislation
Insurance services	Federal Insurance Law No. 6 of 2007
Telecommunications	Federal Law by Decree No. 3 of 2003 regarding the organization of the telecommunication sector, the amended Federal Law of 1991, and the Executive Order of the Supreme Committee No. 3 of 2004
Postal services	Federal Law No. 4 of 1985 and Federal Law No. 8 of 2001
Legal services	Federal Law No. 23 of 1991 concerning the practice of the advocate profession and amending laws, respectively, No. 20 of 1987 1997 and No. 5 of 2002
Information technology	Federal Law No.1 of 2006 concerning Electronic Transactions and E-Commerce
Consumer Protection	Federal Law No. 24 of 2006 concerning Consumer Protection

Source: Information provided by the UAE authorities.

(4) TRADE POLICY OBJECTIVES

(i) General trade policy objectives

17. The UAE has a relatively liberal trade regime, although a number of limitations and conditions are set on foreign investment. The broad strategy set by the Ministry of Foreign Trade aims to, *inter alia*, promote the UAE's trade relations with its trading partners; increase the contribution of foreign trade to GDP; maintain the commercial and investment interests of the country; and increase foreign investment flows to its markets.[13] Improved market access for its products through multilateral trade liberalization and bilateral and regional trade agreements is a main trade policy objective. The UAE coordinates its engagement in regional agreements with its participation at the multilateral level through relevant committees, which hold regular meetings. For example, GCC trade and customs officials conduct regular meetings in Geneva to discuss and coordinate their trade policies and negotiating positions at the WTO level.

18. As part of its Vision 2021 strategy, the UAE is striving for sustainable development by moving towards economic diversification away from oil.[14] In order to achieve this long-term vision, a tri-annual government strategy is implemented; the current strategy is for 2011-13. The UAE aims to transform its economy into one that is knowledge-based, highly productive, and competitive. It aims to do so by upgrading the regulatory framework of existing key sectors, while supporting the development of new ones, mainly high value-added industrial sectors, as well as by empowering nationals to take the lead in developing the economy. Trade will be a key component of this strategy, as it will help expand the UAE's diversified exports.

19. The Federal Government is responsible for the broad framework of policymaking in the UAE. Each emirate, however, sets its own strategy, which is integrated into the overall federal plan. The emirates of Abu Dhabi and Dubai have formulated long-term development plans, Abu Dhabi Economic Vision 2030 and Dubai Strategic Plan 2015, each providing a roadmap to modernize and diversify their economies. The future strategic growth of Dubai is based on six key economic sectors: tourism, trade, transportation, finance, construction, and professional services. To achieve its Vision 2030 objectives, Abu Dhabi will continue to diversify its economy, investing in capital-intensive, export-oriented sectors in which it has or can build a competitive advantage in regional and international trade. Abu Dhabi also plans to set up an export promotion agency. Abu Dhabi's economic vision focuses also on a number of strategic sectors, *inter alia*: oil and gas;

[13] The Ministry of Foreign Trade, in coordination with the Ministry of Foreign Affairs, has set up commercial offices for the UAE in China, Germany, India, Switzerland, and the United States.

[14] See UAE 2021 online information. Viewed at: http://www.vision2021.ae

petrochemicals; metals; aviation, aerospace, and defence; pharmaceuticals and biotechnology; tourism; transportation; and telecommunications.

(5) TRADE AGREEMENTS AND ARRANGEMENTS

(i) Participation in the WTO

20. A contracting party to the GATT since 8 March 1994 and a WTO Member since 10 April 1996, the UAE is a strong supporter of the multilateral trading system. The UAE grants at least MFN treatment to all WTO trading partners, except Israel. The GCC customs tariff does not discriminate between WTO Members and non-members; MFN treatment is granted to all. The UAE does not participate in any of the WTO plurilateral agreements, with the exception of the Information Technology Agreement. The UAE has not been involved in any WTO dispute settlement cases since it became a WTO Member in 1996.

21. In the current Doha Round of multilateral negotiations, the UAE is seeking meaningful liberalization in the area of industrial products under the non-agricultural market access (NAMA) negotiations, and further liberalization of trade in services. In NAMA, the UAE sponsored a proposal in 2003 to eliminate tariffs and non-tariff barriers (NTBs) on raw materials, mainly primary aluminium.[15] In March 2009, Australia co-sponsored the UAE's proposal[16], and in January 2011, both Members tabled a proposal on draft modalities for sectoral tariff elimination for raw materials.[17] The UAE also submitted its initial offer on trade in services.[18] The UAE is an active participant in the Arab Group.

22. The UAE's notifications to the WTO between January 2005 and October 2011 are listed in Table II.2.

Table II.2
Notifications to the WTO, January 2005 to October 2011

WTO Agreement	Description of requirement	Most recent notification	Comment
Agreement on Implementation of GATT Article VI (Anti-dumping)			
Article 16.4	Anti-dumping	G/ADP/N/209/Add.1 26 April 2011	No AD actions taken during 1 July-31 December 2010
Article 16.5	Competent authority	G/ADP/N/14/Add.30 22 October 2010	Anti-dumping, subsidies & countervailing duties and safeguards
Agreement on Sanitary and Phytosanitary Measures			
Article 7, Annex B	Sanitary and phytosanitary Measures	G/SPS/N/ARE/13-21	Emergency measures
Agreement on Subsidies and Countervailing Measures			
Article 25.11	Countervailing measures	G/SCM/N/219/Add.1 26 April 2011	No countervailing action during 1 July-31 December 2010
Article 25.12	Competent authority	G/SCM/N/18/Add.30 22 October 2010	Anti-dumping, subsidies and countervailing duties, and safeguards

Table II.2 (cont'd)

[15] WTO document TN/MA/W/37, 20 May 2003, and Adds.1, 2, 3, 4, and 5.
[16] WTO document TN/MA/W/37/Add.6, 23 March 2009.
[17] WTO document TN/MA/W/37/Add.7, 7 January 2011.
[18] WTO document TN/S/O/ARE, 4 July 2005.

WTO Agreement	Description of requirement	Most recent notification	Comment
Agreement on Technical Barriers to Trade			
Article 2.9	Proposed and adopted technical regulations	59 notifications made during period 28 February 2006-8 March 2011	
Article 5.6	Conformity assessment	G/TBT/N/ARE/14 G/TBT/N/ARE/16 G/TBT/N/ARE/53 1 November 2011	
Article 15.2	Implementation and administration of Agreement	G/TBT/2/Add.96 11 September 2007	
Annex 3C	Code of Good Practice	G/TBT/CS/N/166	
Agreement on Trade-Related Investment Measures (TRIMs)			
Article 6.2	Laws and regulations	G/TRIMS/N/2/Rev.20/Add.3 18 January 2011	

Source: WTO Secretariat.

23. Notifications in a number of areas were pending as at end-October 2011, including: agriculture (export subsidies and domestic support, for which the last notifications to the WTO date from 2002), subsidies (new and full notification due in 2009), intellectual property, import licensing, and services.

(ii) Preferential trade agreements

24. The UAE attaches great importance to regional trade agreements as a valuable complement to, though not a substitute for, a rule-based and non-discriminatory multilateral trade system. The UAE is a founding member of the Gulf Cooperation Council (GCC). In addition, through its participation in the GCC, the UAE has signed preferential trade agreements with Singapore and the European Free Trade Association (EFTA). The UAE is part of the Pan Arab Free Trade Agreement (PAFTA). In 2010, the UAE's total preferential trade amounted to US$38,531.5 million (18.8% of the UAE's total trade), of which almost 73% was with PAFTA (Table II.3).

Table II.3
Trade under preferential agreements, 2010
(US$ million)

FTA	Exports	Imports	Total	Percentage of total FTAs	Percentage of total trade
PAFTA[a]	16,441.7	11,657.1	28,098.7	72.9	13.7
GCC	8,812.8	6,082.1	14,894.9	38.7	7.3
GCC-EFTA	5,143.1	3,329.7	8,472.8	22.0	4.1
GCC-Singapore	578.6	1,381.3	1,960.0	5.1	1.0
Total preferential agreements	22,163.4	16,368.1	38,531.5	100.0	18.8
UAE total trade	73,231.0	132,175.3	205,406.3	..	100.0

.. Not available.

a Includes GCC members.

Source: UNSD, Comtrade database.

(a) Gulf Cooperation Council (GCC)

25. The Gulf Cooperation Council (GCC) is a political and economic union of six Arab Gulf states: Bahrain, Kuwait, Oman, Qatar, Saudi Arabia, and the UAE. Established in May 1981, its main objectives are regional cooperation and integration in areas such as economy, finance, trade, investment, Customs, tourism, and transport. In 2006, the GCC Agreement was notified to the WTO under Article XXIV of GATT 1994, and in March 2008 a notification was made under paragraph 4 (a) of the Enabling Clause. In November 2009, another notification was made pursuant to Article XXIV: 7(a) of GATT 1994.[19]

26. The GCC member states set up a free-trade area in 1983, whereby originating goods were exempt from customs tariffs. Since January 2003, the GCC states have been applying a common external tariff (CET) of 5% across the board on most products, and have followed common customs regulations and procedures based on the GCC Common Customs Law of 2003 and 2007. However, some products, for example alcoholic beverages, are prohibited for import in some GCC countries, (Chapter III(2)(vi)).

27. In January 2008, the GCC liberalized the flow of services, allowing their free movement between the members. The services component of the GCC Agreement is yet to be notified to the WTO. In addition, customs controls between GCC members have been maintained for security and other reasons (e.g. statistics, and to avoid piracy and commercial cheating).

28. Under the GCC Agreement, each member state has its own shortlist of restricted and prohibited products. Restricted products may transit the territory of members who restrict their importation but with the required documentation. Customs duties on goods imported into the UAE and destined for another GCC market are collected at the first point of entry only. However, GCC members are still in the process of reaching a formal agreement on how to allocate customs revenues from applied tariffs. Currently, customs revenue is distributed among the GCC states through a new Electronic Clearing Customs System. The GCC aims to achieve a common market, with equal treatment of GCC citizens in each member state with respect to freedom of movement, work, residence, ownership of real estate, and movement of capital, as well as financial and monetary coordination.

29. In December 2005, an initiative was launched for the adoption of a common currency by 2010. The five macroeconomic and convergence criteria were: a limit on budget deficits as a share of GDP; a limit on public debt as a share of GDP; adequacy levels for foreign exchange reserves; and convergence criteria on inflation; and on interest rates. However, in May 2009, the UAE announced its withdrawal from the monetary union project.[20] In December 2009, Bahrain, Kuwait, Qatar, and Saudi Arabia ratified an agreement to establish a monetary union. In mid 2011, the common currency project had not yet been implemented and the date to achieve a single currency was to be determined.[21]

30. The GCC, as a group is quite an open economy, with trade (imports and exports) representing some 48% of GDP in 2010. However, intra-regional trade among GCC countries is fairly low,

[19] WTO documents WT/REG222/N/1, 20 November 2006, and Corr.1, 31 March 2008; WT/COMTD/N/25, 31 March 2008; and WT/REG276/N/1/Rev.1, 17 November 2009.

[20] Oman had already announced in December 2006 that it would not be able to meet the target date.

[21] *Khaleeji* has been proposed as a name for this currency. If realized, the GCC monetary union would be the second most important supranational monetary union in the world in terms of GDP, after the euro area.

accounting for an average of about 5% of exports and 6% of imports. This is partly explained by the similar factor endowment of the members.[22]

31. As a group, the GCC signed free-trade agreements with Singapore in December 2008, and the EFTA states in June 2009.

32. The GCC-EFTA FTA covers trade in goods and services, investment, competition, government procurement, and intellectual property rights. The agreement covers practically all products in HS Chapters 25 to 97, with a few exceptions. As part of the general FTA framework, the GCC and each EFTA State have concluded agreements on trade in agricultural products on a bilateral basis. Most customs duties on originating goods within HS Chapters 25-97 will be abolished by the GCC at the date of entry into force of the agreement, except those listed in Annex VI.[23] The GCC is to eliminate duties after a five-year transition period on 37 lines at the HS 8-digit level (category B); another 11 lines are not covered by the Agreement (category X, mostly restricted goods in the GCC countries: mixtures of odoriferous substances, retreaded or used pneumatic tyres of rubber, and hides and skins of swine); while the importation of 7 HS lines is prohibited (category P, mainly cocaine and crocidolite, and materials containing asbestos).[24]

33. The chapter on services contains lists of specific commitments tailored after the GATS. The GCC countries' list includes concessions in 11 GATS sectors. Although the coverage is broad, investment limitations are inscribed. Also, the agreement does not contain specific provisions on investment in other sectors. Parties agreed to negotiate on business establishment in non-services sectors within two years after the entry into force of the agreement. Although growing, trade between EFTA and the GCC countries remains small, representing only some 4% of GCC trade. In October 2011, the EFTA-GCC FTA had not yet entered into force; it had not yet been ratified.

34. The GCC-Singapore FTA covers trade in goods, customs procedures, rules of origin, government procurement, and trade in services. Under the agreement, the GCC countries committed to eliminate customs duties on products under 99% of HS headings originating in Singapore, either immediately after the entry into force of the agreement (Group A products), or after a five-year transition period (Group B products). Goods originating in Singapore classified under Group C will not be subject to any elimination or reduction of WTO bound rates under this agreement.[25]

35. The GCC and Singapore agreed to liberalize various services sectors beyond their WTO commitments; in particular, Singapore service suppliers will benefit from preferential access in professional services, for example legal, accounting, and engineering services, as well as business services, such as construction, distribution, and hospital services.

36. Negotiations for an FTA between the GCC and New Zealand were concluded on 31 October 2009, but in late October 2011, the agreement had not yet been signed. The agreement covers nearly 95% of the tariff lines of the Harmonized System (HS), including agricultural products,

[22] Sturm and Siegfried (2005).

[23] Under the agreement, origin is conferred on wholly produced goods or on manufactures in which the value of non-originating materials does not, in general, exceed 60% of the ex-works price of the product; for the products set out in Appendix 2 of the agreement, the percentages are specified for the maximum value of non-originating materials.

[24] For more information on this agreement see EFTA online information. Viewed at: http://www.efta.int/free-trade/free-trade-agreements/gcc.aspx.

[25] This includes, for example, poultry meat, some fish and seafood, used tyres, ammonium products, alcoholic beverages, and beer). Singapore Ministry of Foreign Affairs online information. Viewed at: http://www.fta.gov.sg/fta_C_gsfta.asp?hl=30.

with a few exceptions (mostly restricted goods in the GCC countries: mixtures of odoriferous substances, retreaded or used pneumatic tyres of rubber, and hides and skins of swine). Most customs duties on originating goods will be abolished by the GCC and by New Zealand on the date of entry into force of the agreement, except for a limited number of items on which they will be abolished within 4-7 years. The GCC states are currently negotiating FTAs with Australia, China, the EU, India, Japan, Korea, MERCOSUR, Pakistan, and Turkey. In addition, the GCC has received requests for FTA negotiations from the Association of Southeast Asian Nations (ASEAN); Azerbaijan; Chile; the Common Market for Eastern and Southern Africa (COMESA); Georgia; Hong Kong, China; Malaysia; Peru; and Ukraine.

(b) The Pan Arab Free Trade Area Agreement (PAFTA) (also referred to as GAFTA)

37. The Pan Arab Free Trade Area Agreement (PAFTA), signed on 19 February 1997 to implement the Agreement on Facilitation and Development of Trade among Arab Countries[26], entered into force on 1 January 1998. This agreement encompasses all the members of the Arab League[27], and had as an objective to create a free-trade area by 2007 by dismantling customs tariffs by 10% annually over a decade. On 1 January 2005, all tariffs were eliminated among its members. Therefore, originating goods, including agricultural goods are traded duty free under PAFTA. However, non-tariff barriers, such as customs and administrative procedures and transit fees, still have a negative impact on intra-regional trade. For products imported from PAFTA countries, local value-added of at least 40% is required in order to qualify for preferential treatment. The principal entity responsible for implementing the agreement is the Economic and Social Council of the Arab League. In addition, the Union of Arab Chambers of Commerce has been tasked to produce a half-yearly report on the difficulties encountered by traders with the customs administration and regulatory agencies of individual member countries. Currently, 17 members are implementing the Agreement.[28] The PAFTA was notified to the WTO under GATT Article XXIV.[29]

(c) Bilateral agreements

38. The UAE has signed bilateral trade agreements with Syria, Jordan, Lebanon, Morocco, and Iraq. All tariffs are eliminated for all agricultural and industrial goods traded under the ambit of these agreements. The agreements were made to accelerate the conclusion of PAFTA. The UAE also has a Trade Investment Framework Agreement (TIFA) with the United States. Negotiations to establish a free-trade agreement between the UAE and the United States were launched in 2005 but came to a halt in 2006 and have not resumed. The UAE has bilateral economic agreements with 50 countries/territories.

(d) Other preferential arrangements

39. The UAE does not grant or receive autonomous preferences under the Generalized System of Preferences (GSP) and does not participate in the Global System of Trade Preferences (GSTP) among developing countries.

[26] This agreement dates from 27 February 1981.

[27] The 22 members are: Algeria, Bahrain, Comoros, Djibouti, Egypt, Iraq, Jordan, Kuwait, Lebanon, Libyan Arab Jamahiriya, Mauritania, Morocco, Oman, Palestinian Authority, Qatar, Saudi Arabia, Somalia, Sudan, Syrian Arab Republic, Tunisia, United Arab Emirates, and Yemen.

[28] Bahrain, Egypt, Iraq, Jordan, Kuwait, Lebanon, Libyan Arab Jamahiriya, Morocco, Oman, Palestinian Authority, Qatar, Saudi Arabia, Sudan, Syrian Arab Republic, Tunisia, United Arab Emirates, and Yemen.

[29] WTO document WT/REG223/N/1, 20 November 2006.

(6) FOREIGN INVESTMENT REGIME

40. The UAE's economic environment is generally liberal and business-oriented and its trade regime open. However, despite some modifications in its regulations, its investment policy continues to limit foreign investment and competition between local and foreign investors, except in the Free Zones, where 100% foreign ownership is allowed. Outside free zones, industrial licences are granted only to domestic companies that are majority-owned by UAE nationals (at least 51%-owned by UAE nationals), or by 100% foreign-owned branches that appoint a local services agent or "sponsor". The purpose of the UAE's investment policy is to maintain a balance of preserving business opportunities for UAE citizens while receiving foreign investment and know-how and promoting dynamism in specific areas. Although FDI flows have been substantial, despite the ownership rules (see Chapter I), the effects of the global financial crisis have been felt in terms of a decrease in investment flows, especially in Dubai, and the Government is currently intent on revising the foreign investment framework (see below).

41. Investment policy is coordinated between the Federal Government and the respective emirates. The Federal Department for Investment, established in 2008 at the Ministry of Economy, is the government entity responsible for assisting both foreign and domestic investors and promoting investment. The Department conducts its main task of promoting foreign investment in coordination with the competent authority at emirate level.[30] It provides advice and technical support regarding the application of the investment regulations, including for the registration and licensing of foreign investment projects, and settles any disputes between the investor and the competent authority with regard to registration, licensing, and the operations of the investment project.

42. Licences are the basic requirement to engage in any kind of business in the UAE. Procedures for local and foreign companies are generally the same, except in the case of branches of a foreign company, for which specific rules apply. Licences may be granted at the federal or at the emirate level, depending on the type of activity. Licensing procedures may vary from emirate to emirate. For example, in Dubai there are three categories of licences for all business activity: (i) commercial licences covering trading activities; (ii) industrial licences, covering an industrial or manufacturing activity; and (iii) professional licences to provide professional services, and for craftsmen and artisans. To obtain a licence, official approval from the Ministry of Economy and the local authority is required.

43. Under the Federal Commercial Companies Law (No. 8 of 1984) and its amendments, UAE nationals must hold at least 51% of the capital of any company established in the UAE.[31] Exceptions to this provision include: (i) nationals of other GCC countries who are granted national treatment and may have up to 100% ownership in most activities; (ii) investment in companies located in free zones (Chapter III(3)(iv)), where up to 100% foreign ownership is allowed; and (iii) companies registered as branches or representative offices of foreign companies established in Dubai. Under Cabinet Resolution Number No. 4 of 2008, five activities require majority 51% UAE ownership, and may not be carried out by other GCC nationals: Haj and Umra services, commercial agencies, social services,

[30] In Abu Dhabi, the authority in charge of foreign investment is the Department of Economic Development. For more information see: http://www.adeconomy.ae/english/pages/home.aspx. In Dubai, the competent entity regarding foreign investment is the Department of Economic Development. For more information see: http://www.dubaided.gov.ae/english/pages/default.aspx.

[31] Article 22 of Federal Company Law No. 8 of 1984.

cultural activities, and importing labour. The Federal Commercial Companies Law sets out the regulations governing the operations of a foreign business and defines seven types of companies.[32]

44. Under the Federal Commercial Companies Law, foreign companies may also exercise their main activity in the UAE by opening a branch or a representative office. A foreign branch may exercise only the activities for which it is licensed by each emirate. The company must apply to the Ministry of the Economy for this licence, and once approved by the Ministry, the application goes to the economic department of each emirate in which the business is to be undertaken. Some 3,788 branches of foreign companies operate in the UAE, mostly in construction, petroleum, insurance, accounting, tourism, courier, and air transport services.

45. In order to open a representative office or branch of a foreign company in the UAE, a local services agent or "sponsor" must be appointed, which must be a UAE national or company. Regulated by Federal Trade Agencies Law No. 18 of 1981 and its amendments, the local service agent has no capital share or management power but is paid a lump sum and/or share of profits. The agent helps to obtain the required licences and authorizations but is not responsible for any of the financial obligations of the company's branch or representative office within the UAE or abroad.

46. Foreigners may form sole proprietorships to practice certain activities in some emirates in some professional services, such as medical services, engineering consultancies, legal consultants, computer consultants, and non-trading activities. A foreign sole proprietor is required to appoint a local services agent.

47. Changes were introduced in 2009 to Federal Law No. 13 of 2006 (Commercial Agencies Law), which previously restricted the number of agents a foreign principal could appoint, as well as the terms of the agency relationship. The amendment, among other things, introduced modifications to make contracts more easily enforceable for example, it: (a) limited an agency contract to a fixed time period; (b) required mutual consent to renew an agency agreement; (c) allowed either party to file for damages; (d) allowed the importation of liberalized goods (not subject to restrictions) without the agent's approval; (e) eliminated the Ministry of Economy's Trade Agencies Committee, which handled agency disputes; (f) required that a commercial agency may only be deregistered by mutual agreement or pursuant to a court order; and (g) determined that either party (not only the agent) may request compensation for prejudice caused by the termination of the agency contract. The amendments sought to balance the relationship between the parties to an agency contract, as the situation was unbalanced in favour of the agent. Once an agency agreement had been registered, it could not be terminated, under any circumstances, without the agent's approval (except after a decision by the Commercial Agencies Committee of the MOE), even if the agreement was for a limited time-period.

48. Federal Law No. 2 of 2010 introduced further amendments to the Commercial Agencies Law, which seem to have partly reverted changes introduced in 2009. The new amendment stipulates that, a client (i.e. foreign investor) may terminate an agency contract or fail to renew it, only if there is a fundamental reason that would justify its termination or non-renewal. Additionally, under the amendment, it is not permissible for a company to register a new agent contract in the Registry of Commercial Agents even if the previous agent had a fixed-term contract, unless it was cancelled through mutual consent between the agent and the client, or if there were substantial grounds to justify the termination of the services of the agency, or not renewing it, or if there was a judicial verdict for its cancellation. Cabinet Resolution No. 3 of 2011 established a Commercial Agencies Committee to be formed by Ministerial Council, to review disputes that may arise relating to an agency registered

[32] A general partnership, limited partnership, joint-venture, public shareholding (joint stock), private shareholding (joint stock), limited liability, and limited share partnership company.

with the Ministry. Parties to the dispute may not go to court before first presenting it to the Committee, which must examine it within 60 days. Only the Committee's decisions may be challenged at the relevant court, within 30 days of notification of the decision. If not challenged within this period, the decision would be final and cannot be appealed.

49. The UAE's hydrocarbon industry is specifically excluded from the provisions of the Federal Commercial Companies Law. The industry is owned and controlled by the respective emirates, and foreign participation must take the form of joint-ventures. Similarly, electricity, gas, and water utilities are supplied by state monopolies, although the Emirate of Abu Dhabi has announced the partial privatization of several electricity and water plants.

50. Investment in the industrial sector, other than in free zones, is governed by Federal Law No. 1 of 1979 organizing industrial affairs. This law regulates the establishment of all industrial undertakings in the UAE and the incentives provided for industrial undertakings. It requires a prior industrial licence to be obtained in order to engage in any industrial activity in the country. Investors are expected to fulfil three conditions to obtain the industrial licence: (a) a national entity must hold at least 51% of the shares of the company; (b) the company must have at least 10 employees; and (c) the invested capital must be at least AED 250,000. All companies licensed as industrial companies enjoy duty-free importation of materials needed for the industrial project's licensed production (versus a general tariff rate of 5%). This duty exemption is granted automatically to all companies licenced as industrial companies in the UAE. On 1 June 2009, the Federal Company Law No. 8 of 1984 was amended to allow business partners seeking to establish a limited liability company to determine freely the capital requirements of their new company; previously, there was a minimum capital requirement of AED 150,000for the establishment of such companies. The authorities noted that in mid 2011, Federal Law No. 1 of 1979 was being reviewed, to streamline the licensing process and encourage investment.

51. Certain economic activities are reserved for UAE nationals: (a) Agriculture services; (b) Audio-visual services; (c) Car rental/leasing services; (d) Commercial agencies; (e) Hunting and forestry-related services; (f) Fishing services; (g) Investigation and security services; (h) Natural resources, including oil and gas, electricity, water treatment and distribution; (i) Real estate services; (j) Recreational, cultural and sporting services; (k) Passenger and freight road transport; (l) Pharmacies; (m) Travel agencies and tour operator services; (n) Warehouses for medicines and preventative medicine centres.

52. Foreign suppliers can provide studios for artistic and cinematographic production and photography, theatrical troupes, movie halls, theatres, halls for artistic exhibitions, and sporting activities.

53. Land ownership and property-related transactions in the UAE are in general restricted to UAE nationals, with some exceptions for GCC nationals depending on the emirate. In Dubai, the registration of real estate is regulated under Property Law No. 7 of 2006, under which UAE and GCC nationals are allowed to own freehold property in Dubai. Non-UAE nationals however, are only allowed to hold an interest over land in designated areas; and this may take the form of a freehold or a 99-year leasehold interest. There are currently over 30 designated zones in Dubai in which foreign ownership is permitted.

54. In Abu Dhabi, Law No. 19 of 2005 allows UAE nationals to own a freehold title to land anywhere in Abu Dhabi, while GCC nationals may only own land in certain areas designated by the Government known as "investment areas". In February 2007, the law was amended to permit non-UAE nationals to own floors (excluding the land) of buildings situated in any of the investment zones.

The law also permits non-UAE nationals a right to a 99-year usufruct (similar to a lease) or a 50-year renewable right of *musataha* (right to build) in respect of land situated within the investments zones. There are currently three investment areas in Abu Dhabi.

55. Other emirates have their own regulations and decisions governing land/property ownership, some more liberal than others. For example, Ras Al-Khaimah offers freehold property ownership rights allowing expatriates to purchase in selected developments. In Sharjah, on the other hand, the owner of a property is not permitted to sell it to non-GCC citizens without approval by the Ruler of the Emirate.

56. Since the last review of the UAE in 2006, the Ministry of Economy has been mandated by the UAE Cabinet to implement a National Investment Reform Process aimed at making the UAE more conducive to investments. The authorities indicated that in mid 2011, the Ministry of Economy was preparing a federal law on foreign investment, to serve as a one-stop-shop law reflecting government policies on foreign investment. The new law will regulate foreign investors' rights, protect and promote foreign investments, and give national treatment to foreigners. According to the authorities, the new investment law will also provide incentives for foreign investors, including allowing an investment with 100% foreign equity. The proposed law is aimed at creating favourable conditions for foreign investment and transfer of know-how.

57. Other measures to facilitate FDI will include the registration and licensing of projects within 14 days, and issuance of visas and permanent residency approvals for investors and foreign labour needed for the project.

58. In May 2011, the UAE had signed 39 bilateral investment agreements[33], and 58 treaties on avoidance of double taxation.[34] In 2004, the UAE signed a bilateral trade and investment framework agreement (TIFA) with the United States. The UAE is a member of the Multilateral Investment Guarantee Agency (MIGA).

[33] Algeria, Armenia, Austria, Azerbaijan, Bangladesh, Belarus, Belgium, China, Czech Republic, Egypt, Estonia, Finland, France, Germany, Italy, Jordan, Lebanon, Malaysia, Mongolia, Morocco, Pakistan, Poland, Republic of Korea, Romania, Russian Federation, Singapore, Sudan, Sweden, Switzerland, Syria, Tajikistan, Tunisia, Turkey, Turkmenistan, Ukraine, United Kingdom, Uzbekistan, Viet Nam and Yemen. See Ministry of Finance online information. Viewed at: http://www.mof.gov.ae/En/Publication/Pages/encourageinvestment.aspx.

[34] Algeria, Armenia, Austria, Azerbaijan, Bangladesh, Belarus, Belgium, Bosnia and Herzegovina, Bulgaria, Canada, China, Cyprus, Czech Republic, Egypt, Estonia, Finland, France, Georgia, Germany, Greece, India, Indonesia, Ireland, Italy, Kazakhstan, Lebanon, Luxembourg, Malaysia, Malta, Mauritius, Mongolia, Morocco, Mozambique, the Netherlands, New Zealand, Pakistan, Philippines, Poland, Portugal, Republic of Korea, Romania, Seychelles, Singapore, Spain, Sri Lanka, Sudan, Switzerland, Syria, Tajikistan, Thailand, Tunisia, Turkey, Turkmenistan, Ukraine, Uzbekistan, Bolivarian Republic of Venezuela, Viet Nam and Yemen. See Ministry of Finance online information. Viewed at: http://www.mof.gov.ae/En/Publication/Pages/doubletaxationavoidanceagreements.aspx.

III. TRADE POLICIES AND PRACTICES BY MEASURE

(1) INTRODUCTION

1. Since its previous Review in 2006, the United Arab Emirates has given high priority to trade facilitation. In this respect, the authorities have streamlined the procedures to prepare documents and have reduced the time required to clear customs, mainly by introducing fully electronic clearance procedures around the clock, and by allowing the use of electronic signatures (at present only possible at the Dubai Customs). Also, a risk assessment system has been introduced. However, despite this progress, imports must still be processed by a designated trade agent, who is subject to nationality restrictions. A trade agent requires a trading licence, and licences are granted only to UAE nationals or to companies that are at least 51% owned by UAE nationals.

2. The UAE applies the Gulf Cooperation Council's (GCC) Common External Tariff (since 2003). The tariff structure is relatively simple, with a low dispersion: it comprises four *ad valorem* tariff rates: zero; 5%, which is the general tariff rate; and 50% and 100%, which are applied on alcohol and tobacco, respectively. Some 97% of all tariff lines are *ad valorem*; duties are levied on the c.i.f. value of imports. Alternate or specific duties apply to 0.3% of all tariff lines. Since the last Review of the UAE, the average tariff rate has come down somewhat, from 5.1%, to 4.9%. The UAE has bound all tariff lines. Bound rates are in general considerably higher than applied rates, ranging from zero to 200%, giving scope for their reduction. Some three quarters of lines are bound at 15%, three times the general applied tariff rate. The UAE does not apply other duties and charges on imports.

3. Import prohibitions apply on some 30 HS tariff lines, and another 244 lines at the HS 8-digit level are considered restricted goods. Restrictions and prohibitions are mostly applied on safety, religious or moral grounds. No import licensing regime is in place, and the transaction value of goods is generally used for valuation purposes.

4. In 2005 the UAE issued national legislation to adopt and implement the provisions on anti-dumping, countervailing, and safeguards measures contained in the GCC Treaty. No anti-dumping or countervailing measures were taken during the period under review; no investigations were initiated. The GCC initiated two safeguard investigations in November 2009 regarding uncoated paper and paper board, and steel angles, channels and beams. However, the investigations were terminated on 31 May 2010 because injury could not be determined.

5. The Emirates Standardization and Metrology Authority (ESMA), established in 2001, is the standardization body in the UAE. The ESMA develops and adopts standards, which are prepared by its technical committees at the request of the Government, industry, and consumers. In general, standards are developed according to existing international and regional standards; however, if no international standards are available Dubai develops its own standards. Drafts are circulated to the relevant bodies for comments. There is no central body in charge of preparing technical regulations in the UAE. These may be developed by the ESMA, initially in the form of a standard and then made mandatory, or may be devised directly by a Ministry; all technical regulations are approved by Cabinet decision for legal implementation. The ESMA monitors the application of standards and technical regulations. In mid 2011, there were 6,000 standards, mostly based on GCC standards, in the UAE. It is estimated that, at present, some 65-70% of the applied standards are in conformity with international standards. During the period under review, the UAE made over 90 notifications to the TBT Committee.

6. The Ministry of Environment and Water is responsible for sanitary and phytosanitary (SPS) issues at the federal level in the UAE. Additionally, each emirate has its own responsible agency. The UAE has an extensive body of national legislation to regulate SPS measures, most of the laws are based on GCC standards. All plants and plant products entering the UAE are subject to quarantine, and require a phytosanitary certificate. Similarly, all animals and animal products are subject to quarantine and require a sanitary certificate. All shipments of food are inspected to ensure compliance with labelling and shelf-life regulations.

7. In general, the UAE does not apply export taxes, charges, and levies, with the exception of a tax on steel scrap exports. Exports of dual-use goods require a licence. The UAE applies a number of programmes to promote exports, including an extensive free-trade-zones (FTZ) programme, established in 1980 to attract foreign capital by offering incentives. Foreign ownership in firms established in FTZs may be up to 100%, and investors are exempt from personal income taxes and corporate taxes for 15 years, renewable for an additional 15 years. Goods may be imported into an FTZ duty free. Companies located in FTZs are exempted from agency/distributorship, sponsorship, and national ownership requirements. There are some 26 FTZ operating in the UAE, with investments of US$4 billion. FTZs produce goods and provide services.

8. During most of the period under review, the Emirate Industrial Bank (EBI), a majority-government-owned institution administered by the Ministry of Finance provided credits to both new and existing companies, mostly private and semi-private, engaged in industrial activities. To be eligible, the project was required to have a minimum of 51% UAE or GCC equity participation and be located in the UAE. The loan financed up to 70% of the project's total cost at a preferential interest rate. In October 2011, the EIB was restructured and converted into the Emirates Development Bank; its scope and policies were still to be defined at the time of the Secretariat's visit in November 2011.

9. The UAE economy would benefit from the adoption of a competition law, given the relative concentration of producers/suppliers in some sectors. A draft UAE competition law including restrictive agreements, abuse of a dominant position, and mergers and acquisitions, is under consideration by the Ministerial Cabinet.

10. The UAE is not a party or an observer to the WTO Plurilateral Agreement on Government Procurement. The procurement policy continues to give preference to local companies and suppliers, as foreign participation is limited by nationality requirements. However, there is a strong reliance on foreign companies, particularly for major projects for which local expertise is not always available. An offset programme is in place for defence contracts. Given the federal nature of the UAE, the majority of procurement (by value) is at emirate level.

11. Domestic laws relating to intellectual property rights protection are supplemented with laws issued by the GCC. In recent years, the UAE has implemented programmes to increase awareness of intellectual property protection. The goal is to establish an environment that promotes innovation, and to attract investment in intellectual-property-related areas in the UAE. All main intellectual property laws provide measures to prevent violation of intellectual property rights, including preventive seizure, confiscation, removal or destruction of products and equipment, as well as elimination of the effects of the illegal acts, and compensation, and imprisonment in certain instances.

(2) MEASURES DIRECTLY AFFECTING IMPORTS

(i) Customs procedures

12. Importers and exporters require a trading licence to operate in the UAE. Trading licences are granted to UAE nationals and to companies that are at least 51% owned by UAE nationals. Licences

specify the commodities that may be imported and the region; they may be emirate specific. Importers intending to supply the free-trade zones are exempt from the licensing requirement.[1] Imported goods must be distributed by a trade agency. Ownership of these agencies is restricted to UAE nationals or domestic companies fully owned by UAE nationals. In addition, only UAE nationals or judicial persons fully owned by UAE nationals may act as trade agents (see also Chapter II(6)).[2] Trade agents are entitled to an exclusive territory encompassing at least one Emirate for the specified products (Article 5(1) of the Commercial Agencies Federal Law).

13. Trade (also called commercial) agencies must be registered in the Registry of Commercial Agents. Applications for registration must be submitted to the Ministry of Economy and are subject to a fee. The relationship between the agent and importer must also be registered (currently with the UAE Ministry of Economy). Termination or refusal to renew a contract with a trade agency is not permitted unless the importer can present to the Commercial Agencies Committee and/or court (as applicable) "a material reason justifying its termination or non-renewal".[3] Termination of the contract is then decided by the Committee or the Court, as applicable. The limitations on exiting the market or changing agents may act as a deterrent for foreign companies and individuals to undertake foreign trade operations.

14. Despite these remaining obstacles to trade, since the previous Review of the UAE, trade facilitation has been a high priority in the UAE, which has undertaken a number of steps in this direction.[4] For example, it has streamlined the procedures to prepare documents and reduced the time required to import (export) with the launch of new clearance systems used at local Customs; the main ones were launched by Abu Dhabi Customs and Dubai Customs. Dubai's new customs system, Mirsal 2, allows clients to complete clearance procedures electronically around the clock, and allows the use of electronic signatures. The system also features a Risk Assessment Engine linking Dubai Customs with local, regional, and international organizations to help ensure the global trading process's security. In general terms, the UAE gives high priority to trade facilitation, due to the importance of re-exports and to its position as a global hub.

15. Customs are not authorized to release imported items other than through the designated trade agent, unless permission is granted by the Ministry ((Article 23) of the Trade Agencies Federal Law). The right of trade agents to exclusive distribution (including area of distribution), and the impediment to terminating a contract with an agent act as a barrier to trade at the border and between the emirates, as goods cannot be moved freely from one emirate to another unless the agent has the right to do so. This seems to be in contradiction with the aim of free movement of goods within the GCC and the single entry principle.

16. Imports entering the UAE require a customs declaration that must be submitted to the appropriate customs authorities when goods enter the country. The import declaration must be accompanied by: a bill of lading in its original copy[5]; an original commercial invoice (legalized); a packing list; a certificate of origin legalized by a UAE Consulate; a sanitary or phytosanitary

---

[1] Dun and Bradstreet (2006).

[2] The Trade Agencies Federal Law (Federal Law No. 18 of 1981) has been amended by: Federal Law No. 14 of 26 December 1988; Federal Law No. 13 (To amend certain provisions of the Federal Law No. 18 of 1981 Apropos the Regulations of Commercial Agencies) of 3 June 2006; and by Federal Law No. 2 of 2010.

[3] Federal Law No. 2 of 2010. This law amended Federal Law No. 18 of 1981, which is the law regulating commercial agencies in the UAE.

[4] World Bank and the International Finance Corporation (2010).

[5] The bill of lading must include the following information: port of shipment, country or origin, name of consignee or notifying party and address, all container marks and numbers, a description of the goods, and quantity, weight, and volume.

certificate as required; and for restricted imports a permit and a letter of exemption from the competent authority. Imported meat and poultry products require a health certificate from the country of origin and a halal slaughter certificate issued by an approved Islamic Centre in the country of origin.[6] Each customs office (in each emirate) has its own electronic clearance system.

17. The authorities indicated in the course of this Review, that the UAE is working on applying a single window for import procedures (and for exports).

18. Consular fees of US$15 per document are charged to legalize certificates of origin, commercial invoices, packing lists, original bills of lading, airway bills, etc. An additional fee of US$15 is charged for legalization of each additional copy.

19. The inspection of goods and other customs procedures are conducted at all customs offices, generally based on the results of risk assessment (see below) or for goods subject to an import licensing requirement, sanitary or phytosanitary certificate, or any other restriction. However, Customs has the authority to inspect any inbound cargo at any time in any place, to confirm that it has been correctly declared, that it is eligible for entry, and to determine the value. Customs inspections are generally made at the receiving port before the goods are delivered to the consignee. If the consignee wishes to unpack the container in his own warehouse, Customs will seal the container and make the inspection at the warehouse, upon request. Inspections done within a port are free of charge; however, those made elsewhere incur a fee.

20. In accordance with the Customs Law, the Administration may use Electronic Data Interchange (EDI) system in customs clearance.[7] The customs clearance systems were upgraded at the Abu Dhabi and Dubai's Customs to enable business partners to submit customs declarations online from the client's own system for processing and e-payment.

21. The UAE uses a risk-management system for inspection at Customs, rather than 100% inspection. It uses the Authorized Economic Operators (AEO) concept, which facilitates customs clearance, with the aim of unifying the database federally. However, the authorities indicated that the AEO system is used only by Abu Dhabi and Dubai in mid 2011. The Federal Customs Authority is developing a Federal Risk Analysis Mechanism to exchange risk indicators at the federal and local level.

22. The UAE has signed customs cooperation agreements with several trading partners; those with Algeria and Pakistan have been ratified.[8] In addition, as a signatory of the Kyoto Convention (in April 2011), the UAE is working with the GCC members and secretariat to review the GCC Common Customs Law, including the procedures outlined in the Convention.[9] The UAE signed the Istanbul Convention in 2010 and started implementing it in April 2011. The authorities indicated that, as of June 2011, a unified trader code (UTC) is applied across the UAE. Previously, traders had to register separately in each emirate. The introduction of the UTC allows traders (importers or exporters) to operate throughout the UAE. The authorities indicated that the UTC may be obtained online, and is used as a means of assuring that information in made readily available to the trader. The authorities consider that the use of the UTC facilitates risk management, and constitutes an important step towards the adoption of a single window system.

[6] Dun and Bradstreet (2006).

[7] Common Customs Law.

[8] Information provided by the UAE authorities.

[9] Cabinet Decree No. 33 of 2011.

23. There is no advance ruling system in place. In the context of this Review the authorities indicated that implementation of an advance ruling system would require further assistance due to the complications posed by the UAE's particular federal system.

24. The UAE applies four import regimes: transit, temporary admission, warehousing, and goods imported into the free-trade zones. Customs duties do not need to be paid on goods in transit but a deposit or bank guarantee is required, equal to the customs duties that would be payable upon import plus some nominal charges.[10] The deposit is refundable in full while the charges are not. Goods in transit must be transported through specified routes, which are set by a resolution of the Minister or the competent authority.[11] The Customs Administration prohibits the transit of goods for which importation into the UAE is restricted or prohibited. The transit of goods infringing intellectual property rights through the UAE is also prohibited.[12]

25. Certain goods may be imported temporarily with approval from Customs, provided they are re-exported within six months, with the exception of capital goods, which may remain up to three years, upon payment of a deposit in lieu of duty or a bank guarantee (Table III.1). The deposit or guarantee is refundable on proof of export. The materials and articles that enter under temporary admission may not be used, allocated or disposed of for purposes and objectives other than those for which they were imported as stated in the declaration submitted.[13] Customs is allowed to inspect the use of goods that enter the UAE temporarily. There is a fee for the on-site inspection.[14] Goods remaining in the UAE over six months are liable for duty payment.

Table III.1
Goods that may be imported under temporary admission, 2011

Goods that may be imported under temporary admission
Heavy machinery and equipment for completion of projects or for conducting the experiments and tests relating to such projects
Foreign goods imported for completion of processing.
Items temporarily imported for playgrounds, theatres, exhibitions, and like events
Machinery and equipment imported into the country for repair
Containers and packing imported for refilling
Animals admitted for grazing
Commercial samples for exhibition

Source: Article 90 of the Common Customs Law.

26. Warehouses may be established by a resolution of the Minister in charge of Customs or the competent authority inside or outside the Customs Office. Goods may be deposited with the warehouses without payment of customs duties and taxes for storage.

27. At the time of clearance, even if exempted from customs taxes and duties, a detailed customs declaration, conforming to the requirements of the GCC member states, must be submitted to the Customs Office, containing all the information that would enable the levying of customs taxes and duties.[15]

[10] Charges include: AED 30 for a customs transportation card; AED 10 if the customs transportation card needs to be amended; AED 50 for the transit declaration; and AED 20 for a temporary admission plate for vehicles (Decrees No. 45 of 2009 and No. 1 of 2011).
[11] Common Customs Law.
[12] Common Customs Law.
[13] Common Customs Law.
[14] Article 92 of the Common Customs Law.
[15] Common Customs Law.

28. When goods are to be inspected, the designated customs officer must examine the goods wholly or partially after registering the customs declarations at the Customs Office (Article 53); in certain cases, when goods require special handling, examinations may be conducted outside the Customs Office. Examinations are conducted in the presence of the owner of the goods or his representative. However, if a customs officer suspects the presence of prohibited or illegal merchandise, packages may be opened for inspection in the absence of the owner or his representative, and the customs officer may inspect and analyse the goods prior to notifying the owner. If goods prove through inspection or analysis to be harmful or do not conform to the approved specifications, the Director General of Customs may order their destruction (or re-export) at the expense and in presence of their owners or their representatives.

29. Prior authorization from the appropriate government body is required to import specific goods, including weapons and ammunition, all alcoholic beverages, pork products, tobacco products, publications, visual and audio tapes, telecommunication equipment, all foodstuffs, animals and their products, animal feeds, additives, living bees and bee queens, fireworks and explosives. Other goods are regulated or require registration, as is the case for pharmaceuticals.

30. Some restrictions apply with respect to the transport and unloading of goods. Vessels irrespective of their load capacity, are prohibited from anchoring at any harbour other than those designated for receiving them. Vessels loaded with prohibited or restricted goods, of a loading capacity of less than 200 marine tons may not enter or be involved in shipping activities within the marine customs zone, except in emergency situations. This restriction excludes vessels transporting goods within the UAE's various ports for which customs procedures have been finalized at the port of entry.

(ii) Customs valuation and rules of origin

(a) Customs valuation

31. Imported goods are valued on the basis the transaction value. If the transaction value of the imported good cannot be determined the transaction value of a similar or identical good is used. If neither of these values can be determined, the valuation methods used are: the deductive value, the computed value or the flexible method. The importer may request application of the computed value method before the deductive value method.[16] This request must be made at the time of submitting the Customs Declaration.[17]

32. Customs duties are levied based on the transaction value declared in the customs declaration. If, following the physical inspection, a discrepancy is found between the value of the goods and what is stated in the customs declaration, customs taxes and duties will be levied on the basis of this finding. In this case, Customs has the right to levy a fine.

33. Imported goods are subject to the duties applicable on the date of registering the customs declaration with the Customs Office. Goods taken from the free zones and duty-free shops into the local markets are subject to the customs tariff effective at that time.

34. The Valuation Committee is in place to settle any disputes between importers and the Customs Office about the value of imported goods. Importers may appeal a customs decision before the Valuation Committee within 15 days following registration of the customs declaration or from the

[16] The United Arab Emirates invoked paragraph 3 of Annex III of the Agreement on Customs Valuation (WTO document G/VAL/2/Rev.24, 27 April 2007).

[17] Rules of Implementation of the GCC Common Customs Law.

date of the valuation notice sent by registered mail. The importer is informed in writing of the decision taken by the Committee. Importers may also appeal before a judicial court. The authorities indicated that no cases have been taken to court.

35. Customs may release the goods in dispute, if not prohibited, after collecting a deposit in an amount equivalent to customs duties and taxes determined by the Customs Office. Samples of the goods are maintained temporarily for reference, when necessary; they are returned unless they are used during the inspection and analysis purposes.

(iii) Rules of origin

36. The UAE does not apply non-preferential rules of origin. Preferential rules of origin apply to goods produced in the GCC and in PAFTA members (Table III.2). Under PAFTA and the GCC, the certificate of origin must be issued by the producer, and be authenticated by the competent authorities in the country of origin. The authorities indicated that, in mid 2011, new legislation with respect to rules of origin was being drafted.

Table III.2
Preferential rules of origin, 2011

Agreement/country	Rules
Goods of GCC origin	Wholly obtained
	Substantial transformation, with at least 40% of local value-added, and produced in plants that are at least 51% owned by GCC nationals
PAFTA	Value added no less than 40% when there is substantial transformation
	Value added no less than 20% for assembly industries

Source: WTO Secretariat.

(iv) Tariffs

(a) Applied tariff

37. The UAE adopted the Gulf Cooperation Council (GCC) common external tariff (CET) on 1 January 2003. The CET is mainly *ad valorem* except for duties levied on tobacco. The CET is a five-year tariff. The current CET is for 2007-2012. Tariff changes require approval from the other GCC countries.

38. Under the "single port of entry" principle, customs duties are collected at the first point of entry to the GCC states.[18] The authorities indicated that the distribution of duties is through quarterly electronic transfers between GCC countries, through the "Electronic Clearing Customs". Duties are collected at the first point of entry but allocated to the country where the imported good is finally used. The authorities noted that the GCC has a special committee to deal with problems that might emerge from the redistribution of tariff proceeds. Complaints are lodged first with the respective national Customs Administration which, in turns, transfers the matter to the GCC.

39. The 2011 applied tariff (HS2007 nomenclature) has 7,101 tariff lines at the eight-digit level, comprising four *ad valorem* tariff rates: zero; 5%, which is the general tariff rate; 50%, applied on alcoholic beverages; and 100%, applied on tobacco (Chart III.1). Some 99.7% of all tariff lines are *ad valorem*; duties are levied on the c.i.f. value of imports. Alternate or specific duties apply to 0.3% of all tariff lines, a slight decrease from 2005 (0.4%) (Table III.3).

[18] Gulf Cooperation Council (undated).

Table III.3
Structure of MFN tariff, 2011
(%)

		MFN applied		
		2005[a]	2011	Final bound[a]
1.	Bound tariff lines (% of all tariff lines)	100.0	100.0	100.0
2.	Duty-free tariff lines (% of all tariff lines)	5.9	9.4	2.7
3.	Non-*ad valorem* tariffs (% of all tariff lines)[b]	0.4	0.3	0.0
4.	Non-*ad valorem* tariffs with no AVEs (% of all tariff lines)[b]	0.4	0.3	0.0
5.	Tariff quotas (% of all tariff lines)	0.0	0.0	0.0
6.	Simple average tariff rate	5.1	4.9	14.6
	Agricultural products (WTO definition)	6.2	6.3	25.0
	Non-agricultural products (WTO definition)	4.8	4.6	12.7
	Agriculture, hunting, forestry and fishing (ISIC 1)	3.3	3.2	16.7
	Mining and quarrying (ISIC 2)	5.0	4.9	15.0
	Manufacturing (ISIC 3)	5.2	5.0	14.5
7.	Domestic tariff "spikes" (% of all tariff lines)[c]	0.5	0.5	0.9
8.	International tariff "peaks" (% of all tariff lines)[d]	0.5	0.5	0.9
9.	Overall standard deviation of applied rates	5.6	5.7	17.8
10.	"Nuisance" applied rates (% of all tariff lines)[e]	0.0	0.0	0.2

a Based on WTO (2006).
b Final bound rates are based on the 2005 tariff schedule in HS02 nomenclature. Calculations on bound averages are based on 7,143 bound tariff lines.
c In the 2011 tariff schedule no rates are available for 28 tariff lines, of which 24 tariff lines are denoted as "prohibited".
d Domestic tariff spikes are defined as those exceeding three times the overall simple average applied rate (indicator 6).
e International tariff peaks are defined as those exceeding 15%.

Source: WTO Secretariat calculations, based on data provided by the authorities.

40. The simple average applied MFN tariff was 4.9% in 2011 (2007/12), slightly lower than in 2005. The non-agricultural average tariffs declined, but protection for agriculture (6.3% according to the WTO definition) rose and remains higher than for non-agricultural goods (4.6%) (Table III.4).

Table III.4
Summary analysis of MFN tariff, 2011

	Number of lines	Average (%)	Range (%)	Standard deviation	Duty free (%)
Total	7,101	4.9	0-100	5.7	9.4
HS 01-24	1,198	6.0	0-100	13.6	25.0
HS 25-97	5,903	4.7	0-5	1.2	6.3
By WTO category					
WTO agricultural products	1,122	6.3	0-100	14.0	21.6
Animals and products thereof	145	3.1	0-5	2.4	37.9
Dairy products	33	5.0	5.0	0.0	0.0
Fruit, vegetables, and plants	329	3.7	0-5	2.2	26.1
Coffee and tea	38	3.7	0-5	2.2	26.3
Cereals and preparations	172	3.6	0-5	2.2	27.3
Oils seeds, fats, oil and their products	90	4.8	0-5	0.9	3.3
Sugars and confectionary	38	3.6	0-5	2.3	28.9
Beverages, spirits and tobacco	83	36.5	0-100	39.7	1.2
Cotton	5	5.0	5.0	0.0	0.0
Other agricultural products, n.e.s.	189	4.5	0-50	3.8	15.3

Table III.4 (cont'd)

	Number of lines	Average (%)	Range (%)	Standard deviation	Duty free (%)
WTO non-agricultural products	5,979	4.6	0-5	1.3	7.1
Fish and fishery products	162	3.2	0-5	2.4	35.8
Minerals and metals	1,189	4.9	0-5	0.7	2.1
Chemicals and photographic supplies	1,249	4.5	0-5	1.5	9.3
Wood, pulp, paper, and furniture	428	4.6	0-5	1.4	8.9
Textiles	725	5.0	0-5	0.4	0.6
Clothing	255	5.0	5.0	0.0	0.0
Leather, rubber, footwear, and travel goods	212	5.0	5.0	0.0	0.0
Non-electric machinery	636	4.6	0-5	1.3	7.7
Electric machinery	307	3.8	0-5	2.1	24.1
Transport equipment	233	4.4	0-5	1.6	11.2
Non-agricultural products, n.e.s.	549	4.7	0-5	1.3	6.7
Petroleum	34	5.0	5.0	0.0	0.0
By ISIC sector[a]					
ISIC 1 - Agriculture, hunting and fishing	430	3.2	0-100	9.7	53.3
ISIC 2 - Mining	123	4.9	0-5	0.8	2.4
ISIC 3 - Manufacturing	6,547	5.0	0-100	5.4	6.7
By stage of processing					
First stage of processing	831	3.9	0-100	7.1	30.4
Semi-processed products	2,120	4.8	0-5	1.0	4.1
Fully processed products	4,150	5.2	0-100	6.7	7.9

a International Standard Industrial Classification (Rev.2). Electricity, gas, and water are excluded (1 tariff line).

Note: Calculations for averages are based on national tariff line level (8-digit).
For non-*ad valorem* rates (19 tariff lines), calculations include the *ad valorem* part used for mixed duty rates. No duty rates are provided for four tariff lines.

Source: WTO Secretariat estimates, based on data provided by the UAE authorities.

Chart III.1
Frequency distribution of applied MFN tariff rates, 2011

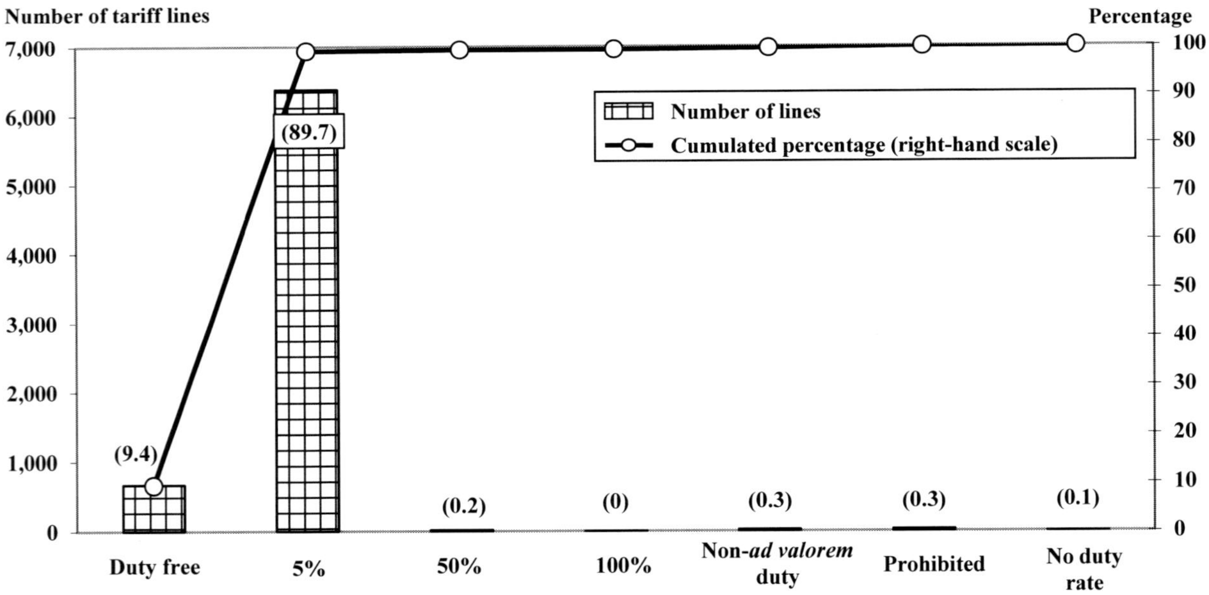

Note: The figures in brackets correspond to the percentage of total lines.

***Source*: WTO Secretariat calculations, based on data provided by the UAE authorities.**

41. There have been no major changes in the tariff distribution. In 2011, tariffs range from zero to 100% (Table AIII.1). The majority of lines (89.7%) carry a rate of 5%, while 9.4% of total lines have a tariff rate of zero (up from 5.9% in 2005). Non-*ad valorem* tariffs (0.3% of tariff lines) and higher tariff rates (100%) apply to alcoholic beverages and tobacco products.

(b) Bound tariffs

42. The UAE has bound all tariff lines in the WTO. Bound rates are all *ad valorem* and range from zero to 200% (Chart III.2). Most tariff lines (74%) are bound at 15%. The highest bound rates of 200% apply to swine meat, alcoholic beverages, and tobacco products, which are also "restricted" or "prohibited" goods.

Chart III.2
Frequency distribution of bound tariffs

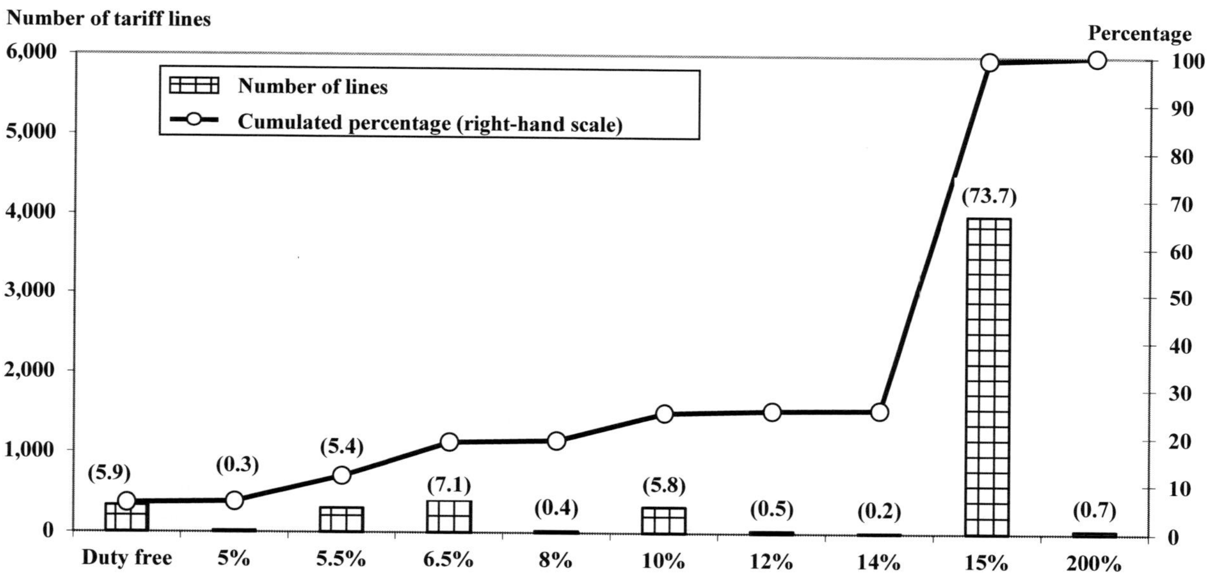

Note: The figures in brackets correspond to the percentage of total lines.

Source: WTO Secretariat calculations, based on data provided by WTO, CTS database.

(c) Preferential tariffs

43. The United Arab Emirates is a member of the Gulf Cooperation Council (GCC), comprised of Bahrain, Kuwait, Oman, Qatar, Saudi Arabia, and the United Arab Emirates. Under the GCC, duty-free access is provided to all goods produced in GCC states that meet GCC content requirements (at least 40% value added within GCC, in plants that are at least 51% owned by GCC nationals). On 1 January 2003, the GCC established a customs union with a common external tariff (CET). The GCC fixed the CET at 5% for most imports from outside of the GCC. Essential products are zero rated. Where importation is permitted, tariffs on alcohol and tobacco may be 50% or 100%. Appendix No. 1 of the Implementing Procedures for the GCC Customs Union lists 417 subheadings that are to be exempt from customs duties. There is a list of special goods at the GCC level, and each member state is allowed to decide whether these goods are subject to a tariff and restricted or prohibited; hence each member can issue its own list of prohibited and restricted goods. Goods produced in free-trade zones within the GCC are taxed at the applied MFN tariff. Goods entering one

GCC member state are allowed to be transported to any other member state without further inspection or duty payments.

44. The UAE is a member of the Pan Arab Free Trade Area Agreement (PAFTA) (see Chapter II(5)). Under the PAFTA all customs duties on goods produced by members were eliminated on 1 January 2005.

(d) Duty and tax concessions and exemptions

45. Tariff exemptions apply to goods imported under various import regimes (e.g. goods in transit, goods in temporary admission, warehoused goods, and goods imported into free-trade zones). Imports by international organizations, diplomatic missions, personal effects and household items, philanthropic societies, and the military forces and internal security forces continue to be exempt from import duties.

46. Goods produced in the UAE that have been exported may be re-imported into the UAE within one year of exportation. Goods that have been temporarily exported for finishing or repair are subject to the customs duties in an amount equivalent to the value addition resulting from such finishing or repair.[19]

(v) Other charges affecting imports

47. There are no transit duties amongst the emirates, or any other additional duty, according to the UAE authorities. In general, no other duties are applied on imports, with the exception of alcoholic beverages, which may be subject to municipality taxes; e.g. liquor is subject to a 30% municipality tax in Dubai.

(vi) Import prohibitions, restrictions, and licensing

48. The GCC Common Customs Law distinguishes absolute import prohibitions from restricted imports. There is a Common GCC prohibited and restricted list of goods. However, each member has the right to have its own list. The UAE applies the GCC prohibited and restricted list and has an additional list.

49. Imports are prohibited in the UAE based on environmental, health and safety, and religious and moral considerations, and to implement international conventions.[20] Thus, the UAE prohibits: imports of goods that are incompatible with the Islamic faith and morals; goods originating in Israel or with Israeli slogans and flags; any equipment devoted to gambling games of all kinds; candy in the form of cigarettes and stored in boxes similar to cigarettes; and any goods contaminated with radiation or nuclear dust. In addition the UAE prohibits imports of products classified in around 30 tariff lines at 8-digit level (Table III.5).

[19] Article 105 of the Customs Law (Returned goods).

[20] The UAE is a signatory to the Convention on International Trade in Endangered Species (CITES), the Basel Convention, Rotterdam Convention, and the Kimberly process for trade in diamonds.

Table III.5
Prohibited goods, 2011

HS code[a]	Description
01 03 00 00	Live swine
01 06 19 10	Camels
05 07 10 00	Ivory natural
06 02 20 10	Palm tree seedlings
09 08 20 00	Mace
12 07 91 00	Poppy seeds
12 07 99 10	Poppy
12 07 99 20	Hemp seeds
12 11 30 00	Coca leaf
12 11 40 00	Poppy straw
12 11 90 20	Black poppy
12 11 90 60	Cannabis sativa
13 02 11 00	Opium
13 02 19 10	Hashish
24 03 99 20	Chopped or pressed tobacco for chewing
25 24 00 00	Asbestos
29 39 91 10	Cocaine
40 12 00 00	Retreaded or used pneumatic tyres of rubber; solid or cushion tyres, interchangeable tyre treads and tyre flaps, of rubber
56 08 11 00	Made-up fishing nets of man-made textile materials
56 08 19 00	Knotted netting of twine, cordage or rope; made-up fishing nets and other made-up nets, of textile materials of man-made textile materials
56 08 90 00	Knotted netting of twine, cordage or rope; made-up fishing nets and other made-up nets, of textile materials
68 11 40 00	Containing asbestos
68 12 80 00	Fabricated asbestos fibres; mixtures with a basis of asbestos or with a basis of asbestos and crocidolite
68 12 93 00	Compressed asbestos fibre jointing, in sheets or rolls
68 13 20 00	Containing asbestos
72 04 10 00	Waste and scrap of cast iron (imports from Iraq only)
72 04 21 00	Waste and scrap of alloy steel: of stainless steel (imports from Iraq only)
72 04 29 00	Waste and scrap of alloy steel: other than stainless steel (imports from Iraq only)
72 04 30 00	Waste and scrap of tinned iron or steel of stainless steel (imports from Iraq only)
72 04 41 00	Turnings, shavings, chips, milling waste, sawdust, filings, trimmings and stampings, whether or not in bundles (imports from Iraq only)
72 04 49 00	Waste and scrap other than turnings, shavings, chips, milling waste, sawdust, filings, trimmings and stampings, whether or not in bundles (imports from Iraq only)
72 04 50 00	Re-melting scrap ingots (imports from Iraq only)
..	Organic fertilizers untreated and non-sterile
..	All the goods that are incompatible with the Islamic faith and morals
..	Goods originating in Israel or with the slogans and Israeli flags
..	Tools, machinery and equipment devoted to gambling games of all kinds
..	Goods contaminated with radiation and nuclear dust
..	Children's candy in the form of cigarettes and stored in boxes similar to cigarettes
..	Waste, and hazardous industrial waste

.. Not available.

Source: Information provided by the authorities.

50. Imports and transit of rough diamonds are prohibited unless these are accompanied by a Kimberly certificate and imported in a tamper-resistant sealed container. Imports and exports of

diamonds must enter and exit through designated points.[21] Imports permitted in one GCC member state may not transit through a member state in which they are prohibited.[22]

51. In addition to import prohibitions, imports of 244 tariff lines at the 8-digit level were restricted in 2011; these comprise mainly swine and alcohol products.[23]

52. During the period under Review the UAE made no notifications to the Committee on Import Licensing Procedures. The UAE does not appear to have an import licensing regime in place.

(vii) Import-related operations of state enterprises

53. The UAE has no state trading enterprises in the sense of Article XVII of the GATT 1994.

(viii) Contingency measures

54. In 2005, the UAE issued Federal Law No. 7 to adopt and implement the provisions on anti-dumping, countervailing, and safeguards measures contained in the GCC Treaty.[24] Thereafter, the UAE adopted the GCC's Anti-dumping and Countervailing Measures and Safeguards Act, as amended in December 2010, and its Rules of Implementation. Both the Act and the Rules are compulsory within member states, which are mandated to establish local enforcement bodies. The Directorate of Anti-Dumping at the Ministry of Economy is the UAE institution in charge of contingency trade remedies.[25]

55. The GCC Anti-dumping and Countervailing Measures and Safeguards Act is implemented by the Ministerial Committee (MC), the Permanent Committee (PC), which is a body in charge of dealing with injurious trade practices at the regional level, and the Bureau of the Technical Secretariat of the PC.[26] All complaints must be submitted to the Technical Secretariat, which examines the accuracy and adequacy of the complaint within 30 days, and submits a preliminary report to the PC with its recommendation to initiate an investigation or reject the complaint. The PC issues a decision to initiate or reject the complaint within 15 days, and this decision is notified to the complainant within 7 days. Provisional trade measures may be imposed by the PC, and do not need to be decided by the MC. The MC, is the competent authority for the imposition of definitive measures; it receives recommendations from the PC. Decisions may be appealed to the MC, within 30 days from their date of publication in the *Official Gazette* issued by the Technical Secretariat. The MC must decide on the petition within 60 days of its submission.

56. GCC member states have agreed on a definition of domestic industry to encompass the regional aspect of the investigations. Domestic industries eligible to submit complaints are the GCC producers of "like products" or "directly competitive products" as a whole, or those producers whose collective output represents a major proportion of the GCC production of those products.[27] In trade

[21] Federal Law No. 13 Regarding Supervision of Import/Export and Transit, 20 July 2004.

[22] Implementation Procedures for the GCC Customs Union. Viewed at: http://www.gcc-sg.org/eng/index9038.html?action=Sec-Show&ID=93.

[23] At the four-digit level 165 tariff lines are considered restricted (information provided by the authorities).

[24] GCC Common Law on Anti-dumping, Countervailing, and Safeguard measures, 21 December 2003 and Rules of Implementation 11 October 2004.

[25] WTO documents G/ADP/N/14/Add.30 and G/SCM/N/18/Add.30, 22 October 2010.

[26] The Ministerial Committee refers to the GCC Industrial Cooperation Committee, which consist of the members' Ministers of Industry.

[27] This definition follows the Anti-dumping Agreement, adapting it to the (GCC) regional level. Consequently, an application is considered to have been made "by or on behalf of the domestic industry" if it is

remedy investigations, the GCC market is considered as one market, and all GCC producers of the "like products" or "directly competitive products" within the GCC are treated as a single domestic industry. Contingency trade measures are applied throughout the customs union.

57. The UAE has not applied any anti-dumping measures during the period under review, although notifications to the WTO for this period are not complete. The UAE notified to the WTO that no anti-dumping measures were imposed during 1996, 1998, first half of 1999, and in July-December 2010.[28] No countervailing actions have been taken, although here, too, notifications are incomplete; the UAE has only notified to the WTO that no countervailing actions were taken in 1998, January-June 1999, in 2010, and in January- June 2011.[29]

58. The GCC initiated two safeguard investigations in November 2009 regarding uncoated paper and paper board, and steel angles, channels and beams.[30] However, these investigations were terminated on 31 May 2010 because injury could not be determined.[31] In 2010, a Notice of termination was published in the *Official Gazette* of the Bureau of the Technical Secretariat. The UAE has not imposed any safeguards since 2005.

(ix) Standards and other technical requirements

(a) Standards, testing, and certification

59. The Emirates Standardization and Metrology Authority (ESMA), established under Law No. 28/2001, is the sole standardization body in the UAE. The ESMA is chaired by the Minister of Environment and Water and comprises representatives of the main parties involved in the standardization in the UAE.[32]

60. The ESMA is in charge of drafting, formulating, and issuing standards, as well as adopting international standards and technical regulations issued by binding resolutions of the Cabinet. Standards are developed based on demands of the Government, industry, and consumers, through the work of the ESMA's ten technical committees.[33] Draft standards are prepared by the technical committees based on existing international and regional standards. The draft is circulated for comments to the stakeholders in the relevant field; these must be provided within 60 days. Draft standards are circulated abroad for comments if they are not based on an existing international standard. The technical committee studies the comments and suggestions received, and amends the draft standard as required. Once approved, a standard is numbered and published in the *Official Gazette*. Thereafter, it is printed and is available for sale. Technical regulations are approved

---

supported by those domestic (GCC) producers whose collective output constitutes more than 50% of the total production of the like product produced by that portion of the domestic (GCC) industry expressing either support for or opposition to the application. No investigation may be initiated when domestic (GCC) producers expressly supporting the application account for less than 25% of total production of the like product produced by the domestic (GCC) industry.

[28] WTO documents G/ADP/N/16/Add.1/Rev.12, G/ADP/N/22/Add.1/Rev.9, G/ADP/N/41/Add.1/Rev.9 and G/ADP/N/47/Add.1/Rev.6, and G/ADP/N/53/Add.1/Rev.7, all dated 27 April 2009; and G/ADP/N/209/Add.1, 26 April 2011.

[29] WTO documents G/SCM/N/40/Add.1/Rev.9, 28 April 2009; G/SCM/N/52/Add.1/Rev.1, 2 May 2000; G/SCM/N/219/Add.1, 26 April 2011; and G/SCM/N/228/Add.1, 20 October2011.

[30] WTO document G/SG/Q2/ARE/1, 19 November 2010.

[31] WTO document G/SG/Q2/ARE/2, 2 February 2011.

[32] The main parties involved are the Federal Government, industrial sector, traders, laboratories, and calibration bodies.

[33] For more information see ESMA online information. Viewed at: http://www.esma.ae/en-us/aboutesma/ Pages/VisionMissionObjectives.aspx.

by Cabinet decision for legal implementation by all state agencies (see below). The ESMA monitors the application of standards and technical regulations.

61. In mid 2011, there were 6,000 standards in the UAE, mostly based on GCC standards. When there are no national or GCC standards, the ESMA will follow international standards that are suitable for the UAE environment, as mandated by Ministerial Decision No. 114/2 of 2004. It is estimated that some 65-70% of the applied standards are in conformity with international standards.

62. Since 2005 the ESMA has been the UAE national enquiry point for standards information; it represents the UEA in regional and international conferences and organizations. The ESMA is a member of several international standards organizations including the International Organization for Standardization (ISO), the International Electrotechnical Commission (IEC), the International Laboratory Accreditation Cooperation (ILAC), the GCC Standardization Organization (GSO), the Arab Industrial Development and Mining Organization (AIDMO), the International Organization of Legal Metrology (OIML), and Codex Alimentarius.

63. The ESMA is responsible for metrology and calibration in the UAE. Under the national system of measurement (NMS), established in 2006[34], the ESMA is responsible for regulating the use of measuring instruments. The authorities indicated that the ESMA is planning to establish a National Metrology Institute.

64. The UAE has implemented the Emirates Quality Mark Scheme since 2007 to ensure that products comply with the approved standards and to give consumers confidence in the products that carry this mark for sale locally or exported. The Emirates Quality Mark, granted to a certain product by the ESMA, proves that the product meets the approved standards and its production system meets the quality management system requirements as per ISO 9001. The conformity assessment process for granting the mark verifies that the approved standard is implemented, which is similar to granting a product conformity certificate.

65. In 2004, the ESMA started operating the National Accreditation System (ENAS) in accordance with Decision of Council of Ministers No. 22 of 1 June 2004. Institutions seeking accreditation must to apply to the ESMA; after an assessment, the ESMA decides whether to grant; accreditation. Once accredited institutions are surveyed. The authorities have noted that accreditation in the UAE follows international requirements and procedures, and that the ENAS operates in accordance with the international practices for accreditation bodies (ISO/IEC 17011). In the context of this Review, the authorities indicated that there are 31 accredited laboratories, 8 inspection bodies and 2 certification bodies in the UAE.[35]

66. The UAE does not implement the GCC International Conformity Certification Programme (ICCP). It implements the Emirates Conformity Assessment Scheme (ECAS) as a mandatory product certification scheme, which applies to products that affect health and safety or have an impact on the environment, such as low-voltage equipment and toys.[36] The authorities indicated that the ECAS' aim is to ensure the safety and quality of products and to protect consumers. The ECAS may also cover

---

[34] Cabinet Resolution No. 31, 2006.

[35] For more information, see: http://www.esma.ae/en-US/OurServices/ENAS/Pages/CABs.aspx.

[36] The "mandatory" products are: electric storage water heaters; electric power extension cords and adaptors; electric irons; microwave ovens; washing machines and clothes dryers; electric cooking stoves; refrigerators, chillers and freezers; room air-conditioner; household cooking appliances; electromechanical kitchen appliances; vacuum cleaners; fans and fan systems including air-purifiers. ESMA online information. Viewed at: http://www.esma.ae/SiteCollectionDocuments/ECAS/EMPro.pdf.

products subject to (voluntary) standards for which interested parties may request certification.[37] The conformity assessment process verifies that the product complies with the approved standards and an effective quality management system is implemented. The process involves sampling and testing products, as well as visiting and auditing the factory to ensure that products and system requirements are satisfactorily complied with. If successful, ESMA issues a license to use the Emirates Quality Mark on the product and the Certificate of Conformity (COC) for the product, to the producer or trader. Locally manufactured products as well as imports are included in this scheme.

(b) Technical regulations

67. There is no central body in charge of preparing technical regulations in the UAE. They may be developed by the ESMA, initially in the form of a standard and then made mandatory, or may be devised directly by a Ministry. According to the authorities, the former is the more common, and the standard is made mandatory by Cabinet resolution. In the context of this Review, the authorities noted that the decision whether a standard will become a technical regulation is generally taken before the standard is drafted. However, in some cases, however, an existing standard may be the base for issuing a technical regulation. The final draft of the standard must be approved by the ESMA Board of Directors before being sent to Cabinet for approval.

68. During the period under review the UAE made 90 notifications to the Committee on Technical Barriers to Trade. Most (86) relate to draft technical regulations distributed for comments. The measures notified relate to food and tobacco products, motor vehicles, cosmetics, detergents, toys, and natural gas. Comments by Members or other interested parties on these proposed measures are sent to the ESMA, who channels them to the appropriate Committee for consideration.

69. The UAE notified its acceptance of the WTO TBT Code of Good Practice for the Preparation, Adoption and Application of Standards in 2006.[38] In 2007, the UAE designated the Emirates Authority for Standardization and Metrology (ESMA) as the national enquiry point to implement the Agreement on Technical Barriers to Trade.[39] In September 2011, there were 632 technical regulations in place.

(c) Labelling and packaging requirements

70. Labelling requirements in the UAE apply mainly to toys, cigarettes, and food. All warning labels on toys are required to be in Arabic or in Arabic and English. Cigarette packages require a special health warning in Arabic.

71. Food labels must also include: product and brand names in Arabic or Arabic and English; ingredients listed in descending order of proportion, as well as additives, using their "E" numbers; the origin of all animal fats; net content, expressed in metric units; and country of origin. The labels for specialty items such as diet, health or baby foods must contain detailed nutritional information.

72. The production and expiry dates (best use-before date) must appear on food products as a fully integrated part of the packaging (i.e. printed on the label or embossed on the can). The production date must be preceded by the word "Production" or the letter "P". Stickers and rubber stamping are not acceptable for date markings.

---

[37] ESMA online information. Viewed at: http://www.esma.ae/en-us/ourservices/ecas/Pages/Home.aspx.

[38] WTO document G/TBT/CS/N/166, 2 May 2006.

[39] WTO document G/TBT/2/Add.96, 11 September 2007.

73. GMOs are not specifically banned in the UAE; however, food labels should indicate if any of the ingredients used are genetically modified.[40]

(x) Sanitary and phytosanitary requirements

74. The Ministry of Environment and Water is responsible for sanitary and phytosanitary (SPS) issues at the federal level in the UAE. Additionally, each emirate has its own responsible agency. The UAE's SPS enquiry point and national notification authority is the Protection and Agricultural Quarantine Department in the Ministry. The Review, Notification and Inquiry Unit in the Ministry maintains a data base of notifications, both by the UAE and its trading partners, and receives comments from partners.[41] The UAE made 12 notifications under the Agreement on the Application of Sanitary and Phytosanitary Measures during 1 January 2006 to 1 September 2011; most (11) were emergency measures submitted in 2006.

75. In general, UAE federal regulations on SPS requirements are based on GCC standards. The UAE's has an extensive body of national legislation to regulate sanitary and phytosanitary measures (Table III.6). The main national laws are Federal Law No. 5 of 1979 on agricultural quarantine, as amended, and Federal Law No. 6 of 1979 on veterinary quarantine, as amended. All main federal laws, executive by-laws, and ministerial decrees with respect to SPS issues are available at the Ministry of Environment and Water's website.[42] The UAE applies the GCC laws on veterinary quarantine and plant quarantine, which were implemented by ministerial resolutions and by-laws and apply at the federal level.[43]

76. In addition to federal laws, executive by-laws and ministerial decrees, each emirate has the authority to issue regulations on SPS measures to implement federal laws and regulations. Also, each emirate has its own authority responsible for SPS issues. For instance, the Abu Dhabi Food Control Authority (ADFCA) is responsible for the emirate's food safety and agriculture, including animal health.[44]

77. Under Federal Law No. 5 of 1979 on agricultural quarantine, all plants and plant products entering the UAE are subject to quarantine. Plants and plant products in transit are subject to plant quarantine regulations and must stay in quarantine centres for at least seven days. It is prohibited to introduce plants and plant products affected with pests before their disinfection. Federal Law No. 5 of 1979 specifies insects and diseases that may not enter the UAE. In general, it is prohibited to import living insects, bacteria, virus, parasites, and agricultural materials infected by any pests without previous authorization from the relevant authority. To protect plant and animal health and the environment, the Minister in charge, may at any point prohibit or restrict the importation, sale, cultivation, propagation or movement of any plant, soil or any item that can spread a pest. In these cases, the Minister must issue an Administrative Decision to enforce the restriction or import prohibition.

---

[40] Articles 2, 6, and 7 of Technical Regulation UAE.S GSO 9/2007 (Labelling Of Pre-packaged Foodstuffs).

[41] Ministry of Environment and Water online information. Viewed at: http://uaeagricent.moew.gov.ae/msps/index_e.htm.

[42] Ministry of Environment and Water online information. Viewed at: http://uaeagricent.moew.gov.ae/msps/index_e.htm.

[43] Ministerial Resolution No. 248 of 2003 issuing the Implementing Regulation of the Law (Regulation) on agricultural quarantine in the GCC states, and Ministerial Decree No. (460) of 2001, concerning the executive by-law of the veterinary quarantine in the GCC states.

[44] Law No. 02 of 2008 in respect of food within the Emirate of Abu Dhabi, and food hygiene throughout the food chain, Regulation No. (6) of 2010 of the Abu Dhabi Food Control Authority.

Table III.6
Rules and regulations related to SPS issues

Federal Law No. (5) of 1979 concerning agricultural quarantine
Federal Law No. (6) of 1979 concerning veterinary quarantine
Federal law No. (6) of 1992 concerning the amendment of some provisions of the Federal Law No. (5) of 1979 regarding agricultural quarantine
Federal Law No. (7) of 1992 on the amendment of some provisions of the Federal Law No. (6) of 1979 regarding veterinary quarantine
Federal Law No. (38) of 1992 regarding the establishment of nurseries and regulating of production, importing and circulation of seedlings
Federal Law No. (39) of 1992 concerning production, importing and circulation of fertilizers and agricultural conditioners
Federal Law No. (41) of 1992 concerning pesticides
Federal Law No. (23) of 1999 regarding the exploitation, protection and development of the living aquatic resources in the waters of the State of the United Arab Emirates
Ministerial Decision No. (434) of 2001 concerning veterinary medicine stores
Ministerial Decree No. (458) of 2001 concerning the Convention on International Trade in Endangered Species of Wild Fauna and Flora (CITES)
Ministerial Decree No. (460) of 2001, concerning the Executive By-law of Veterinary Quarantine in the Cooperation Council for the Arab States of the Gulf
Federal Law No. (10) of 2002 on practicing the veterinary medicine profession
Federal Law No. (11) of 2002 concerning regulating and controlling international trade in endangered species of wild fauna and flora
Federal Law No. (223) of 2002 concerning importation of honey bees
Ministerial Decree No. (170) of 2003 concerning issuance of the executive by-law of the Federal Law No. (10) of 2002 regarding the practicing of veterinary profession
Ministerial Decree No. (255) of 2003 concerning investigation procedures of infectious abortion disease (brucellosis)
Ministerial Decree No. (383) of 2005 on adopting precautionary measures to avoid the infection of bird flu in the country
Ministerial Decree No. (44) of 2006 on banning importation of all kinds of live, tamed, wild, ornamental birds, their products and their offal from the Republic of Nigeria
Ministerial Decree No. (45) of 2006 on banning importation of all hoofed, live animals, and their products from some provinces in Argentina
Ministerial Decree No. (90) of 2006 on banning importation of all kinds of live, tamed, wild, ornamental birds, their products and their offal from the Republic of Albania
Ministerial Decree No. (91) of 2006 on banning importation of all kinds of live, tamed, wild, ornamental birds, their products and their offal from the State of Cameron
Ministerial Decree No. (96) of 2006 on banning importation of all kinds of birds, live, slaughtered, tamed, wild, bred in captivity, their products and their offal from the Republic of Niger
Ministerial Decree No. (112) of 2006 concerning banning importation of all kinds of live, slaughtered, domestic, wild, bred in captivity birds, and products and offals from Burkina Faso
Ministerial Decree No. (175) of 2006 on banning importation of all species of live, domestic, wild ornamental birds, their products and offal from Fuon Town in Denmark
Ministerial Decree No. (276) of 2006 concerning banning importation of all kinds of live, domestic, slaughtered, wild, ornamental birds, their products and offal from Alava province in Spain

Source: Information based on UAE Environmental and Agricultural Information Centre online information. Viewed at: http://uaeagricent.moew.gov.ae/RULES_REGULATIONS/rules_regulations_e.stm.

78. The Ministry of Environment and Water issues requirements and conditions for the importation (exportation) of plants and plant products prior to shipment of the consignment, for the exporting country. No agricultural consignments may be introduced in the UAE without a sanitary or phytosanitary certificate issued by the relevant authority in the country of origin, certified by the UAE Embassy. All imports (exports) of plants and plant products are subject to control and inspection. If an imported item presents any risk of introducing or spreading pests, in the absence of an appropriate treatment, the merchandise may be re-exported or destroyed.

79. The Department of Veterinary Quarantine in the Ministry of Environment and Water must authorize the importation of animals and their products, animal feeds, and additives. Under Federal Law No. 6 of 1979 on veterinary quarantine, as amended, the introduction of imported live animals, meat, animal products, and animal residues that have not undergone quarantine measures is

prohibited. Imported animals, meat, animal products, and animal residues may enter only through specific border crossing points. Importers of live animals and animal products require a licence issued by the competent veterinary body. Imports of live animals, meat, animal products, and animal residues also require: an official veterinary certificate from the country of origin; a report of the captain of the vessel transporting them attesting that the animals did not enter into contact with sick animals; a certificate of origin certified by the UAE Embassy; a certificate attesting that the animals were slaughtered following the Islamic method; and a certificate attesting that the animal or animal products are free from radiation. Consignments of animals and their products are retained for observation and to conduct the necessary tests prior to entry. Live animals imported to be slaughtered are quarantined. Importation of vaccines and serums without prior authorization is prohibited.

80. All animals and animal consignments in transit are subject to control and inspection. The veterinary authority has the right to confiscate and destroy any consignment that upon examination would appear to cause harm to human health. Sperm used for industrial insemination and hen eggs for hatching may be imported only if accompanied by an attested certificate of origin that they stem from animals free from disease.

81. The Ministry of Environment and Water regulates the importation of food. All shipments of food are visually inspected to ensure compliance with labelling and shelf-life regulations. Imported and locally produced food products are treated equally regarding food safety regulations and labelling requirements. Food products may also be subject to random laboratory testing at the time of importation and at the point of sale, except for edible oils and baby food, which are subject to 100% testing. These shipments are stored under bond (for about 7 to 10 days) until the laboratory results are given. If the food imported is found unfit for human consumption it will either be destroyed or returned to the country of origin within 30 days, according to the importer's preference, and, depending on the severity of the infraction, fines may be levied.

82. The UAE enforces Gulf Standard No. 150/1993, Part I, which regulates shelf-life duration for approximately 120 food products, including labelling requirements. A product must have at least half of its shelf-life remaining at the time of importation. Under specific circumstances some plant and animal imports may require a statement that the products are not contaminated by radiation.

83. The UAE notified to the WTO the GCC Guide for Control on Imported Foods, which has not yet been implemented.[45] The guide describes the requirements that the exporting country and the importing GCC countries must follow to assure the safety of imported food. It provides a list of the animal and plant health certificates needed, and aims at harmonizing the requirements and procedures to import food amongst GCC members. According to the authorities, the new requirements are based on risk analysis and conform to international standards including the Codex Alimentarius, the World Organization for Animal Health (OIE), and the International Plant Protection Convention (IPPP), particularly where no GCC requirements are available.

(3) MEASURES DIRECTLY AFFECTING EXPORTS

(i) Procedures

84. Exports must be cleared at Customs, which requires a customs declaration and other documentation (i.e. international air waybill and commercial invoice) issued by the Ministry of Economy as well as by the various chambers of commerce in the respective emirates.[46] Specific

[45] WTO document G/SPS/N/ARE/22, 6 June 2011.

[46] Commercial invoices must include: complete shipper and consignee information, the quantity of the goods exported, a complete description of the goods, the value of each of the commodities in the shipment, the

export permits or licences are required for commodities subject to export controls, for instance under CITES. Exports of meat, seeds, fruit, vegetables, and marine goods require phytosanitary certificates.

85. Imported goods may be re-exported under specific circumstances within 180 days of importation; shipments must be inspected before re-export.[47] Reimbursement of the duties is possible within 30 days of re-export.

(ii) Export taxes, charges, and levies

86. In general the UAE does not apply export taxes, charges, and levies. However, since 2004 exports of steel scrap have been subject to an export tax of AED 250 per tonne.[48]

(iii) Export prohibitions, restrictions, and licensing

87. Exports are prohibited or restricted on safety, security, environmental, and moral grounds, and to ensure compliance with international treaties and conventions. Prohibited exports include: psychotropic substances; endangered fish and wildlife species; items that are offensive to Muslim culture; items that cause corruption and disorder; and irradiated food products.

88. Licenses are required for exports of dual-use goods (goods that may be used in both military and civilian application). Licence requirements depend on an item's technical characteristics, the destination, the end-use, end-user, and other activities of the end-user. Export licences are also required for: controlled substances and precursor chemicals, endangered fish and wildlife species (Ministry of Environment and Water), defence and nuclear material, fuel, and drugs and medical devices.

(iv) Export support

89. During the period under review the UAE made no notifications to the WTO Committee on Agriculture regarding subsidies.[49] In accordance with Articles 25.1 and 25.2 of the Agreement on Subsidies and Countervailing Measures and Article XVI:1 of the GATT 1994, the UAE notified the Committee on Subsidies and Countervailing Measures that the UAE does not grant or maintain any subsidy within the meaning of Articles 1.1 and 2 of the Agreement, or that operates directly or indirectly to increase exports from or reduce imports into its territory within the meaning of Article XVI:1 of the GATT 1994. However, the last notification was made in 2000.[50]

90. The UAE has free-trade-zone (FTZ) regime, which was established in 1980 to attract foreign capital by offering incentives. In contrast to the general investment regime, which places limitations on foreign investment, foreign ownership in firms established in an FTZ may be 100%, and investors are exempt from paying corporate taxes for 15 years, renewable for a further 15 years. Additionally, goods are imported into an FTZ duty free. Companies located in the FTZs are exempted from agency/distributorship, sponsorship, and national ownership requirements.

91. Each free zone is governed by an independent FTZ authority which is responsible for issuing FTZ operating licences and assisting companies to establish their business in the FTZ. Investors may

---

country of origin for each of the commodities in the shipment, currency type, and signature of shipper with date and title.

[47] GCC Customs Law Article 95.

[48] Cabinet Ministerial Decision No. 262/4 of 2004.

[49] WTO CRN database.

[50] WTO document G/SCM/N/38/ARE, G/SCM/N/48/ARE, G/SCM/N/60/ARE, 18 April 2000.

either register a new company in the form of a Free Zone Establishment (FZE) or establish a branch or representative office of their existing or parent company based within the UAE or abroad in the FTZ. An FZE is a limited liability company governed by the rules and regulations of the free zone in which it is established. Under Federal Law No. 15 of 1998, the provisions of the Commercial Companies Law (CCL) do not apply to FZEs, provided that the free zones have special provisions regulating such companies. Each free zone has its own regulations.

92. Goods prohibited from entering the UAE may not enter an FTZ.[51] Other products prohibited from FTZs include: flammable goods, except fuels necessary for the operation of industries; radioactive materials; arms, ammunition, and explosives, of any kind, except those licensed by the competent authorities; narcotic drugs and derivatives thereof; and any good prohibited from entering the country. Customs officials may inspect the FTZ to detect the presence of any prohibited goods.

93. Imported goods may be transported from one FTZ to another without payment of taxes. However, once goods are taken out of the free zones into a Customs Office, they are treated as foreign goods even if they incorporate local raw materials. Goods imported from the free zones into the UAE are treated as foreign goods and hence subject to duties and any other charges. There is no limit regarding the percentage of FTZ products that may be sold in the national territory, provided that import duties are paid. To import products from an FTZ to the national territory an agent is needed.

94. Most FTZs are located near major ports and have large warehousing and storage facilities available to facilitate trade. The FTZs have been successful in attracting a large number of companies and foreign direct investment to the UAE, as well as expanding net non-oil exports. In September 2009 (latest available information) there were 26 FTZs operating in the UAE, with investments of US$4 billion. FTZs produce goods and provide services. In 2010, the volume of total trade (exports plus imports) in UAE free zones grew by 23% year on year, to AED 352.8 billion, of which imports accounted for AED 201.4 billion, and exports and re-exports accounted for AED 151.4 billion. In 2010, the major exports from FTZs were telephones and reception apparatus (HS84.43, 85.25, 85.27, and 85.28), and the major markets were Saudi Arabia and Iran; in 2009 the major markets were China and India.[52]

95. The Jebel Ali Free Zone Authority (Jafza), built around Dubai's Jebel Ali Port, is one of the largest and fastest growing export processing zones, as well as an important trans-shipment centre. The authorities have indicated that over 6,000 businesses from over 110 countries operate at Jafza: some three-quarters are involved in trading, warehousing, and distribution; 20% in manufacturing; and the rest in services. Jafza functions as a commercial organization but is supported financially by its only shareholder, the Government of Dubai, to which it submits quarterly performance reports. A number of other FTZs are dedicated to specific services subsectors, including Dubai Internet City, Dubai Media City, Dubai Health Care City, and Knowledge Village. Twelve FTZs are under development, and Dubai has announced the launch of several more.

96. The UAE does not have a duty drawback system in place; however, any customs duties "taxes" collected on the imports are totally or partially refunded if the good is re-exported.

(v) Export finance, insurance, and guarantees

97. During most of the period under review exporters had access to funding from the Emirates Industrial Bank (EIB), through the export credit facility. Loans were provided for up to 80% of the value of the export contract, as long as the value of the loan did not exceed 7% of the paid-up capital

---

[51] Each emirate may have its own list.

[52] Federal Customs Authority (2010) and (2011b).

and reserves of the EIB for a single project or 14% for a group of projects. Loans were granted until the exporter was paid. The exporter could be the actual manufacturer or an agent. To be eligible, the operation needed to have a minimum 51% UAE or GCC ownership and to be established in the UAE.[53] According to the authorities, exporters did not use this facility during the period under review.

98. The Export Credit Insurance Company of the Emirates (PSC-ECIE), wholly owned by the Government of Dubai, is the only trade credit insurer with in the UAE. The PSC-ECIE offers short-term credit insurance of not more than 180 days, which may cover up to 90% of the gross invoice value. However, in certain cases, credits for a longer term, of up to 360 days, may also be considered. The risks covered include: buyer's insolvency; non-payment; delay in payment, due to the imposition of foreign exchange controls in the purchasing country; cancellation or imposition of import licence in the purchasing country or export licence in the UAE; and political risk.[54]

(vi) Export promotion and marketing assistance

99. Export promotion and marketing assistance is the responsibility of the federal authorities as well as of each emirate.

100. The Dubai Export Development Corporation, is an autonomous organization established in 2006[55], to facilitate exports.[56] The services provided by EDC include: information about existing markets and new market opportunities; advice to first time exporters; identification of market development opportunities for non-traditional exports; organization of local exhibitions and trade fairs and participation in international ones; assistance in identifying new export opportunities, including matching buyers with exporters; and provision of legal and regulatory advice to assist exporters.

(4) Measures Affecting Production and Trade

(i) Incentives

101. The UAE's most recent "new and full" notification regarding subsidies dates back to 2000 (section (3)(iv) above). At that time the UAE notified that no subsidies were granted.[57]

102. Under Federal Law No. 1 of 1979, the Council of Ministers may provide certain incentives to industrial undertakings. However, according to the authorities these provisions are not applied. The only incentive available to all licensed industrial undertakings is the granting of the right to import duty free all materials included in the industrial project's licence.

103. The UAE is planning to enact a Foreign Investment Law, which will provide further incentives and benefits to foreign investors.

104. At the federal level, the Emirate Industrial Bank (EIB), a specialized state-owned institution founded in 1982 to promote the economic diversification in the UAE, provided financing for the industrial sector during the review period. At the time of completing this report (November 2011),

[53] EIB online information. Viewed at: http://www.eib.ae/index.php.

[54] ECIE online information. Viewed at: http://www.ecie.ae/who-we-are.html.

[55] Law No. 10/2006, 1 May 2006.

[56] DEDC online information. Viewed at: http://www.dedc.gov.ae/en/2/.

[57] WTO document G/SCM/N/38/ARE, G/SCM/N/48/ARE, G/SCM/N/60/ARE, 18 April 2000.

the EIB was undergoing a process of reform and was being transformed into the Emirates Development Bank (EDB), created by Federal Law No. 7 of 2011.

105. The aims of the EIB were to promote economic growth in the UAE through economic diversification, by assisting in the development of the industrial structure. EIB credits were directed towards both new and existing companies and targeted mainly private and semi-private companies engaged in industrial activities. To be eligible, the project required a minimum of 51% UAE or GCC equity participation and had to be located in the UAE.

106. The EIB's loan amount for any project could not exceed 20% of the bank's subscribed capital and reserves or 70% of the project's total cost (including three months working capital), whichever was lower. The borrower was charged an annual interest rate of EIBOR plus a profit margin to be determined by the management. In the context of this review, the authorities noted that this translated into rates of 3-5%. The EBI provided short (less than 2 years), medium (2-5 years), and long-run credits. The grace periods could be between six months and three years. The withdrawal period was of 12 months. In its lending, the EBI gave priority to industries that employed modern technology and adopted a capital-intensive approach; industries that depended on local resources (capital, energy) and marketed their products locally and abroad; and import substitution industries.[58]

107. The authorities indicated that during 2006-10 an average of 29 projects were financed each year, and that most were replacement projects, rather than new investments. The EIB's annual average budget amounted to some AED 321 million.

(ii) Role of state-owned enterprises, and privatization

108. In October 1996, the UAE notified the WTO that it did not maintain any state-trading enterprises within the meaning of Article XVII of the GATT.[59] However, a number of state-owned companies appear to be engaged in international trade, for example in the hydrocarbon subsector. Wholly or partially government-owned companies that engage in trade include: Etisalat; the Abu Dhabi National Oil Company (ADNOC); the Dubai Petroleum Company; the Emirates National Oil Company; the Sharjah Oil Refining Company; and the Dubai Aluminium Company.

109. In general, although the Government has an open approach towards the economy, the federal state or the governments of the emirates are involved in a number of important economic sectors, and their participation in the economy is considerable. Privatization has been limited by the foreign ownership limit of 49% maintained outside of free zones. The only significant steps towards privatization since the UAE's WTO Membership in 1996 have been in Abu Dhabi's electricity and gas subsectors (Chapter IV(3)), although Abu Dhabi has also initiated plans for the sale of certain companies in the manufacturing sector. Some of the state-owned companies have significant presence abroad through foreign investments. Some of these companies (e.g. in electricity and air transport) act as both operators and regulators of their respective sectors.

110. Among the main state-owned enterprises are: (a) the Abu-Dhabi Investment Authority (ADIA), which is one of the largest investment funds in the world and has several investment arms abroad[60]; (b) the Abu Dhabi Investment Council (ADIC), a joint-stock company, spin-off from

[58] Emirates Industrial Bank (EBI) (2011).

[59] WTO document G/STR/N/1/ARE, 14 October 1996.

[60] ADIA was originally established in 1967 as Abu Dhabi's Financial Investments Board, under the Department of Finance. In 1976, the Government of Abu-Dhabi decided to make ADIA an independent institution. Following a period of organization, ADIA started investing in private equity in 1989. In 1998, ADIA started investing in inflation-indexed bonds. ADIA continued to expand its scope of activities and, in

ADIA, which specializes in providing investment and corporate finance in addition to advisory services, and invests in private equity, real estate, asset management, and infrastructure. ADIC owns some 73% of the equity of the National Bank Abu Dhabi; (c) the Emirates Investment Authority (EIA), a federal fund established in November 2007 and mandated to manage the sovereign wealth of the UAE Federal Government; (d) the International Petroleum Investment Company (IPIC), an Abu Dhabi state enterprise established in 1984 and responsible for all foreign investments in the oil and chemicals sector[61]; (e) the Investment Corperation of Dubai (ICD), which owns Emaar, Dubai Holding, and Borse Dubai, constituted in 2006 and which is Dubai's sovereign wealth fund and is composed of several operating investment companies; (f) Dubai World, which owns Nakheel, DP World, Drydocks World, Economic Zones World, and Istithmar; (g) Mubadala, a public joint-stock company established in October 2002 and wholly owned by the Emirate of Abu Dhabi, which seeks to diversify Abu Dhabi's economy. Mubadala comprises nine separate business units: energy, industry, aerospace, information and communication technology, services ventures, real estate and hospitality infrastructure, healthcare, and acquisitions; and (h) the Investment and Development Office (IDO) in Ras Al Khaima, set up in January 2004 with the aim of identifying new investment opportunities and facilitating setting up new businesses in Ras Al Khaimah.

(iii) Competition policy and regulatory issues

111. The UAE does not have a competition law, but the authorities noted that a draft UAE competition law is under consideration by the Ministerial Cabinet. The Ministry of Economy has the mandate to develop and implement the competition law.

112. The draft law covers three major areas: restrictive agreements, abuse of a dominant position; and mergers and acquisitions. It includes a general clause that allows the competition authority to exempt anti-competitive practices and agreements if such practices and agreements help to improve the production or distribution of goods or services or to promote technical or economic progress. The violation of the law may result in the imposition of fines. The authorities indicated that the law will apply to all enterprises operating in the UAE with the exception of state-owned enterprises and SMEs, and enterprises operating in sectors that are subject to specific competition regulations (e.g. telecommunications, the financial sector, petroleum and gas, and distribution of water and gas).

113. A draft GCC competition law is also under consideration by the GCC member states. This law would only cover anti-competitive practices arising from cross-border trade between GCC member states. The authorities have noted that the law will apply to all enterprises engaged in commercial activities in the GCC.

114. There are no price controls in the UAE. The Ministry of Economy only monitors the price of food products.

(iv) Government procurement

115. The UAE is not a party or an observer to the WTO Plurilateral Agreement on Government Procurement. Government procurement continues to favour local companies and suppliers, as foreign participation is limited by nationality requirements. However, there is a strong reliance on foreign

2007, started investing in infrastructure. In 2008 ADIA was appointed to co-Chair with the IMF the International Working Group of Sovereign Wealth Funds. ADIA is a founding member of the International Forum of Sovereign Wealth Funds (IFSWF). The extent and amount of ADIA's investments are not disclosed.

[61] The IPIC portfolio includes investments in Austria, Egypt, Germany, Japan, Oman, Pakistan, Portugal, Spain, South Korea, and the UAE. Its investments are in areas such as downstream hydrocarbon operations, petrochemical plants, pipelines, power utilities, and shipping.

companies, and companies established in free zones, particularly for major projects for which local expertise is not always available. In this case, the foreign company or company operating in the free zone must open a branch in the UAE and employ a local agent. For defence contracts, an offset programme is in place. Given the federal nature of the UAE, the majority of procurement (by value) is at emirate level. The importance of the public sector, including state-owned companies, means that public purchases are particularly large in relation to total expenditure. National accounts data show that consolidated government expenditures on goods and services amounted to AED 11.1 billion (US$3 billion), or 3.7% of the UAE's GDP in 2010. These figures exclude purchases in the context of development projects (AED 1.2 billion), or procurement by government bodies, estimated at AED 13.8 billion (US$3.8 billion), or 4.6% of GDP.

116. The main regulations with respect to federal government procurement are contained in the Federal Regulation of Conditions of Purchases, Tenders and Contracts, Financial Order No. 16 of 1975 (the Public Tenders Law), Ministerial Decision No. 20 of 2000 on the administration of the contracts system, as well as Amendment Decision No. 90 of 2009. These regulations do not apply to purchases by the Ministry of Defence or acquisitions and tenders of the State Security System, which are conducted pursuant to Decree No. 12 of 1986 of the Deputy Supreme Commander of the Armed Forces (the Armed Forces Procurement Regulations). Also excluded from the scope of the regulations are purchases for any "projects" handled by the Permanent Project Committee, as well as any project explicitly excluded from the ambit of the regulation by a resolution or law passed by the Council of Ministers. The Public Tenders Law and the decisions relate to federal government procurement and not to procurement by the governments of the individual emirates, which have their own procurement systems, although these generally follow the federal regulations.

117. Procurement is decentralized. The federal ministries and governmental authorities are authorized to contract directly their procurement, including purchases, imports of materials, works or service contracting. Each ministry audits its own procurement process and reports to the Ministry of Finance.

118. Under the Decision of 2000, the main modality for purchases of products, services, and construction works is "general tender" (open tender). Under the general tender, bids are to be advertised publicly. The use of other tendering modalities is allowed depending on the circumstances, and, in practice, most procurement takes place under modalities other than the general tender (see below).

119. Under the "practical participation" method, a committee requests quotations from selected contractors without any tendering process. This method is used: (a) when the product is only available from a certain dealer or agent; (b) the product required is hard to describe in detail; (c) for works that require technical assistance or a specialist to be appointed; (d) for urgent procurement of products or contracting works; (e) when the procurement requires confidentiality due to public interest (the approval of the relevant Minister must be obtained in this case); (f) for low-cost products, not commensurate with the cost of preparing a general tender; (g) in case of products produced under monopolistic conditions; (h) when two or more suppliers have provided similar price and condition quotations in the tendering process; (i) for products or works that have already been tendered under the general tender method, but have received only one quotation or none, or when the quotation that has been provided has not been accepted and it is not possible to open another tendering process; (j) for the completion of the remaining work in a contract that has been terminated before completion. The "limited tender" method is generally used when only a limited number of suppliers is available; in this case, bids are requested from a list of pre-approved suppliers. The "direct order" method is used in exceptional circumstances, such as the absence of competitive markets (e.g. monopoly).

120. The vast majority of procurement takes place under practical participation procedures. In 2010, some 60% of total procurement was under this method, 20% was under the general tender method, while 10% of procurement was under limited tender, and 10% under direct order.

121. The UAE procurement regulations contain nationality restrictions. Any bidder must be a GCC citizen or a company with maximum foreign equity of 49%. This must be proven by an official, notarized contract showing the partnership shares in the company capital, with the exception of contracts ratified abroad or that take place through correspondence. The bidder must also be registered in one of the municipalities or chambers of commerce and industry or one of the economic departments in the UAE, or in the Commercial Agents Registry of the Ministry of Economy in the case of an agent. The bidder is required to be registered in the Suppliers and Contractors Registry at Ministry of Finance for tenders and auctions invited by federal ministries and departments. In some cases, tenders may be exempted from the nationality conditions and opened to foreign companies and establishments, mainly when these are the only available suppliers, or for foreign companies established in free zones. In these cases, the foreign company must open a branch and employ a local service agent (Chapter II(5)).

122. The UAE's e-procurement system continued to develop during the review period. A procurement notice is usually posted electronically for one month by the Ministry of Finance or the relevant ministry, and is published twice in two widely disseminated newspapers. Access to the electronic system requires registration with the Ministry of Finance and payment of AED 1,000 the first year and AED 500 for renewal.[62] The notice includes a description of goods and services to be procured, the authority receiving tenders, the period of validity of tenders, and the deadline for submission of tenders. Specifications and conditions of the procurement must be in Arabic but, if necessary, they may be translated into one or more foreign languages.

123. For tenders above AED 100,000, bidders must place a bid bond of 5% of the bid value with a UAE bank; this bond acts as an initial guarantee, in accordance with Article 32 of the Decision. The letter of initial guarantee is returned to non-accepted bidders automatically upon expiry of the tender or earlier if the final guarantee has been collected from the successful bidder. The evaluation of tenders is done by the Tenders committee of the relevant procuring ministry. Tenders Committees are expected to assess the tenders and select the "best and lowest" bid. The selected company must provide a performance bond, generally of 10% of the bid value, to finalize the contract. Majority-government-owned companies are exempt from the two bond obligations.

124. Tenders committees must post their procedures in an official *procès verbal* stating all the facts of the tender, its remarks, and recommendations. Final approval of the tender is granted by different authorities, depending on the value of the tender. Approval by the Chairman of the Tenders Committee is required for tenders of up to AED 3 million; tenders between AED 3 million and AED 10 million must be approved by the undersecretary of the relevant ministry, and tenders above AED 10 million by the competent minister.

125. There is no standard system for suppliers to challenge the award of a contract. In accordance with the Decision, a committee formed within the Ministry of Finance analyses claims submitted by the bidders regarding faults in the tenders or in decisions by the tenders committee.

126. Defence purchases are centralized at the federal level and conducted by the Ministry of Defence. Under the UAE offset policy, all purchases by the UAE armed forces or elements thereof are subject to the offset obligation. In general, all contracts with a cumulative value exceeding

[62] UAE Government online information. Viewed at: www.uae.gov.ae and egov.uae.gov.ae (Arabic only).

US$10 million in any five-year period are subject to an "offset programme", by the UAE Offset Program Bureau (OPB). The OPB was created in 1992, and is mandated to set up joint ventures, as well as to invest in commercial, industrial, financial, and educational projects and to create investment funds in the UAE and abroad. In 2007, the OPB created a fully-owned subsidiary, Tawazun Holding, to contribute substantially in diversifying the UAE's oil-dominated economy by focusing on the development and expansion of selected emerging companies across a wide range of industrial and commercial areas. The OPB is also entitled to require offsets on other than military public purchases, but does not do this at present. OPB purchases are conducted through direct negotiation with contractors.

127. The procurement and offset processes start in parallel. A defence contractor is informed of the requirement to enter into an offset agreement during the bidding process; the contract award process is linked to the signing of the agreement. Suppliers (domestic or foreign) that sign a defence procurement contract must undertake to set up a joint-venture with the private sector that will generate returns equal to an agreed-upon share of the contract, over a specified period. An investment agreement is reached on an "offset programme" with each foreign defence supplier. Under the programme, the foreign company undertakes to "fulfil its offset obligation", i.e. it is required to add economic and commercial value to the UAE's economy equivalent to 60% of the supply contract value. The level of obligation does not directly correspond to investments made in an offset venture but to the value created by an offset venture in terms of contributions and profits generation over time. The UAE Offsets Group (UOG) measures the output of an offset project through its profits. Typically, all defence contractors are expected to fulfil their offset obligations over a period of seven years. Certain projects may be granted an additional grace period depending on the level of complexity, sophistication, and infrastructure requirements.

128. A certain level of obligation is expected at the end of each year, specifically: 5%, 10%, 10%, 15%, 15%, 20%, 25% in each of the seven years, respectively.[63] Investors may also use a hybrid programme consisting of input and output-based activities to generate the expected value added. Input credit generating activities are limited to 30% of the total contribution, while output credit generating activities should not be less than 70% of the value added created. In case of non-performance of the obligations, damages of 8.5% of the unfulfilled portion of the obligation are charged.

129. Offset projects cover a wide range of economic activities, including advertising, fish farming, language centres, shipbuilding, leasing and financial services, and medical services. In the future, to align with the Abu Dhabi Vision 2030, the OPB will be focusing on building capabilities in the manufacture of end-user products (systems) and all their components.[64]

130. Apart from the federal regulations, each emirate has specific provisions regulating government procurement activities. In Abu Dhabi, Law No. 4 of 1977 regulates contracts between a foreign company and an Abu Dhabi government department. Under the law, only local companies or local agents of foreign companies that are registered in Abu Dhabi may submit tenders. A bid bond

[63] Offset Program Bureau online information. Viewed at: http://www.offset.ae/EN/Menu/Index.aspx?MainMenuID=&MenuID=84&mnu=&LeftImage=62420101106458731250.jpg&TopImage=62420101106459356250.gif&division=Cat&CatName=Offset+Policy+Guidelines&PriID=34&Rmnu=OUR+PROGRAM&URL=&CatID=&SubName=.

[64] Offset Program Bureau online information. Viewed at: http://www.offset.ae/EN/Menu/Index.aspx?MainMenuID=&MenuID=85&mnu=&LeftImage=62420101106458731250.jpg&TopImage=62420101106459356250.gif&division=Cat&CatName=Area+of+Focus&PriID=34&Rmnu=OUR+PROGRAM&URL=&CatID=&SubName=.

must accompany all tenders for government contracts, and the bond is automatically forfeited if a bid is withdrawn before the date for the opening of the tenders.

131. Dubai Law No. 6 of 1997 contains provisions regulating contracts between Dubai government departments and companies, including the preparation of tender documents, issuing the tender, bid-bond requirements, and performance-bond requirements. The Dubai Government also requires a foreign company to employ a service agent. Certain governmental purchases may be handled electronically (since 2000).[65]

(v) Intellectual property rights

(a) Overview

132. The intellectual property regime in the UAE is still developing; the first intellectual property (IP) laws were enacted in 1992 and replaced or amended in 2002. Domestic laws relating to intellectual property rights protection are supplemented with laws issued by the Cooperation Council for the Arab States of the Gulf. The authorities indicated that the UAE is currently drafting legislation to protect layout-designs (topographies) of integrated circuits and undisclosed information. The UAE does not have laws to protect geographical indications.

133. The UAE has been a member of WIPO since 1974, and is a member of: the Paris Convention (1996); the Patent Cooperation Treaty (1999); the Berne Convention (2004); the Rome Convention (2004); the WIPO Copyright Treaty (WCT) (2004); and the WIPO Performances and Phonograms Treaty (WPPT) (2005). The UAE is party to the Gulf Cooperation Patent Treaty.

134. The Ministry of Economy is the federal authority responsible for implementing and enforcing IP laws regarding patents, industrial designs, and copyright, and it is the UAE contact point in the WTO.[66] Enforcement at the border is mainly dealt with by the Federal Customs Authority. The Ministry of Justice is responsible at the federal level, for any IP related matters referred up by local courts.

(b) Patents

135. The Patent and Design Law No. 17 of 2002 provides for the protection of patents and industrial designs. Patents are granted for any invention that is the result of an innovative idea, or for an innovative improvement on a patented invention, whether in relation to a new industrial product, an industrial process or method or to the application of a known industrial process or method. The term of patent protection is 20 years (non-renewable) from the date of filing the application.

136. The Patent and Design Law extends protection to innovations in all fields of technology, including pharmaceuticals and agricultural chemical products, and it covers both products and processes. Micro-organisms are patentable. However, exceptions from patentability exist for: plant and animal research, or biological processes for the production of plants or animals, with the exception of microbiological processes and products; scientific principles and discoveries; diagnostic, therapeutic, and surgical methods for the treatment of humans or animals; inventions related to national defence; or inventions that would be contrary to public order and morality.

[65] In the Emirate of Dubai, Tejari.com is used to advertise public purchases of information technology equipment.

[66] WTO document IP/N/3/Rev.4/Add.3,12 September 2000.

137. Law No. 17 of 2002 enables a patent holder to prevent others from manufacturing, importing, offering for sale, selling, using or otherwise keeping for the purpose of selling or using the product, or using the method.

138. Patent applications must be filed with the UAE Patent Office. Applications are examined with respect to compliance with formalities and patentability under the Patent Law, including novelty, inventiveness, and industrial applicability. In case of refusal, an applicant has the right to appeal to the Committee in the Patent Office. Accepted applications are published in the *Official Gazette*, and any interested party has the right to appeal to the Committee within 60 days of publication. In the absence of opposition, the letters-patent or the utility certificate is issued.

139. The law allows for the granting of compulsory licences, where the right-holder does not satisfy the stipulated working requirements within three years from the grant date of the patent.[67] Compulsory licences may also be granted if exploitation of the patent is stopped for two consecutive years, or if the owner refuses to license it voluntarily under a contract. To obtain a compulsory licence, an applicant must prove that efforts have been made to obtain a licence from the patent owner on reasonable conditions. No compulsory licences have been granted during the period under review. There are no provisions on parallel imports of patented products and there has been no jurisprudence in the UAE in this regard.

(c) Industrial designs

140. Industrial designs are protected by the Patent and Design Law (Law No. 17 of 2002). Industrial designs must be registered to be protected. Applications to register a design are filed with the Patent Office once examined for compliance with the law. If accepted, the application is published in the *Official Gazette*. The examination procedure for designs and industrial models is the same as that for patents. There is a 60-day period for any interested party to oppose registration. In the absence of any opposition, a certificate of registration is issued.

141. The term of protection for a design is 10 years. The holder is accorded exclusive rights over imports of any product related to the industrial design, or processing of such a product for the purpose of offering it for sale or selling it. A special register is kept by the Ministry of Economy as per Law No. 31 of 2006.

(d) Copyright and related rights

142. Copyrights and Neighbouring Rights Law No. 7 of 2002, as amended by Federal Law No. 32 of 2006, is the main legislation protecting copyright. The law provides for the exclusive right to exploit, under the rental right, literary works, including computer programs and cinematography work (Table III.7). Copyright protection is in general for 50 years. Registration with the Ministry of Economy is not required for the work to be protected.

143. Registration with the competent authority is optional, but is regarded as the authoritative reference to the copyrighted information. However, non-registration does not mean that the work is not protected.

144. An author's rights are protected for life plus 50 years. Holders of copyrights and neighbouring rights may assign their economic rights to specialized professional societies to administer them, or authorize other bodies to practice these rights.

---

[67] The authorities have indicated that the working of a patent refers only to commercial exploitation and does not include importation.

Table III.7
Protected works under the Copyright and Neighbouring Rights Law, 2011

- Books, booklets, articles and other literature
- Computer software and applications, databases and similar works defined in a decision to be issued by the Minister
- Lectures, speeches, sermons and other works of similar nature
- Plays, musicals and pantomimes
- Musicals accompanied by dialogue and musicals which are not accompanied by dialogue
- Audio and video work or audio visual work
- Architectural work and architectural plans and drawings
- Work involving drawing, painting, sculpturing, etching, lithography, screen printing, relief and intaglio prints and other similar works of fine art
- Photographic work
- Works of applied art and plastic art
- Charts, maps, plans, 3-D modelling for geographical and topographical applications and architectural design etc.
- Derivative works, subject to the protection afforded to the work(s) upon which they are based. The protection shall extend to the title of the work if created as well as the creative concept devised for broadcast material
- Translations, summaries, editorials, modifications and commentaries which have been carried out with the consent of the author
- Any other works whose means of expression are writing, sound, drawing, photography or movement

Source Federal Law No. 7 of 2002 concerning Copyrights and Neighbouring Rights.

145. Performers and their successors also have literary and economic rights (Table III.8). The economic rights of performers and producers of phonograms are protected for 50 years from the beginning of the calendar year following that in which the performance was accomplished. If the performance was fixed in a phonogram, the period is calculated from the end of the year in which the fixation was made. The rights of broadcasting organizations are protected for 20 years, calculated from the beginning of the calendar year following the year of first transmission.

Table III.8
Protection of neighbouring rights, 2011

Performers enjoy the right to:

- transmit their unfixed performance and communicate it to the public
- fix their performance on a phonogram
- reproduce their fixed performance on a phonogram
- fix live performances on a phonogram for direct or indirect commercial revenue, rental, transmission

Producers of phonograms enjoy the right to:

- prohibit any exploitation of their phonograms by any means without their authorization
- copy, rent, broadcast, or re-broadcast
- disseminate their recordings via wire, wireless, computer or other means

Broadcasting organizations enjoy the right to:

- grant licences for exploitation of their recordings and broadcast programmes
- prohibit any communication of their programmes or recordings to the public without their authorization

Source: Federal Law No. (7) of 2002 concerning copyrights and neighbouring rights.

146. Applications for a compulsory licence for either copying or translating any protected work may be submitted to the Ministry of Economy three years after the date of publication in case of a translation licence and five years for photocopying.

147. There are no provisions on parallel imports in the copyright legislation.

(e) Trade marks

148. Federal Law No. 37 of 1992 on trade marks, as amended by Law No. 19 of 2000 and Law No. 8 of 2002, provides protection for registered trade marks in the UAE. The law includes the definition of trade marks, signs that cannot be registered as trade marks, trade mark registration and cancellation procedures, transfer of ownership and mortgage of trade marks, licensing others to use trade marks, penalties for trade mark law infringement and general and transitory provisions.

149. Federal Law No. 37 defines a trade mark as any distinguishing form of names, words, signatures, letters, figures, graphics, logos, titles, hallmarks, seals, pictures, patterns, announcements, packs or any other marks or group of marks used or intended to be used either to distinguish goods, products or services from whatever sources or to indicate that certain services, goods or products belong to the owner of the trade mark because of their provision, manufacturing, selection or trading. The law also contains provisions on the protection of well-known marks. The trade mark law also specifies signs that may not be registered (Table III.9).

150. Trade marks may be registered with the Ministry of Economy, which is in charge of registration in the UAE. Once an application is filed, it is examined to assess the trade mark's registrability. Applications accepted by the Registrar are published in the *Trade mark Journal* and two local Arabic newspapers. There is a 30-day period for filing an opposition by any interested party. In the absence of opposition, the published trade mark is registered, and a certificate of registration is issued. Approved trade marks are published in the *Trademark Journal* and two Arabic newspapers at the expense of the applicant. Applications for renewal must be submitted during the last year of the protection period. There is a three-month grace-period for late renewal, upon payment of a fine. Renewals are also published in the *Trademark Journal* and in two local Arabic newspapers. Trade mark registration is valid in all the emirates for ten years, renewable for consecutive periods of ten years.

Table III.9
Signs that may not be registered as a trade mark, 2011

- Signs without any distinctive character or property or that use common names of goods, products and services or ordinary drawings or pictures of goods and products
- Signs that offend public morals or are contrary to public order
- Signs using or imitating public symbols, flags and other logos of the UAE or any Arab or international organization or any foreign country without their authorization
- The emblem of the Red Crescent or the Red Cross or any similar symbols or signs or their imitations
- Signs that are identical or similar to symbols with absolutely religious character
- Geographical names if their use can cause confusion about the origin or source of the goods, products or services
- The name, title, image or logo of a third party unless he or his heirs agreed to their use in advance
- Particulars of degrees of honour that do not prove that the applicant is legally entitled thereto
- Signs that may mislead the public or contain false statements or descriptions about the origin or source of products or services, as well as marks that contain a fictitious, imitated or forged trade name.
- Trade marks owned by individuals or legal entities with which any deal is prohibited
- Signs whose registration could result in undervaluation of other products or services distinguished by such signs
- Trade marks that contain words or expression such as Concession, Concessionaire, Registered, Registered Drawing, Copyright, or other similar words and phrases
- National and foreign medals, coins or bank notes
- Trade marks that are merely a translation of a renowned or already registered trade mark if the registration would confuse consumers about the products distinguished by the trade mark

Source: Law No. 8 of 2002.

151. The Ministry may remove a registered trade mark after notifying the concerned party of the reasons for removal. Affected parties may appeal the removal decision in the relevant civil court within 30 days of notification of removal. Trade marks may be cancelled by any interested party who

can prove that the trade mark was not actually used for five consecutive years. There have been no such cases during the period under review.

152. Violations of the trade marks law, such as: forging or imitating a registered trademark, the deliberate use of a forged or imitated trade mark, and the sale, display, promotion or possession (with the intent of selling) of products with a forged, imitated or illegally placed trade mark may lead to imprisonment and/or a fine of at least AED 5,000. A person giving the false impression that he holds a registered trade mark is also subject to imprisonment and a fine.

153. The trade mark law does not contain provisions with respect to parallel imports or to national or international exhaustion of rights. However, the owner of a trade mark may, by a written notarized contract, grant to any person a licence to use the trade mark. The licence has no effect on third parties unless it has been recorded in the Register and published as prescribed in the Executive Regulations. According to the authorities, the trademark law could, as a result, be invoked by the owner of the trade mark to prevent parallel imports; no such case has so far been filed in the UAE.

(f) Enforcement

154. The UAE has implemented programmes to increase awareness regarding IP protection. According to the authorities, this is in order to establish an environment that promotes innovation, which could help attract investment in IP-related areas in the UAE.

155. The laws on copyright, patents and designs, and trade marks provide for measures to prevent violation of intellectual property rights, including preventive seizure, confiscation, removal or destruction of products and equipment, as well as elimination of the effects of the illegal acts, and compensation, and imprisonment in certain instances.

156. The trade marks law defines penalties with regard to counterfeit, imitation, misleading practices, and fraudulent use of registered trade marks. Fines of at least AED 5,000 may be levied, as well as prison sentences of up to three years, depending upon the crime. The copyrights law lays down similar procedures, with minimum detention of two months, fines of AED 10,000-500,000 and/or closure of the premises. Articles 60-62 of the patent and design law also lay down criminal sanctions and monetary penalties in the range of AED 5,000-100,000, according to the crime.

157. Customs is entitled to take measures at the border to prevent any violation of IPRs, in accordance with the above-mentioned laws as well as under customs regulations. These measures may be taken upon demand of the right-holder, based on a judicial order or by the customs authorities on their own initiative.

IV. TRADE POLICIES BY SECTOR

(1) INTRODUCTION

1. The UAE economy continues to be dominated by the oil sector and connected industries. However, attempts are under way to diversify the economy, particularly into the areas of services and manufacturing. The petroleum sector accounted for 31.5% of GDP and 59.5% of export revenues in 2010. The UAE's estimates of proven crude oil reserves are 97.8 billion barrels, equivalent to almost 8.5% of the world's reserves, while production reached 2.32 million barrels/per day in 2010. Some 95% of petroleum production is in the emirate of Abu Dhabi.

2. In accordance with the Constitution[1], natural resources in the UAE are vested in each individual emirate and not with the Federal Government. Foreign equity in projects is determined by the competent authorities of the local government of the emirate where the natural resource is located.

3. Agriculture represents a small share of the UAE's economy, accounting for just 1% of GDP. Total cultivated land has decreased in recent years. Lack of arable land, intense heat, periodic locust swarms, and limited water supplies are the main obstacles to agricultural development in the UAE, which remains a major net food importer. Foreigners, other than GCC nationals, are not allowed to own agricultural land, but may own up to a 49% stake in agri-business companies. Fishing is restricted for UAE and GCC nationals. Notifications to the WTO on agriculture remained pending as at December 2011. The last notification with respect to domestic support dates from 2002, and corresponds to the years 2000 and 2001; the measures notified were exempt from reduction commitments.

4. During the period under review, the UAE has continued to seek to develop its manufacturing sector, in its quest to diversify away from oil. However, some of the main manufacturing industries, such as petrochemicals, remain linked to the oil industry. Nevertheless, this, there have been important developments in aluminium production and pharmaceutical products. As per the GCC Common External Tariff, most manufactured imports face a 5% tariff. However, all materials used in the production of a licensed industrial project enter the UAE duty free.

5. The services sector is experiencing fast growth, particularly in air and maritime transport, telecommunications, and tourism. However, development in the services sector would benefit, in general, from some flexibility in the current foreign investment limitations.

6. In financial services, the emirate of Dubai was particularly affected by the global financial and economic crisis. There was a sharp contraction in equity markets: as a result of the crisis, market capitalization and the general share price index decreased in 2009 and continued falling in 2010. The Emirates Securities and Commodities Authority responded to the crisis by stepping up regulation, as did the Central Bank. Minimum capital adequacy ratios for banks were raised from 10% to 12% in 2010. Other measures adopted to counter the financial crisis included a moratorium on new licences for commercial banks, and placing a limit on the number of branches permitted to licensed foreign banks. The Central Bank also issued guidelines for implementation of the Basel II Capital Accord in November 2009. Locally incorporated banks in the UAE are well capitalized, with a minimum capital-adequacy ratio well above the legal requirement, reaching an average of 21.2% at the end of September 2011.

---

[1] Article 22.

7. Foreign banks must open branches in the UAE to provide services there. In 2010 a limit was imposed on the number of branches they may open; they must not exceed eight branches in the UAE. Subsidiaries of foreign banks are not allowed. Foreign banks are granted national treatment for paid-up capital requirements, but not with respect to the taxation of profits, for which foreign banks are subject to a 20% tax on profits, which is not applied to national banks.

8. National and foreign insurance companies wishing to establish in an emirate must first apply to the Insurance Authority for an establishment procedure, then for licensing. Conditions for the granting of licences include economic needs criteria and the appointment of a minimum number of UAE nationals as staff. Eligible foreign insurance companies may open a branch, appoint a local insurance agent and/or enter into an agency contract with a local insurance agent representing them.

9. Competition in the telecommunications sector remains low; however, since the last review, the monopoly in telephony services has been terminated. Despite this, as a duopoly with relatively high pricing policies, the market could benefit from increased competition.

10. The UAE has one of the world's largest air transport industries. It has five airlines, two of which are major international carriers, and two major airports, one of which is among the busiest in the world (Dubai). The airline industry benefits from the "open skies" policy adopted by the UAE, state-of-the-art civil aviation infrastructure, and competition between the emirates. The authorities are expecting the sector to continue to grow rapidly in the near future through the role of the two main airports and airlines as hubs and transfer carriers. The UAE's domestic market is relatively small.

11. There are ambitious plans to increase the capacity and activities of ports in the UAE. However, despite the policy of granting concession to private service providers in some areas, port management remains a prerogative of the different emirates. As in other service areas, despite coordination to some extent, at the federal level, the fact that each emirate is launching policies in the same area could lead to overcapacity. Further coordination among emirates could assure that investment projects are complementary and lead to a more integrated development policy.

12. Prior to the 2008-09 global financial crisis, the UAE had witnessed a construction boom, which helped sustain the emergence of conglomerates in this sector. However, in the aftermath of the crisis, the construction sector suffered a major downturn, with values falling by 50% in Dubai and 40% in Abu Dhabi. The effects of the crisis were exacerbated by the large number of new units on the market, resulting from the boom, and the reduction in the number of new buyers.

13. Tourism is of growing importance in the UAE; particular efforts have been made to build infrastructure, and there have been several developments in the area. The National Council for Tourism and Antiquities (NCTA) was established in 2008 to help align UAE tourism-related policies at the federal level. However, tourism licences are issued by each emirate. The creation of the NCTA is expected to boost the promotion of tourism.

(2) AGRICULTURE

(i) Features

14. Agriculture represents a small share of the UAE's economy, accounting for just 1% of GDP in 2009 and 0.9% in 2010, and employing around 3.8% of the workforce. Total cultivated land has decreased in recent years, and has been assigned to other uses, due partly to lack of irrigation water. Most of the UAE's cultivated land is in the emirate of Abu Dhabi. Lack of arable land, intense heat, periodic locust swarms, and limited water supplies are the main obstacles to agriculture in the UAE.

15. According to the authorities, total agricultural production increased from 494,000 tonnes in 2005 to 1.25 million tonnes in 2009. The main agricultural products are dates, tomatoes, and fresh vegetables. Livestock production comprises mainly chickens, goats, sheep, camels, and cattle, (Table IV.1).

Table IV.1
Agricultural and livestock production, 2005-10

Production	2005	2006	2007	2008	2009	2010
Crops and livestock primary ('000 tonnes)	1,554	1,526	1,522	1,570	1,513	1,609
Subtotal of items	*1,488*	*1,478*	*1,485*	*1,529*	*1,476*	*1,570*
Dates	760	750	758	758	758	759
Tomatoes	240	229	202	202	202	205
Vegetables fresh n.e.s.	100	96	135	140	124	136
Cow milk, whole, fresh	12	12	12	12	13	101
Camel milk, whole, fresh	39	41	40	41	41	40
Goat meat	22	16	29	25	37	37
Goat milk, whole, fresh	35	36	36	37	38	36
Chicken meat	35	34	29	26	36	36
Hen eggs, in shell	17	16	18	25	25	26
Soybean oil	45	67	55	95	38	24
Pumpkins, squash, and gourds	21	22	20	21	19	21
Camel meat	15	8	22	20	20	20
Cucumbers and gherkins	26	27	17	17	17	18
Onions (including shallots), green	16	16	17	13	13	15
Sheep milk, whole, fresh	12	13	14	14	12	12
Mangoes, mangosteens, guavas	4	5	6	11	11	11
Cauliflowers and broccoli	13	13	10	10	10	11
Fruit juice	13	10	10	10	10	10
Cabbages and other brassicas	15	16	9	9	9	10
Carrots and turnips	2	2	9	9	9	9
Citrus fruit, n.e.s.	5	5	7	7	7	8
Potatoes	7	7	7	7	7	7
Sheep meat	8	13	11	7	7	7
Eggplants (aubergines)	20	21	7	7	7	7
Fruit fresh n.e.s.	5	6	6	6	6	7
Live animals ('000 head)	**18,455**	**18,467**	**16,645**	**16,763**	**18,263**	**18,272**
Chickens	16,000	16,000	14,000	14,000	15,500	15,500
Goats	1,500	1,520	1,626	1,708	1,708	1,710
Sheep	590	580	600	615	615	620
Camels	250	250	359	378	378	380
Cattle	115	117	59	62	62	62
Horses	0.38	0.38	0.40	0.41	0.41	0.41
Fisheries (tonnes)	**90,000**	**86,735**	**82,500**	**78,300**	**74,075**	**77,705**
Crustaceans	470	512	630	750	870	712
Diadromous fish	60	61	65	70	77	258
Marine fish	89,280	85,977	81,579	77,200	72,803	76,339
Molluscs	190	185	226	280	325	396

Source: FAO, online information. Viewed at: http://faostat.fao.org/.

16. The UAE remains a net food importer, although total exports have more than doubled since 2004. In 2009, the UAE imported around US$9.3 billion of agricultural products; rice, its largest import, represented around 9% of total imports. Other imports include chicken, meat, tea, palm oil, and wheat. The UAE's agricultural exports in 2009 amounted to US$3.3 billion. The main

agricultural exports include dates, fruits and vegetables, and natural flowers. Re-exports comprise mainly rice, cigarettes, and refined sugar.

(ii) Policy objectives for the sector

17. In 2006, the Ministry of Agriculture and Fisheries was dissolved and policies related to agriculture and fisheries became the responsibility of the newly created Ministry of Environment and Water (MOEW). At the federal level, the MOEW is in charge of designing agricultural policies and coordinating with other agencies. MOEW's responsibilities include the sustainability of water security, safeguarding food security, and promoting environmental and bio-security. The Abu Dhabi Food Control Authority (ADFCA) is responsible for food safety and agriculture in the emirate of Abu Dhabi, including animal health.[2] According to the authorities, the UAE's long-term policy objective is to achieve food security, while protecting the environment and scarce water resources. This will be attained by providing new sources of irrigation; disseminating modern irrigation systems; and establishing agricultural research centres in order to improve domestic production of agricultural products, livestock, and fisheries.

18. In the emirate of Abu Dhabi, the ADFCA embarked on a strategy to restructure the agriculture sector. The strategy includes the reduction of water consumption by 40% and of the use of fertilizers by 25% in the emirate's by the end of 2013. According to (Abu Dhabi) Law No. 7 of 2010, the ADFCA offers financial assistance to farmers, and will continue to do so in the future, but subject to conditions. Farmers are granted a financial subsidy of AED 90,000 annually if they accept to: stop cultivating Rhodes grass (a product that consumes around 93 billion gallons of Abu Dhabi's water annually); become members of a farmers services centre (FSC); sign a date service contract with an FSC; and commit not to use their farm and its resources for commercial purposes.[3] Government assistance is also provided in the Northern Emirates.

19. Agricultural land is owned and managed privately by UAE and GCC nationals only, foreigners, except for GCC nationals, are not allowed to own agricultural land. However, foreigners may own up to 49% in agri-business companies. Fishing is restricted for locals. A licence is required for fishing in Abu Dhabi and is obtained from the Environment Authority of Abu Dhabi (EAD).

20. Notifications on agriculture remain pending at end 2011. During the period under review, the UAE has not made any notifications to the WTO with respect to domestic support. The last notification dates from 2002, and corresponds to the years 2000 and 2001. The domestic support measures notified in 2002 were measures exempt from the reduction commitment (green box and development programme measures).[4] The UAE has notified to the WTO that it does not maintain export subsidies in agriculture; however, the latest notification was made in 2002, which pre-dates the period under review.[5]

21. Protection for agricultural products remains higher than for non-agricultural products, with an average rate of 5.6% (WTO definition), compared with 4.6% for non-agricultural goods. MFN applied tariff rates on agricultural products range from zero to 5%, with the exception of alcoholic beverages (50%), and tobacco products (100%).

[2] MOEW online information. Viewed at: http://moew.gov.ae/En/AboutMinistry/Pages/ValuesAims.aspx.

[3] *Khaleej Times*, "Abu Dhabi Seeks To Reduce Usage of Water, Fertilizers", by Anwar Ahmed, 24 October 2010.

[4] WTO document G/AG/N/ARE/5, 22 May 2002.

[5] WTO document G/AG/N/ARE/4, 22 May 2002.

(iii) Fisheries

22. Fishing in the UAE is small-scale and traditional; in the main speed boats and wooden dhows are used. Fishing committees have been established in each emirate to help the fishermen and to ensure proper coordination with other governmental bodies. In order to preserve stocks of fish that are sustainable, the Ministry of Environment and Water has issued several regulations concerning fishing gear, areas and seasons, and the structure of the workforce. According to UAE regulations, all fishing vessels must have a UAE citizen on board. The regulations forbid the catch of undersize fish and the use of fish traps with less than 2-inch mesh. Fishing of various species is subject to restricted periods. Fishing is prohibited in spawning and nursery areas during the restricted period. To improve fish stock, a comprehensive re-stocking programme is in place: juveniles and fingerlings of commercially important local species are released annually.

23. The Government assists local fishermen in procuring marine outboard engines and establishing small-scale fish farms. The MOEW provides fingerlings for the start-ups. Cooperatives assist fishermen in marketing their catch. The UAE Government also provides support for commercial fish-farming activities, through the UAE Offsets Group (Chapter III(4)). The group, for example, helped establish the aquaculture company Asmak.

(3) MANUFACTURING

(i) Features

24. In its attempt to diversify away from oil, the UAE has managed to position itself as an industrial hub in the Middle East in recent years. In 2009, the manufacturing sector contributed 10.1% of GDP and 9.7% in 2010. There were 4,644 industrial establishments in 2009, and total employment was almost 348,000; in 2010, the number of industrial undertakings had risen to 4,960 units.

25. The UAE's main industries are food, beverages and tobacco; chemicals; mineral products; metal products; equipment; paper products; textiles and clothing; and wood products (Table IV.2). The largest individual manufactured products include aluminium, cabling, petrochemicals, steel, and products of the marine industry. The manufacturing sector was the recipient of 18.9% of total foreign direct investment in 2009.[6]

Table IV.2
Manufacturing output by activity, 2007-10
(AED million)

Industry	2007	2008	2009	2010
Food industries	334	359	379	405
Wood products	489	546	615	656
Paper products	294	317	362	384
Chemical products	679	734	810	857
Metallurgy	516	557	616	653
Metallurgical products	1,042	1,178	1,315	1,437
Spinning and weaving industries	267	277	282	290
Mining and petroleum refining	69	77	82	87
Other industries	162	174	183	191
Total	**3,852**	**4,219**	**4,644**	**4,960**

Source: Information provided by the UAE authorities.

[6] Ministry of Economy (2010).

(ii) Legal framework and policy objectives for the sector

26. The UAE's manufacturing sector is governed by Federal Law No. 1 of 1979. The law applies to all industrial projects in the UAE with the exception of those pertaining to oil and gas extraction and refining; mineral raw materials refining; and projects with a fixed capital of less than AED 250,000 or employing less than ten people. Foreign ownership is limited to 49%, and senior management and at least 25% of employees must be UAE citizens.

27. The Ministry of Economy is the federal authority in charge of implementing the 1979 Federal Law as well as formulating and implementing policies on manufacturing. An industrial licence, issued by the Ministry of Economy, is required to undertake any industrial activity in the UAE. All licensed industrial projects are granted a customs exemption on all materials included in the project, such as the raw material, the machinery, etc. (Chapter III(4)(i)). The emirates and the Council of Ministers may provide various incentives schemes; but the authorities state that these provisions are not applied, except for the import duty exemption mentioned above. During most of the period under review, the Emirates Industrial Bank (EIB) has helped industrial projects in the UAE by providing loans at preferential interest rates in the range of 3% to 5%. The EIB has financed around 65-70 projects each year (Chapter III(4)(i)).[7]

28. During the period under review, an advisory industrial committee was established in the Ministry of Economy, composed of members from the main ministries, a representative of each emirate appointed by the respective ruler, and representatives of the private sector. The committee may call upon experts from any other government agency and may establish sub-committees to analyse particular problems.

29. The Government is expected to continue to pursue its diversification programme through large-scale investments in the industrial sector. A study prepared at the federal level identified the following potential industrial sectors: shipbuilding and vessels; basic pharmaceuticals products; refined petrochemical products; parts and accessories for motor vehicles; and electric power generation, transmission, and distribution.

30. The UAE's largest industrial conglomerate is the state-owned General Holding Corporation (GHC). GHC is also an important player in implementing the of Abu Dhabi government industrial diversification policy. The UAE general policy approach in manufacturing, as in other policy areas, has two levels: the federal level and the emirate level. As a consequence, each emirate holds a majority stake or is the sole shareholder in key manufacturing companies. In Abu Dhabi, the Higher Corporation for Specialized Economic Zones and Khalifa Industrial Zones are the key players in developing and promoting industrial zones and investments in manufacturing activities. Dubai is developing Dubai Industrial City, a new manufacturing zone that will focus on six industrial sectors: machinery and mechanical equipment; transport equipment and parts; base metals; chemicals; food and beverages; and mineral products.

31. MFN applied tariffs on manufactured goods, except for agricultural food are generally at 5%, with a few exceptions, which are zero-rated. For example, imports of pharmaceutical products are duty free. Imports of all inputs are also duty free. The average MFN tariff rate in 2011 for non-agricultural products (WTO definition) was 4.6%. Protection is slightly higher than average for textiles and clothing, metals, and leather goods; however, tariff dispersion is very low.

[7] In September 2011, under Federal Law No. 7 of 2011, the Emirates Industrial Bank was replaced by the Emirates Development Bank, which is in charge of real estate and industrial activities.

32. In the context of the Doha Round, under the Non-Agricultural Market Access (NAMA) negotiations, the UAE sponsored a proposal in 2003 to eliminate tariffs and non-tariff barriers (NTBs) on raw materials, mainly primary aluminium.[8] In March 2009, Australia co-sponsored the UAE's proposal[9] and in January 2011, both Members tabled a proposal on draft modalities for the sectoral tariff elimination in the raw material sector.[10]

(iii) Selected industries

(a) Petrochemicals

33. The petrochemicals industry continues to be of considerable importance in the UAE, despite attempts at diversifying the economy by venturing into new sectors. The UAE accounts for around 3% of total petrochemical and chemical output in the Gulf region.[11] It currently produces 3.4 million tonnes of petrochemicals annually, which is expected to more than double, to 7.8 million, by 2015.

34. The UAE's petrochemicals activities are concentrated in Abu Dhabi, with the majority of olefin and polymer production capacity in that emirate. Dubai is the second largest petrochemical producer in the UAE, and is especially important in terms of exports, as it accounts for around 70% of the UAE's foreign trade in petrochemical products. In its 2030 Economic Vision, Abu Dhabi plans to make petrochemicals one of its prime growth sectors. It aims to spend around US$100 billion by 2030 to further develop the sector.

35. Petrochemical production in Abu Dhabi is managed by three subsidiaries of the state-owned Abu Dhabi National Oil Company (ADNOC): Ruwais Fertilizer Industries (Fertil), a joint venture between ADNOC (with a shareholding of 66%) and TOTAL (33%), which operates ammonia and urea plants; Abu Dhabi Polymers Company (Borouge), a joint venture between ADNOC (60%) and the European plastics company Borealis (40%), which processes and produces ethylene and polyethylene; and ADNOC Linde Industrial Gases Company Ltd. (ELIXIER), which supplies industrial gases for oil, gas and to petrochemical companies in Ruwais, and other oil areas.

36. Several petrochemical projects are under way in the city of Taweelah. Projects are frequently undertaken in collaboration with foreign players, with expansion plans currently more prominent than plans to set up new petrochemical plants. Borouge is expected to expand its polyolefin operations by entering the FEED (front-end engineering and design) stage of its Borouge 3 project, which includes the construction of an ethane cracker, second generation Borstar polypropylene and polyethylene units, LDPE, and butane units. This facility is expected to boost capacity by 2.5 million tonnes per annum by the fourth quarter of 2013. In addition, in 2009, Ruwais Fertilizer Industries (Fertil) signed a US$1.2 billion contract with Samsung Engineering to construct a second fertilizer complex to boost its production and export capacity. The facility will produce urea and ammonia and is expected to be operational in 2012. Another petrochemicals complex to be developed in Abu Dhabi is Chemaweyaat, which will be the only plant in the region to use naphtha instead of ethane as feedstock.

---

[8] WTO document TN/MA/W/37, 20 May 2003, 37 Add.1, Add.2, Add.3, Add.4 and Add.5.

[9] WTO document TN/MA/W/37/Add.6, 23 March 2009.

[10] WTO document TN/MA/W/37/Add.7, 7 January 2011.

[11] This includes the five GCC countries and Iran (see: http://m.gulfnews.com/business/oil-gas/petrochemicals-industry-to-get-55b-infusion-in-the-gulf-1.787932).

(b) Aluminium

37. The aluminium industry is one of the UAE's main manufacturing activities. Several state-owned companies operate in the sector, most notably, Dubai Aluminium Company (Dubal). Dubal is the world's seventh largest producer of high-quality primary aluminium, and exports more than 92% of its production. Another significant aluminium producer is Emirates Aluminium (Emal), a joint venture between Abu Dhabi's Mubadala Development Company and Dubal. Situated in the Khalifa Port Industrial Zone in Taweelah, Abu Dhabi, Emal is expanding its production, which will make it the world's largest single-site aluminium smelter.

(c) Pharmaceutical products

38. Imports of pharmaceutical products are generally duty free. Federal Law No. 4 of 1983 is the main law regulating the pharmaceutical industry. The Ministry of Health is responsible for licensing pharmaceutical manufacturers in the customs territory of the UAE; the Ministry also inspects the production of pharmaceutical manufacturers in the free zones, for quality and good manufacturing practice (GMP) compliance. Licensing of pharmaceutical companies in free zones is by the free zone authorities as per their applicable laws. Most production takes place in six companies outside the free zones, and in two companies in the free zones. The authorities indicated that in late 2011 ten new pharmaceutical manufacturers were in the process of establishment or of obtaining a licence.

39. The largest company, in terms of capital and of sales, is the Gulf pharmaceuticals company (Julphar) based in Ras Al Khaimah. A public listed company, with majority ownership from the emirate of Ras Al Khaimah, Julphar manufactures around 518 types of pharmaceuticals adding up to around 3,780 products with sales of AED 935 million in 2010.[12] Neopharma, another main manufacturer located in Abu Dhabi Industrial City, produces medicine tablets, syrups, capsules, and suspension medicines.

40. All other pharmaceutical producers are privately owned. An important producer, Gulf Inject, set up by a group of local and Gulf business interests in the Jebel Ali Free Zone, specializes in the production of intravenous solutions, also mostly for the export market.

(d) Other industries

41. In recent years, the UAE has been developing its cable manufacturing industry, although growth has declined since the 2008 slump in the construction sector. Large investments in the industry include a joint venture between Abu Dhabi Basic Industries Corporation (ADBIC) and Midal Cables Limited, one of the world's largest manufacturers of aluminium rods and conductors, to set up an aluminium rod plant at Taweelah, with a combined investment of around AED 368 million. In December 2009, the production capacity of Midal Cables Limited was 110,000 tonnes of aluminium rods.

(4) ENERGY AND WATER

(i) Petroleum

42. The UAE is the world's seventh largest oil producer and fourth largest exporter of crude oil. The petroleum sector accounted for 31.5% of GDP and 59.5% of export revenues in 2010. The UAE's proven crude oil reserves are estimated at 97.8 billion barrels, equivalent to almost 8.5% of the world's reserves. Production was 2.32 million barrels/per day in 2010 (Table IV.3). The UAE has

[12] For more information see: http://www.julphar.net.

been a member of OPEC since 1974 and a member of the Organization of Arab Petroleum Exporting Countries (OAPEC) since 1970.

Table IV.3
Basic data on the petroleum subsector, 2006-10

	2006	2007	2008	2009	2010
OPEC proven oil reserves (m/b)	97,800	97,800	97,800	97,800	97,800
Crude oil production ('000 b/d)	2,568.0	2,529.0	2,572.2	2,241.6	2,324
Crude oil exports ('000 b/d)	2,420.3	2,342.7	2,334.4	1,953.4	2,103

Source: OPEC (2010), *Annual Statistical Bulletin, 2010/11.* Viewed at: http://www.opec.org/opec_web/static_files_project/media/downloads/publications/ASB2010_2011.pdf.

43. Abu Dhabi holds around 95% of the UAE's oil reserves (around 92.2 billion barrels), followed by Dubai with 4 billion barrels, Sharjah with 1.5 billion barrels, and Ras al Khaimah with 100 million barrels. The majority of the UAE's oil fields are located offshore. Abu Dhabi's main offshore oilfields are Umm Shaif, Lower Zakum, Upper Zakum[13], al-Bunduq, and Abu al-Bukhoosh.[14]

44. According to Article 22 of the Constitution of the UAE, natural resources are vested in each individual emirate, not with the Federal Government. Any foreign equity in projects is determined by the competent authorities of the local government of the emirate where the natural resource is located. The Federal Ministry of Energy has limited powers to set policies and planning at a federal level and is subject to the constitutional rights of the emirates. Its main functions include: the coordination among local authorities on energy matters; the compilation of energy-related data and statistics; and representation of the UAE in international organizations.

45. In Abu Dhabi, the main petroleum producer, the Supreme Petroleum Council (SPC), is the main regulatory body of the sector, it sets policies with regard to the preservation of petroleum resources, decision-making, policy formulation, and implementation. The SPC was established by (Abu Dhabi) Law No. 1 of 1988. The ruler of Abu Dhabi is the Council's chairman and retains final authority over key decisions relating to oil and gas development.[15] The SPC is the highest authority responsible for petroleum affairs in Abu Dhabi, and conducts its policy through resolutions, and is in charge of their implementation and follow-up. The SPC is also responsible for implementing Law No. 8 of 1978 regarding the conservation of petroleum resources.

46. The Abu Dhabi National Oil Company (ADNOC), established in 1971, is the state monopoly in charge of the emirate's hydrocarbon interests around the world. Through its 16 subsidiary companies, ADNOC has become one of the world's largest oil conglomerates, operating in exploration and production of crude oil and natural gas; refining, marketing, supply and transportation; and the manufacture of petrochemicals (Table IV.4).

47. The right to explore, develop, and produce petroleum is typically granted by way of a concession by the relevant emirate. Concessions are often granted on a joint-venture basis; the involvement of international oil companies is limited to minority ownership interests in the project companies that are granted the concession and to the provision of technical services to those project

[13] Upper Zakum is the third-largest offshore oilfield in the Gulf and one of the biggest in the world. It is estimated to contain in excess of 50 billion barrels of reserves, with estimated recoverable resources of around 16 to 20 billion barrels.

[14] Butt (2001).

[15] The SPC is also composed of the UAE Petroleum Minister, and representatives of the Abu Dhabi Finance Department, ADNOC, and the Abu Dhabi Investment Authority (ADIA).

companies. Abu Dhabi does not have specific legislation governing the granting of exploration and development concession rights. However, a number of laws affect the petroleum industry, including the (Abu Dhabi) Gas Ownership Law No. 4 of 1976, the (Abu Dhabi) Petroleum Resources Conservation Law No. 8 of 1978, the (Abu Dhabi) Petroleum Ports Law No. 12 of 1973 and its amendment, and the Abu Dhabi Tax Decree of 1965.

Table IV.4
Abu Dhabi National Oil Company activities, 2011

Main activities	Subsidiaries of ADNOC
Upstream operations for oil and gas exploration and extraction	Abu Dhabi Company for Onshore Oil Operations (ADCO)
	Abu Dhabi Marine Operating Company (ADMA-OPCO)
	Zakum Development Company (ZADCO)
Downstream operations of oil and gas refining and processing	Abu Dhabi Gas Industries Limited (GASCO)
	Abu Dhabi Gas Development Company (ADGAS) Al Hosn Gas
	Abu Dhabi Oil Refining Company (TAKREER)
Distribution of refined products	ADNOC Distribution
Marine transportation	Abu Dhabi National Tanker Company (ADNATCO)
	National Gas Shipping Company (NGSCO)
Chemical and petrochemicals	Ruwais Fertilizer Industries (FERTIL)
	Abu Dhabi Polymers Company Limited (BOROUGE)
	ADNOC Linde Industrial Gases Company Ltd. (ELXIER)

Source: ADNOC online information. Viewed at: www.adnoc.ae.

48. In the other emirates, the respective rulers regulate the oil and gas industry. In Dubai, policy is regulated through the Department of the Ruler's Affairs and Petroleum Affairs, with the Executive Council of the Government of Dubai responsible for approving agreements relating to oil and gas development. Operations are carried out through concessions or contracts concluded between companies and the Government of Dubai. The Sharjah Petroleum Council is responsible for regulating policy regarding the development of oil and gas in Sharjah.

49. It is expected that the UAE will continue to rely on hydrocarbons (oil and gas) for its energy consumption in the next years. Abu Dhabi has formulated a long-term vision to develop its energy sector both in terms of productivity and efficiency, while also enlarging its economic base. Following years of minimal investment in increasing capacity, Abu Dhabi, through ADNOC, is aiming to boost capacity from around 2.3 million barrels per day in 2010 to 3.5 million barrels per day by 2017, the majority of which are targeted for exports.

50. ADNOC has long maintained partnerships with international oil companies (IOCs). This is expected to benefit the UAE as more technologically challenging oil reserves are being exploited. The IOCs benefit from production-sharing rights and are able to book reserves, although they receive a low rate of return. Around 40% of the UAE's oil production is carried out by wholly foreign-owned concessionaires.

51. Several projects are under way to increase crude oil production in Abu Dhabi's oil fields. These include the development of the offshore Upper Zakum field by the Zakum Development Company (Zadco), an ADNOC subsidiary, with an investment of US$1.5 billion, Exxon Mobil on technical-based merit, submitted the winning bid in an SPC tender and acquired 28% of Zadco, with the Japan Oil Development Company holding 12% and ADNOC holding 60%. Another large project is being developed by the Abu Dhabi Company for Onshore Oil Operations (ADCO), with investments of US$1.5 billion, to develop three new fields in Abu Dhabi's north-eastern region:

Al Dabbiya, Rumaitha, and Shanayel, with an initial production of around 100,000 barrels per day (b/d).[16]

52. Downstream petroleum activities (i.e. the processing of crude oil to fuel) are owned and managed by three ADNOC subsidiaries: Abu Dhabi Gas Industries Limited Company (GASCO), Abu Dhabi Gas Liquefaction Company Limited (ADGAS), and Abu Dhabi Oil Refining Company (TAKREER). The UAE has five refineries, with a total refining capacity of 781,250 barrels per day in 2009. The largest two are ADNOC's Ruwais refinery with a capacity of 350,000 b/d and Umm Al-Nar at 150,000 b/d. There are plans to build a new refinery at Fujairah with a capacity to process 500,000 b/d of crude oil. Fujairah has the third-largest bunkering port in the world and is the country's major oil export terminal. About 70% of total refined output is consumed domestically.

53. The UAE levies a corporate tax on companies in oil and gas activities which is regulated by the individual emirates. In Abu Dhabi the corporate tax applies in accordance with the Abu Dhabi Income Tax Decree of 1965, as amended. Although not a petroleum-specific decree, it applies only to chargeable persons "dealing in oil", "chargeable persons" including foreign entities, ADNOC and its subsidiaries, and any other domestic companies involved in petroleum. The tax ranges between 55% and 85% depending on production.[17] The Supreme Petroleum Council grants tax incentives to businesses that benefit Abu Dhabi, for example, through furthering its economic development, investment, technology transfer, and training of UAE nationals.

(ii) Natural gas

54. Natural gas is an increasingly important energy source and accounts for approximately two-thirds of the UAE's total energy consumption, with crude oil accounting for the remainder. The UAE has the world's fifth-largest reserves of natural gas, at 6.09 trillion cubic meters, around 3.5% of the world total. In 2009, the UAE produced approximately 48.8 billion cubic meters of natural gas (Table IV. 5); Abu Dhabi holds about 92% of the UAE's gas reserves. The majority of the UAE's natural gas production is associated gas. In Abu Dhabi, the non-associated Khuff natural gas reservoirs beneath the Umm Shaif and Abu Al Bukhush oil fields are among the largest in the world.

55. Abu Dhabi's gas policy is to develop gas resources to meet growing domestic demand, giving priority to generating water and electricity, supply of gas to new industries, petrochemical projects, and any re-injection needs. Natural gas in Abu Dhabi is managed by two subsidiaries of ADNOC, the Abu Dhabi Industries Company (GASCO), which handles onshore gas operations, with 68% ownership by ADNOC; and the Abu Dhabi Gas Liquefaction Company (ADGAS) for liquefied natural gas (LNG) production, with 70% ownership by ADNOC. Foreign participation by international oil companies accounts for the remaining interests in GASCO and ADGAS; the main players are Total, Royal Dutch Shell Group, Mitsui & Co, BP, and Partex Gas Corporation.

[16] ADCO, in which ADNOC has a 60% interest, operates onshore and in the shallow coastal waters of the Emirate of Abu Dhabi. ADCO produces from six oil fields: Asab, Bab, Bu Hasa, Sahil, Shah, and North East Bab (Dabbiya, Rumaitha, and Shanayel). These fields are linked by more than 450 kilometres of pipeline, with storage and shipping facilities at Jebel Dhanna, where tankers load crude oil for export to many parts of the world. See ADNOC online information. Viewed at: http://www.adnoc.ae/content.aspx?newid=27 &mid=27.

[17] Article 17 of the Abu Dhabi Income Tax Decree of 1965 stipulates that a company must pay a basic income tax at 55%. However, if the production of crude oil during a calendar year reaches an average of 100,000 barrels a day, then the rate increases to 65%, and if production reaches an average of 200,000 barrels a day, the company must pay income tax at 85%.

Table IV.5
Gas production and utilization, 2006-10
(Million cubic metres)

	2006	2007	2008	2009	2010
Gross production	76,194	78,963	80,055	75,840	79,778
Marketed production	48,790	50,290	50,240	48,840	51,282
Flared	950	970	980	967	972
Re-injection	20,984	22,033	23,135	22,051	22,406
Shrinkage	5,470	5,670	5,700	3,983	5,118

Note: Marketed production corresponds to gross production, minus the volumes of gas flared or re-injected into the fields, minus the shrinkage.

Source: OPEC (2010), *Annual Statistical Bulletin, 2010/2011*. Viewed at: http://www.opec.org/opec_web/static_files_project/media/downloads/publications/ASB2010_2011.pdf.

56. Since the 1970s, the UAE has exported liquefied natural gas (LNG), mainly to Japan, but in 2008 it became a net importer of gas, due to a sharp increase in demand through increased electricity consumption (accompanied by a preference for natural gas as the feedstock for power generation and water desalination projects) and a growing petrochemical industry. It is estimated that as much as half of UAE's natural gas production is used for domestic power generation during the peak summer months. Significant quantities of natural gas are also used in re-injection operations for oil reservoir pressure maintenance.

57. Given the increasing demand for natural gas, the UAE addresses the shortfall in domestic gas supply by importing around 30% of its domestic gas demand from Qatar through the Dolphin Energy Project (see Box IV.1). In addition, the UAE has embarked on a substantial investment programme to boost domestic gas production, most notably through sour gas development projects in Abu Dhabi. Sour gas reserves from the Shah Field are expected to produce 10 billion cubic metres per year at an estimated cost of US$12 billion. Al Hosn Gas is a joint venture between ADNOC and Occidental and is expected to be operational in 2013. Another project, undertaken by GASCO, the Integrated Gas Development Project, is due for completion in 2012 and is expected to produce 7.5 billion cubic metres per year of high-pressure gas from the offshore Umm Shaif and Khuff fields for processing through new onshore facilities at Habshan and Ruwais.

Box IV.1: The Dolphin Project a regional energy initiative

Dolphin Energy is a consortium of the Abu Dhabi government-owned Mubadala Development Company (51%) and Occidental Petroleum of the United States and Total of France (each of which holds a 24.5% stake). Dolphin Energy was established in 1997 to further expand the UAE's gas network. The project is the largest energy-related venture undertaken in the GCC region and the first cross-border refined gas transmission project involving the UAE, Qatar, and Oman.

A development and production-sharing agreement (DPSA) was reached in 1999 between the governments of the UAE and Qatar to allow the Abu Dhabi Government and its partners to invest in the appraisal, drilling, and construction of the upstream facilities in the dedicated concession area in the North Field. In return, Dolphin Energy would share with Qatar the income from the by-products extracted at its Ras Laffan Gas Processing Plant, while buying all the natural gas produced for export to the UAE and Oman. The agreements provide for the supply of Dolphin natural gas to each customer for terms of 25 years.

Currently, Dolphin Energy helps meet around 30% of the UAE's energy requirements. The project delivers around 2 billion standard cubic feet of natural gas per day to customers throughout the UAE and Oman. Moreover, Dolphin's natural gas is helping to support the Abu Dhabi Vision 2030 by being a reliable supplier of clean energy.

Source: Information provided by the authorities; and online information at: www.dolphinenergy.com.

58. The UAE continues to export a large amount of gas, at relatively stable levels, notwithstanding the increase in imports to meet its domestic needs. This is largely because: (i) a significant portion of the UAE's natural gas production is committed to long-term LNG export contracts; and (ii) most of its reserves are concentrated in the emirate of Abu Dhabi, and the lack of an integrated gas pipeline distribution network means that the other emirates (particularly the "northern" emirates need to import natural gas.

59. The emirate of Sharjah has its own gas production and investment projects. Its main project, DanaGas, is the region's first privately owned gas exploration company. DanaGas has active investments in the UAE, Saudi Arabia, Iraq, Egypt, and the United Kingdom. DanaGas has been a pioneer in the creation of the "gas cities" concept, which aims to create an integrated natural gas industry cluster in various locations around the world.

60. The UAE is assessing the exploitation and use of alternative renewable sources of energy, in particular solar power, through the Abu Dhabi Future Energy Company (MASDAR), which is wholly owned by the state-owned Mubadala Development Company. The Federal Government's energy policy aims at producing 7% of total capacity by 2020.

61. Nuclear energy has gained priority in recent years, following the establishment of the Emirates Nuclear Energy Corporation, which was set up to act as the government investment arm for the development of nuclear energy.

(iii) Electricity and water

62. The UAE is the second-highest consumer of electricity among the Gulf countries, after Saudi Arabia. In 2010, UAE residents consumed around 89,587GWh of electricity. Plans for economic diversification, coupled with strong population growth, have led to increased demand for electricity. Electricity in the UAE is produced from conventional thermal sources, such as natural gas and diesel oil fuel. Installed generation capacity increased from 15,865 MW in 2006 to 23,215 MW in 2010.

63. Water resources are scarce. Almost 93% of potable water is desalinated, and the rest comes from ground water. In 2010, total desalinated water production was 354,536 million gallons and ground water production 25,000 million gallons. The supply of both electricity and water are highly subsidized in the different emirates.

64. Electricity and water in the UAE remain under the responsibility of four entities: the Abu Dhabi Water and Electricity Authority (ADWEA), the Dubai Electricity and Water Company (DEWA); the Sharjah Water and Electricity Company (SEWA), and the Federal Electricity and Water Authority within the Ministry of Energy, which supplies the four northern emirates. The Ministry of Energy plays a coordinating role among these authorities. ADWEA is the only government entity with domestic and foreign private ownership (40%).

65. The electricity market in Abu Dhabi is based on a "single buyer" model where all generated power is purchased by ADWEA. ADWEA sells the electricity to the Abu Dhabi Distribution Company (ADDC) and Al-Ain Distribution Company (AADC) for distribution. In addition, ADWEA pays a transmission company (TRANSCO) for wheeling charges of its transmission system. This process is regulated by the Regulation and Supervision Bureau (RSB) in Abu Dhabi.

66. The Dubai Electricity and Water Authority (DEWA) is responsible for electricity and energy in Dubai. DEWA is in charge of overall power generation, transmission, distribution, and operation. The Supreme Council of Energy in Dubai is an independent legal entity that aims to guarantee energy supply to end-users in the emirate.

67. The Ministry of Energy represents the UAE in regional and global forums and coordinates between the local authorities on energy matters. The Ministry also supervises the integration of the power grid of local projects in the UAE, known as Emirates National Grid Project (ENG).

68. In order to increase electricity capacity, Abu Dhabi has actively involved the private sector through independent water and power projects; five projects have been concluded. Dubai has recently involved the private sector, and one project is so far under way.

69. Prices of electricity and water are determined at emirate level (including the formula used and the criterion), taking into account the different emirates' government subsidies.

(5) SERVICES

(i) Financial services

70. Prior to the global financial crisis of 2008, the UAE's financial sector had experienced remarkable growth; with Dubai portrayed as the financial hub of the Gulf region. Financial services are of considerable importance to the economy, particularly to Dubai's; they represented 6.8% of GDP in 2010. However, as a result of the crisis, many UAE banks suffered from liquidity shortages and stock markets plunged; the Dubai Financial Market (DFM) and the Abu Dhabi Securities Exchange (ADX) fell by 68.5% and 46.4% respectively in November 2008. The effect of the crisis on the economy in general, and on the financial sector in particular was substantial, particularly for Dubai. The debt of the Dubai Government and its government related entities (GREs) has exceeded 100% of GDP; the greatest risk to the financial sector is the possibility of further debt restructurings by Dubai (Box IV.2).

71. The UAE financial system consists mainly of commercial banks, accounting for over 90% of total lending by the financial sector. Equity and insurance markets are considered small, in comparison to other emerging markets. Banking and financial intermediation services are regulated at federal level, by the Central Bank of the UAE; insurance services are also regulated at federal level under the authority of the Ministry of Economy.

72. Under the GATS[18], the UAE has made commitments on all banking and other financial services, with the exception of settlement and clearing services for financial assets (as there was no stock exchange in the UAE when it became a Member of the WTO in 1996). The UAE has bound measures on all these services for cross-border supply and consumption abroad without limitation. Measures affecting mode 3 (commercial presence) supply remain unbound for new licences to operate bank branches and to expand activities of existing financial entities. In the area of insurance services, the UAE made no specific commitments in its GATS Schedule. Cross-border supply of insurance services is not possible for companies located abroad. All assets and risks in the UAE must be insured domestically. Maximum foreign ownership of domestic insurance companies is set by law at 49%. Representative offices may not engage in business or act as agents.

[18] WTO document GATS/SC/121, 2 April 1996.

Box IV.2: The global financial crisis and its effect on the UAE's financial system

In 2009, the UAE economy slowed down significantly as a result of the global recession, the bursting of the Dubai property bubble, and the post-Lehman shutdown of international capital markets. Dubai World (DW), one of three major holding companies owned by the Dubai Government, reached a debt standstill in November 2009. Other government related entities (GREs) had similar financial difficulties.

The UAE authorities adopted a number of measures to handle the effects of the financial crisis, which led to a liquidity squeeze that began in the third quarter of 2008. The Emirate of Abu Dhabi provided financial support to the Emirate of Dubai, through its participation in a financial support fund (see below). Measures taken by the UAE authorities included, *inter alia,* supporting the banking sector through liquidity injection, recapitalization, and deposit guarantee. More specifically, the Central Bank of the UAE guaranteed all bank deposits for three years and provided an AED 50 billion liquidity support. The Ministry of Finance injected AED 70 billion of deposits, which it later agreed to convert into subordinated debt, and the Government of Abu Dhabi injected AED 16 billion of capital into the five largest banks based in Abu Dhabi.

In July 2009, the Government of Dubai established the Dubai Financial Support Fund (DFSF) to provide financial assistance to GREs of strategic importance. The DFSF manages a US$20 billion bond programme, half of which was subscribed by the Central Bank and the rest by the emirate of Abu Dhabi. Following the DW standstill announcement, the Government of Dubai enacted a special insolvency regime for DW and its Nakheel subsidiary specialized in real estate development. The debt restructuring of DW was agreed by all creditors in late October 2010. The restructuring plan covered US$24.9 billion of debt, of which US$14.4 billion was owed to some 90 domestic and foreign banks and the remaining US$10.5 billion to the Government of Dubai. The bank debt refinancing was at low interest rates (1%) and with long maturity periods (five years for a US$4.4 billion, and eight years for a US$10 billion tranche. The US$10.5 billion government debt was to be converted into equity through the DFSF, which committed to provide new funds up to US$1.5 billion to DW for the company's working capital and interest payments. Through the DFSF, the Government would also provide US$8 billion new equity to Nakheel and convert its existing US$1.2 billion debt into equity. Nakheel was to be separated from DW and owned directly by the Government; its creditors and suppliers to be paid off with a combination of 40% cash and 60% debt security.

According to the IMF, the DW debt restructuring led to an increase in Dubai sovereign debt, with spill-overs to the banking sector and financial markets. Debt due in 2011-12 is estimated at around US$31 billion, of which at least US$5 billion in the real estate sector. Other Dubai GREs have reached or are also in debt restructuring negotiations with banks, such has been the case of Dubai Holding Commercial Operations Group (DHCOG), Dubai Group (DG), and Dubai International Capital (DIC). Also, there are signs that some Abu Dhabi GREs heavily investing in the real estate sector are experiencing financial difficulties. Nevertheless, investor confidence, especially in Dubai has risen as a result of several major GRE's reaching restructuring agreements with their lenders.

Source: International Monetary Fund (2011). *Staff report for the 2011 Article IV Consultation-Staff Report; Staff Supplement; Public Information Notice on the Executive Board Discussion.* IMF Country Report No. 11/111, May. Viewed at: http://www.imf.org/external/pubs/ft/scr/2011/cr11111.pdf.

(a) Banking

73. The UAE's banking sector is the second largest among GCC countries, after Saudi Arabia. Total assets increased by 5.7% from AED 1,519 billion at the end of 2009 to AED 1,605 billion at the end of 2010, but their share of GDP declined from 153% to 144%. Assets were at AED 1,672 billion in September 2011. Bank deposits increased from AED 982 billion at end 2009 to AED 1,049 billion at end 2010, an increase of 6.8%; they reached AED 1,067.3 in September 2011.[19] Loan growth declined in 2009-10 due to the Dubai debt crisis and a collapse in real estate property prices; this was reflected in a lower share of loans to GDP, which declined from 99% in 2009 to 95% in 2010.

[19] UAE Central Bank online information. Viewed at: http://www.centralbank.ae/en/pdf/dataroom/UAEMonthlyBanking Indicators-July11.pdf.

Table IV.6
Selected monetary and banking indicators, 2006 to September 2011
(US$ billion unless otherwise specified)

Indicators	2006	2007	2008	2009	2010	Sept. 2011
UAE Central Bank						
Total assets/liabilities	28.1	77.9	52.8	55.5	62.3	74.5[a]
Foreign assets and gold holdings	27.9	77.8	30.8	24.5	31.8	44.2[a]
Notes and coins issued	7.3	8.6	12.3	12.4	13.0	14.0[a]
Banks						
Total assets/liabilities	225.0	327.4	394.3	414.2	438.2	465.5[a]
Foreign assets	63.2	53.6	55.4	56.7	63.6	71.0[a]
Foreign assets to total assets (%)	28.1	16.1	14.1	13.7	14.5	15.3[a]
Foreign liabilities	48.4	87.4	77.0	68.4	74.0	78.9[a]
Foreign liabilities to total liabilities (%)	21.5	26.7	19.5	16.5	16.9	17.0[a]
Deposits[b]	**141.3**	**195.0**	**248.4**	**267.6**	**285.8**	**306.6**[a]
Residents	127.8	177.4	226.9	243.4	253.0	273.0[a]
Non-residents	13.5	17.6	21.4	24.1	32.8	33.6[a]
Bank credit (net)[c]	**137.0**	**189.6**	**268.2**	**277.0**	**280.7**	**287.5**[a]
Residents	120.1	170.6	251.7	261.0	264.7	267.2[a]
Non-residents	16.9	19.0	16.5	16.0	16.0	20.3[a]
Local banks	**21**	**22**	**24**	**24**	**23**	**23**
Branches	431	507	614	674	732	757
Foreign banks	**25**	**27**	**28**	**28**	**28**	**28**
Branches	81	80	82	82	83	83
Number of workers in banks (in UAE)[d]	**26,963**	**32,142**	**39,589**	**37,704**	**37,403**	**37,291**[a]

a June 2011.
b Excluding inter-bank deposits.
c Excluding loans to banks, net of provisions and interest in suspense.
d Excluding auxiliary staff.

Source: Central Bank of the UAE, *Statistical Bulletin,* various issues. Viewed at: http://www.centralbank.ae/en/index.php; and UAE Banking Indicators. Viewed at: http://www.centralbank.ae/en/pdf/dataroom/UAEMonthlyBankingIndicators-July11.pdf.

74. At the end of September 2011, the UAE had 51 commercial banks (up from 46 in 2006), with 23 national banks (of which 8 are Islamic) and 28 foreign banks (including GCC banks). During 2006-07, the number of GCC banks increased from three to six. There are 20 foreign banks with head offices in Dubai and 8 in Abu Dhabi; 83 branches of foreign banks (including GCC); and 757 branches of national banks.[20] There are 4,053 automated teller machines (ATMs).

75. There are 110 licensed representative offices of foreign banks and financial institutions (42 in Abu Dhabi, 67 in Dubai, and 1 in Sharjah). In addition, two investment banks operate in the country, Arab Emirates Invest Bank, and HSBC Financial Services (Middle East) Limited. In 2009-2010, the Central Bank granted three wholesale bank licences to Deutsche Bank AG and Industrial, Commercial Bank of China, and the Bank of Tokyo-Mitsubishi UFJ Ltd. In 2011 a fourth wholesale licence was issued to the Korea Exchange Bank.

[20] Central Bank online information. Viewed at: http://www.centralbank.ae/en/pdf/bsed/1-1-LB%20br.%20List%2031-10-2010_english.pdf.

76. Union Law No. 10 of 1980 governs the Central Bank, the monetary system, and the organization of banking in the UAE. Under the law, there are five principal categories of banking institutions in the UAE: commercial banks, investment banks, financial institutions, financial and monetary intermediaries, and representative offices, each of which must be licensed by the Central Bank.

77. Foreign banks operating in the UAE are also regulated by the Central Bank and must open branches in the UAE; they must be licensed by the Central Bank and (since 2010), are subject to a maximum of eight branches in the UAE. The typical operation of a foreign bank takes the form of a branch. Subsidiaries of foreign banks are not allowed, but foreign banks are allowed to open representative offices. Foreign banks are granted national treatment for paid-up capital requirements. All commercial banks, including branches of foreign banks are required to have a minimum paid-up capital of AED 40 million, or 10% of risk weighed assets in the UAE, whichever is greater. However, national treatment is not applied as regards the taxation of profits. Foreign banks are subject to a 20% tax on profits, which is not applied to national banks. The authorities indicated that banks were required to adopt Basel II provisions as of 2006.

78. Financial investment companies are regulated by Central Bank Resolution No. 164/8/94, of 18 April 1995. This resolution defines financial investment companies as those conducting one or more of the following business: (a) opening investment accounts and managing portfolios on behalf of others, whether individuals or companies; (b) preparing feasibility studies for projects and marketing allotments and stocks of shareholding companies; (c) establishing and/or managing investment trust funds; (d) establishing and/or managing other investment funds and acting trustee of funds entrusted to it by a trust to manage on behalf of a beneficiary; or (e) underwriting companies' capital and participating in syndicated loans. A financial investment company must be a juridical person with a minimum capital of AED 25 million, subject to increase according to the business the company intends to undertake. The resolution also requires national shareholding of not less than 51% of the paid-up capital, in addition to other terms and conditions in the regulation.[21]

79. UAE banks were expected to follow Basel II guidelines since 2006 as per Central Bank Notice 3,735/2006 "Basel II Implementation in the UAE" of 27 August 2006 and Notice 4,004/2009 "Capital Adequacy". The latter increased the minimum capital adequacy ratio (CAR) from 11% to 12% from 30 June 2010. The CAR measurement of capital allows banks to maintain Tier 2 capital at a maximum of 67% of Tier 1 capital. UAE banks are well capitalized, with a CAR of 21% and Tier 1 CAR of 16.4% in mid 2011.[22]

80. The Central Bank issued guidelines for implementation of the Basel II Capital Accord in November 2009; the guidelines have been in effect since then.[23] As per the guidelines, although BIS standards on Basel II are generally applicable, specific guidelines given by the Central Bank are to prevail. The guidelines mandate the immediate effective application of the standardized approach for credit risk, and encourage "internationally active UAE banks" to migrate to the foundation internal rating based (FIRB) approach in due course. Banks may select any of the market risk and operational risk approaches, with the advanced options requiring explicit approval by the Central Bank. The

---

[21] Central Bank online information. Viewed at: http://www.centralbank.ae/en/index.php?option=com_content&view=article&id=134&Itemid=99.

[22] Central Bank online information. Viewed at: http://www.centralbank.ae/en/pdf/dataroom/UAEMonthlyBankingIndicators-July11.pdf.

[23] The guidelines focus on specific issues of relevance for the UAE banking community; the complete Basel II guidelines include: Bank for International Settlements, "International Convergence of Capital Measurement and Capital Standards", June 2006, and Bank for International Settlements, "Enhancements to the Basel II Framework", July 2009.

Central Bank also expects each bank to develop and document its own internal capital adequacy assessment process (ICAAP), which is to become a key component of its supervisory review. quarterly prudential reporting by banks of their capital calculations under the standardized approach has been required since the quarter ending 30 September 2009.

81. In 2010, the Central Bank implemented a series of regulatory measures to help mitigate future financial crises. They include, *inter alia*: an increase of the minimum capital-adequacy ratio to 12%; a moratorium on new licences for commercial banks; a limit on the number of branches (only eight) permitted to licensed foreign banks; new provisioning rules requiring banks to classify loans as being in default, and make provisions accordingly, after 90 days of delinquency, instead of the previous 6 months (introduced in November 2010)[24]; a limit on personal loans to 20 times the monthly salary or income of a borrower, with a maximum repayment period of four years; and restrictions on processing fees for loans, debit, and credit cards.

82. The banking sector has undergone some mergers and acquisitions as a way of consolidating funds. In 2008, the Emirates Bank and National Bank of Dubai (NBD) merged to form Emirates NBD, the largest bank in the UAE, with a market capitalization of AED 19 billion. In 2011, the Abu Dhabi-based Real Estate Bank merged with the Emirates Industrial Bank (EIB) to create Emirates Development Bank, with an initial market capitalization of up to AED 10 billion.

83. Islamic banking in the UAE accounts for around 14% of total banking assets, with large potential for growth. Islamic banks are governed by Federal Law No. 6 of 1985 and regulated by the Central Bank; the capital adequacy ratio requirements for Islamic banks are the same as for ordinary banks. Islamic banks must take the form of joint-stock companies and may engage in any banking operation. The UAE has eight Islamic banks offering Shariah-compliant products and services such as: *sukuks* (Islamic bonds) and *ijara* transactions, which are used in property purchasing deals.[25]

84. At end September 2011, there were 116 moneychangers (main offices) operating in the UAE with 613 branches, up from 114 main offices and 562 branches at the end of 2010.[26]

85. Foreign banks pay a 20% local emirate tax on profits, governed by specific legislation in each emirate. There are no restrictions on the presence of foreign senior staff in foreign banks. All banks in the UAE are required to employ a minimum of 10% UAE nationals in total staff (excluding auxiliary staff) as per Central Bank regulations. Additionally, in accordance with Council of Ministers Decree No. 10 of 1998, all banks are to increase the number of UAE-national staff by 4% annually, although reportedly this has not been achieved due to lack of domestic workforce.

(b) Securities

86. As a result of the global financial crisis, market capitalization and the general share price index began to decrease in October 2009 and continued to fall in 2010. Market capitalization fell by 4.8%, from AED 404.7 billion at the end of 2009 to AED 385.4 billion at the end of 2010; and the general share price index decreased by 4.2% in 2010. The price earnings ratio (price per share divided by annual earnings per share) was 13.3 at the Abu Dhabi Securities Exchange and 17 at the Dubai Financial Market by the end of 2010.

[24] Notice No. 28/2010, 11 November 2010, Central Bank Revision of the Regulations for Classification of Loans and Determining their Provisions.

[25] According to Islamic banking laws, banks may not charge a fixed interest rate on deposits or loans but only variable interest rates based on a profit/loss sharing model.

[26] Central Bank of the United Arab Emirates (2011).

87. The UAE has three stock exchanges: the Dubai Financial Market (DFM), the Abu Dhabi Securities Exchange (ADX), and NASDAQ Dubai (formerly the Dubai International Financial Exchange (DIFX). NASDAQ Dubai is part of the Dubai International Financial Center (DIFC) free zone; whereas the DFM and ADX are both "on-shore" stock exchanges. In addition to these equity and bond exchanges, the UAE has the Dubai Gold and Commodities Exchange (DCGX), which trades in financial derivatives, and the Dubai Mercantile Exchange (NYMEX), which is the first international energy futures and commodities exchange in the Middle East.

88. The Dubai Financial Market (DFM) was established as an independent public institution by Ministry of Economy Resolution No. 14 of 2000. It operates as a secondary market for the trading of securities issued by public joint-stock companies, bonds issued by the Federal Government or any of the local governments and public institutions in the country, and units of investment funds and any other financial instruments, local or foreign, that are accepted by the Market. The DFM started operations in March 2000. In December 2005, it was converted into a public joint-stock company with a paid-up capital of AED 8 billion allocated over 8 billion shares, with a par value of AED 1 per share; 20% of these shares were offered for public subscription.[27] Market capitalization reached AED 194.9 billion in July 2011[28] (Table IV.7).

Table IV.7
UAE securities market, July 2011

	Abu Dhabi Securities Exchange	Dubai Financial Market	NASDAQ Dubai
Market capitalization, July 2011 (AED million)	275,115	194,880	38,743
Average daily trading value, 2010 average (AED million)	151.2	82.7	18,919
Number of listed companies/bonds, July 2011	65/1	64/7	..
Number of brokerage companies	62	62	..
Ownership	Abu Dhabi Government: 100%	Public: 20% and Borse Dubai (owned by Dubai Government) 80%	Borse Dubai (owned by Dubai Government) 66.7% and 33.3% NASDAQ-OMX

.. Not available.

Source: Information provided by the UAE authorities; Abu Dhabi Stock Exchange. Viewed at: http://www.adx.ae/PublicationAttachments/Aug2011-report_9-11-2011%202_09_55%20PM.pdf; and Dubai Financial Market. Viewed at: http://dfm.ae/documents/Publications/e0724b3f-c1f5-4be1-98a6-90d4d1e8348c.pdf.

89. The Abu Dhabi Securities Exchange (ADX) was established on 15 November 2000 by (Abu Dhabi) Law No. 3 of 2000, the provisions create an autonomous legal entity, with independent finance and management, and the necessary supervisory and executive powers to exercise its functions. These functions are to: provide opportunities to invest savings and funds in securities in order to benefit the UAE economy; ensure the soundness and accuracy of transactions and the proper interaction between demand and supply in order to determine prices; protect investors by establishing fair and proper dealing principles between the various investors; impose controls over securities transactions to ensure sound procedures; and ensure the financial and economic stability and develop the appropriate trading methods needed to ensure liquidity and stability of the prices of the securities listed on the market. The ADX has the authority to establish centers and branches outside the Emirate

[27] Dubai Financial Market online information. Viewed at: http://dfm.ae/pages/default.aspx?c=801.

[28] Dubai Financial Market (2011).

of Abu Dhabi. The Abu Dhabi Securities Exchange board of directors comprises seven members nominated by Decree, for a term of three years.[29]

90. The Emirates Securities and Commodities Authority (SCA) is in charge of regulating the DFM and the ADX, while the Dubai Financial Services Authority (DFSA) regulates NASDAQ Dubai. The SCA is an independent body, chaired by the Minister of Economy, under Federal Law No. 4 of 2000. It is responsible for regulating the licensing, management, membership, and supervision of financial markets and brokerage firms. The SCA is the only agency legally authorized to approve the listing of securities. SCA regulations allow foreign firms to list their securities in these markets after having satisfied certain requirements. Currently, 20 of the 130 companies registered in the SCA are foreign. The ADX and DFM started operating the Delivery Versus Payment (DVP) procedure in May 2011.

91. The number of finance companies licensed to operate in the UAE decreased from 24 in 2009 to 23 in 2010. No new company was given a licence to operate during 2010 or 2011, although there is no moratorium on licensing new financial institutions or on establishing branches of existing ones. Two companies were licensed during 2009: Abu Dhabi Commercial Islamic Finance Company, and Siraj Finance Company, There are also 13 financial consultancies (all locally incorporated), 15 financial intermediaries dealing in currencies and commodities as money market transactions (Forex dealers), and two investment banks.

92. No changes were made to the relevant legislation during the review period. Federal Law No. 4 of 2000 is the main piece of legislation regulating the licensing, management, membership, and supervision of the financial markets and brokerage firms in the UAE, with the exception of NASDAQ Dubai. Brokers seeking to operate on the DFM and ADX exchanges must establish a company with at least 51% national ownership, minimum capital of AED 30 million and the necessary financial guarantees (currently a AED 20 million bank guarantee).

93. Since the last Review of the UAE, the SCA has issued a number of regulations that seek to develop the financial services industry and strengthen supervision and regulation of the financial sector. These include a new Code of Corporate Governance, issued in 2007, to set governance practices and disclosure of listed companies and for regulating initial public offerings (IPOs) and secondary offerings (previously the role of the Ministry of Economy); 2008 regulations concerning margin trading, dual listing, and financial consultation and analysis; 2009 regulations concerning the custody of securities; and 2010 regulations concerning criteria for capital adequacy for brokerage firms in securities and commodity contracts. The authorities indicated that a number of new regulations are in the pipeline, dealing with issues including market makers and mutual funds. The number of licensed brokerage firms decreased from 104 in 2007 to 61 in 2011. Listed securities are tradeable via brokers only.

Offshore financial services

94. Despite the general policy of restricting ownership and limiting the number of banks, the UAE authorities allow individual emirates to maintain free zones specializing in the provision of financial services. In this respect, the Dubai International Financial Centre (DIFC), has independent jurisdiction under the UAE Constitution. The DIFC is the only financial free zone currently within the UAE, although, technically, another could be created. Financial institutions established in the DIFC benefit from: zero tax rate on income and profits; 100% foreign ownership; no restrictions on foreign exchange or capital/profit repatriation; operational support and business continuity facilities.

[29] ADX online information. Viewed at: http://www.adx.ae/English/AboutADX/Pages/MarketEstablishment.aspx.

The DIFC has its own court system, and as well as an independent centre for arbitration to which disputes may be brought. Corporate capital in the DIFC is designated in U.S. dollars rather than UAE dirhams. Institutions wishing to offer regulated financial services must obtain approval from the DFSA, the centre's independent regulatory body.

95. Investments in NASDAQ Dubai, which is housed in the DIFC, are not subject to the laws of the Emirates but to DIFC law. In July 2010, NASDAQ Dubai, made some structural changes to its market by outsourcing its key operational functions to the DFM, in order to help increase liquidity. There is no withholding tax on dividends, except for those on non-domestic dual-listed shares traded in NASDAQ Dubai, which may be subject to a withholding tax depending on the tax regulations in the country of origin. There is no withholding tax on interest on corporate bonds and no capital gains tax.

(c) Insurance services

96. According to the Insurance Authority, total insurance expenditure in the UAE more than doubled between 2006 and 2010, from US$2.7 billion to US$5.9 billion, in terms of total premium value. Non-life insurance accounts for the bulk, around 82% of total insurance expenditure, with the remainder in life insurance.

97. In 2010, 59 insurance companies were licensed in the different emirates, 32 national and 27 foreign. Most companies are based in Abu Dhabi or Dubai, and carry out the full range of insurance business (Table IV.8). Eleven national and two foreign firms operate both life and non-life insurances; two national and eight foreign firms undertake life insurance only, and 18 national and 17 foreign firms carry out non-life insurance activities only. In addition, there are: 11 UAE insurance agents; 170 insurance brokers (163 national and 7 foreign); 68 surveyors and loss adjustors; 22 insurance consultants; and 21 actuaries. Between 2006 and 2011, six foreign companies were licensed. The three largest insurance companies operating in the UAE are: Oman Insurance Company of Dubai, Islamic Arab Insurance Company of Dubai, and Daman Health Insurance Company of Abu Dhabi.

Table IV.8
Insurance premiums and claims, 2010
(US$ million)

	Total		Local		Foreign	
	Claims	**Premiums**	**Claims**	**Premiums**	**Claims**	**Premiums**
Car	772	1,173	582	818	190	355
Cargo and transportation	241	608	184	480	57	128
Fire	309	616	256	460	53	157
Theft	0	2	0	1	0	1
Life	213	1,096	58	374	154	721
Others[a]	1,364	2,496	1,149	2,050	215	447
Total	2,899	5,991	2,230	4,182	669	1,809

a Category comprises: fidelity guarantee, civil liability, cash in safe, cash in transit, worker compensation, engineering, glass breakage, health insurance, miscellaneous.

Source: Insurance Authority, Ministry of Economy.

98. Insurance penetration in the UAE is the highest in the Middle East, although it is still low by global standards. In 2010, insurance penetration accounted for 2.15% of GDP. Abu Dhabi made health insurance mandatory for expatriates in 2007[30], and for nationals in 2008; this helped increase broader awareness of the concept and has resulted in higher penetration. Life insurance policies still account for only a small proportion of overall business, but the popularity of *takaful* insurance has spurred the growth of life premiums in recent years.[31] The oil subsector represents a large share of insurance business.

99. An independent regulatory agency was established in 2007 to regulate the insurance sector in the UAE. The Insurance Authority, under the purview of the Ministry of Economy, has among its functions: formulating and issuing regulations for the insurance industry; approving and processes licences for insurance companies and brokers; determining policies and procedures related to solvency margins, accounting policies, investment rules and reinsurance standards; and implementing a code of conduct for the insurance industry. A new Federal Insurance Law (No. 6 of 2007) was adopted in 2007 to regulate the conditions for the establishment and operation of all insurance-related companies.[32]

100. Domestic and foreign insurance companies wishing to establish in an emirate must apply to the Insurance Authority for licensing. Conditions for the granting of licences are set out in Articles 19 and 20 of the Insurance Law (No. 6 of 2007). They include: economic needs criteria, such as domestic demand for the classes of insurance offered by the applicant; whether the applicant will introduce new classes of insurance coverage; and the appointment of a minimum number of UAE nationals as staff.[33] Eligible foreign insurance companies that meet licensing conditions may open a branch in the UAE and appoint a local insurance agent, it is also possible to open a representative office.

101. National companies and foreign branches must have minimum fully paid-up capital of AED 100 million (US$27 million), and must deposit, with a local bank, a guarantee of AED 6 million for non-life insurance and AED 4 million for life insurance. Combined life and non-life, or non-insurance-related operations are not allowed. As of August 2012, all insurance companies (new and existing) will be required to carry out life and non-life insurance separately. The general manager, authorized manager, and senior employees of an insurance company must have suitable qualifications and experience in the insurance business. The manager of a foreign branch must be a resident of the UAE. An application to open a foreign branch must specify the expected overall volume of retention within the UAE market.

102. Although allowed in principle, no new licences are currently being granted. The Insurance Authority took the decision not to issue new licences in December 2008, due to the relatively large number of insurance companies already operating in the UAE, which is considered to be a small market.

103. No taxes or stamp duty are levied on insurance companies at federal or emirate level on the settlements from life or non-life insurance.

---

[30] Per the Abu Dhabi Health Insurance Regulation Bill of Law 35 of 2005.

[31] Takaful is an Islamic insurance concept grounded in Islamic banking, observing the rules and regulations of Islamic law.

[32] Law No. 6 of 2007 replaced Federal Insurance Law No. 9 of 1984.

[33] To be granted a licence, the foreign company must commit to engage UAE nationals in the following percentages: 10% of the staff or at least two persons in the first year, rising to 25% of the staff or at least 12 persons in the fourth year.

104. The UAE made no specific commitments in its GATS Schedule regarding insurance services. The cross-border supply of insurance services is not permitted for companies located abroad. All assets and risks in the UAE must be insured domestically by a company registered in the UAE; this may be a domestic company, a local branch of a foreign company or an agency. However, UAE-based companies may insure risks located abroad. To protect the interests of policyholders, the maximum foreign ownership of domestic insurance companies allowed by law is 25%. Representative offices may not engage in insurance business or act as insurance agents. This does not apply to reinsurance services, for which commercial presence is not required: UAE insurance companies may reinsure their risks from international reinsurance markets. Insurance agents must be UAE citizens.

(ii) Telecommunications and postal services

105. The UAE has the highest mobile and internet penetration in the Arab world, according to the WEF's Networked Readiness Index (NRI) (Table IV.9).[34] In March 2011, mobile subscriptions per 100 inhabitants were at 196.7, i.e. almost two mobile phones per person; internet subscribers exceeded 1.3 million; and there were around 1.7 million landline users. The main reason for the high penetration rates is the large number of tourists, businessmen, and temporary residents that pass through the country (although a national ID card or passport is required to purchase a prepaid SIM card). Usage of multiple SIM cards is also higher than usual, and there is a high level of cross-border traffic. According to a report published recently by the ITU, the UAE ranks second worldwide in the category "mobile-cellular sub-basket as a percentage of GNI per capita".[35]

106. The telecommunications sector is governed by Federal Telecommunications Law No. 3 of 2003 and its Executive Order No. 3 of 2004, and regulated by the Telecommunications Regulatory Authority (TRA). The main functions of the TRA are to issue, implement and enforce all the regulations pertaining to telecommunications services and licensed telecommunications operators in the UAE. It is responsible for managing the frequency spectrum and numbering resources, and for standardizing type approval for telecommunications equipment. It is also responsible for developing sustainable competition in the sector to protect and promote consumer interests, by regulating interconnection and its pricing as well as retail services and prices.

107. The Supreme Committee for the Supervision of the Telecommunications Sector, set up under the Telecommunications Law, was dissolved in 2008 under Law No. 5 of 2008 amending the provisions of the Federal Law No. 3 of 2003. Under the new law, the functions of the Supreme Committee were transferred to the TRA. These functions include formulating general telecom policies, issuing telecom services and licensing, and fixing licence fees. As a result, the TRA is responsible for all policy formulation and implementation for telecommunications in the UAE.

[34] World Economic Forum (2011). The NRI measures the capacity of an economy to fully leverage ICT for increased competitiveness and development. The NRI study is based on data collected by organizations such as the International Telecommunications Union, the World Bank, and the United Nations. According to the NRI, the UAE is ranked 24th out of 138 for overall country network readiness, reflecting the increasingly central role ICT occupies in the Government's agenda, as an enabling infrastructure for economic diversification and a target sector in itself (the UAE is ranked 3rd for government readiness). The Government's focus in the sector has been matched by an equal interest in and capacity for using the latest technologies by individuals (5th and 21st for individual readiness and usage, respectively), with a rapid increase in ICT penetration rates over the last few years. Other competitive advantages are to be found in the very ICT-friendly market environment (18th) and infrastructure for ICT (28th).

[35] International Telecommunications Union (2011).

Table IV.9
Telecommunications indicators, 2007 to March 2011

Fixed statistics	2007	2008	2009	2010	Mar. 2011
Number of fixed lines[a]	1,324,213	1,454,929	1,561,196	1,460,985	1,722,060
Fixed lines per 100 inhabitations	29.2	30.2	29.9	26.4	30.6
Telephone connection charges	49.01	49.01	49.01	49.01	49.01
Monthly subscription charges	4.1	4.1	4.1	4.1	4.1
Cost of 3-minute local call	0	0	0	0	0
Cost of 3-minute call to U.S. or France	1.12	1.12	1.12	1.12	1.12
Cost of 3-minute call to Kuwait	1.12	1.12	1.12	1.12	1.12
Total fixed telephony revenues (US$ million)	768.9	864.6	1,042.8	878.2	..
Fixed domestic calls revenues (US$ million)	303.5	316.6	347.7	312.3	..
Fixed international calls revenues (US$ million)	333.2	326.4	439.2	324.3	..
Mobile statistics					
Active mobile subscriptions[b]	7,742.164	9,357,735	10,671,878	10,926,019	11,066,525
Mobile subscriptions per 100 inhabitants	164.4	190.4	204.4	197.2	196.7
Post-paid	770,071	824,589	958,685	1,176,435	1,238,273
Pre-paid	6,972,093	8,533,146	9,713,193	9,749,584	9,828,252
Total mobile revenues (US$ million)[c]	3,591.0	4,719.1	4,846.6	5,013.6	-317.1
Internet statistics					
Internet subscribers	832,515	1,201,853	1,404,405	1,374,903	1,366,770
Dial-up subscribers	528,633	642,849	713,981	584,821	553,364
Broadband subscribers	303,882	559,004	690,424	790,082	813,406
Broadband internet subscribers per 100 inhabitants	6.6	11.4	13.2	14.3	14.5
Internet subscribers per 100 inhabitants (both broad-band and dial-up subscriptions	18.5	25.2	26.9	24.8	24.3
Internet users per 100 inhabitants[d]	45.1	61.3	67.3	62.0	60.7
Peak dial-up access cost (US$/hour)	0.49	0.49	0.49	0.49	0.49
Off peak dial-up access cost (US$/hour)	0.27	0.27	0.27	0.27	0.27
Total internet revenues (US$ million)	241.7	474.1	689.9	744.7	..
Investment					
Total investment (US$ million)	2,153.1	2,247.4	2,600.5	2,142.0	..
Staff					
Telecommunications staff	10,695	11,759	11,890	11,528	..

.. Not available.

a Includes ISDN fixed lines.
b Includes active mobile subscriptions only. "Active" is defined by any subscriber who has made or received a voice or video call in the preceding 90 days, or has sent an SMS or MMS during that period.
c Excluding mobile data revenues.
d Penetration rate calculated using the ITU methodology, which assumes there are 2.5 internet users per internet subscription (includes broadband and dial-up usage).

Note: Exchange rate AED 3.6725 = US$1.

Source: Etisalat and Telecommunication Regulatory Authority.

108. Important changes have been introduced with respect to market competition since the UAE's last Review; however competition remains limited and the prices of services high. As a result of the changes, the UAE telecommunications market is no longer a monopoly. In February 2006, Du (Emirates Integrated Telecommunications Company) was awarded a licence to become the UAE's second telecom services operator, therefore ending Etisalat's (Emirates Telecommunications Corporation) 30-year monopoly in the telecoms sector. Both companies are majority owned by the

UAE Government. Etisalat is 60% owned by the UAE Government, and 40% of its shares are publicly traded. Du is owned by several UAE entities, with public-sector ownership of over 50%, followed by the Emirates Investment Authority (39.5%), Mubadala Development Company (19.75%), and the Emirates Communications & Technology Company LLC (19.5%), while 21.25% of its shares are publicly traded. All shareholders must be UAE nationals, as foreign investors are not allowed to buy shares in these companies. The TRA does not plan to licence a third operator as it considers the current competition level in the UAE's telecoms sector as adequate (especially in mobile services).

109. Etisalat is a one-stop shop for mobile and fixed-line voice and data services to individuals, enterprises and international telecommunications companies, ISPs, content providers, and mobile operators. It also offers card manufacturing, clearing house services, peering, voice and data transit, and submarine and land cable services. Etisalat has 525 roaming agreements connecting 185 countries enabling BlackBerry, 3G, and voice roaming.[36]

110. In February 2011, Etisalat was the 16th largest mobile operator in the world, with operations in 18 countries across Asia, the Middle East, and Africa, and over 135 million customers. In 2010, Etisalat reported annual net revenue of AED 31.9 billion, a 2% increase, while net profits decreased to AED 7.6 billion.

111. Du is an integrated telecom service provider offering fixed and mobile telephony, broadband connectivity, and IPTV services to individuals, homes, and businesses, and carrier services for businesses. Du has 40.2% of the mobile market in the UAE, with 4.4 million subscribers at end 2010. In 2009, Du's reported annual net revenue was AED 5.3 billion and net profits of AED 528 million. Its revenue increased 32% in 2010, and net profits were AED 1.22 billion before royalties.

112. Du paid the TRA a licence application fee of AED 300,000 and an initial licence fee of AED 124.5 million. In addition, it pays an annual licence fee of AED 1.5 million. Other fees include radio spectrum authorization fees, number allocation fees and an annual fee for the telecommunications and information technology development fund of 1% of the operator's total revenues. Etisalat pays 50% of its profits in royalties or taxes to the UAE Government, while Du paid 15% in 2010. The authorities explained that this difference reflects the importance of supporting new market entrants through regulatory measures to enable them to become strong competitors, and thus achieve effective and sustainable competition in the long term. There are plans by the TRA to lower Etisalat's royalty amounts.

113. Mobile subscriptions are expected to continue to rise as internet surfing on mobiles increases, although growth will be mostly from business visitors, tourists, multiple SIM cards, and new services such as mobile broadband.

114. In late 2011, a number of developments in the telecoms sector were expected to be completed in the near future, including the introduction by the TRA of mobile number portability; and the TRA's approval for Etisalat and Du to compete on fixed-line voice and broadband services, as both companies offer fixed-line services in the UAE, but not in the same districts.

115. Postal services in the UAE are regulated at the federal level by the Emirates Post Holding Group (EPHG). Established under Federal Law No. 14 of 2007, EPHG has four subsidiaries: Emirates Post; Emirates Cooperation for Commercial Postal Services (EMPOST); Wall Street Exchange Center; and Electronics Documents Center (EDC). There are over 120 post offices in the UAE.

[36] Etisalat has made efforts to roll out its fibre-to-the-home (FTTH) network in the UAE. At end 2009 it had completed the roll-out for 85% of households in Abu Dhabi.

116. Any company (national or foreign) wishing to conduct courier services in the UAE requires a licence: a licence is required for transport of documents, letter items, and parcels. The licensing department at EPHG is responsible for granting and issuing licences against payment of a prescribed fee (AED 100,000), and presentation of the necessary documentation. In 2011, 85 postal companies had been licensed by the EPHG, with 19 new companies registered in 2009.

(iii) Transport

(a) Overview

117. Transport plays an important role in the UAE's economic development. In 2010 transport, storage, and communication constituted 9.05% of GDP. Due to its geographical position, the UAE is strategically located to establish links between Asia, Europe, and Africa. A key component of the UAE's economy, especially in Dubai and Abu Dhabi, has been its logistics and transport infrastructure, with continued investments to fulfil its long-term plans. Plans include: continued expansion of passenger and freight handling capacity at the international airports in Abu Dhabi, Dubai, and Sharjah and construction of the new Al Maktoum International Airport at Jebel Ali port; expansion of port cargo-handling capacity; construction of intra-emirate metro systems or light rail transport systems in Abu Dhabi and Dubai; creation of a rail network covering the UAE, and eventually the GCC countries; and improvements in bus services.

118. Each emirate has an independent emirate-wide transport policy. Various federal authorities, such as the National Transport Authority (NTA) and the General Civil Aviation Authority (GCAA), are responsible for inter-emirate and international transport policy at the federal level. The NTA, which replaced the Ministry of Transport under Federal Law No. 1 of 2006, is in charge of setting general policies and regulations related to inter-emirate and international land (road and railway) transport and international maritime transport. The GCAA was set up in 1996 and is in charge of air transport in the UAE.

119. At the emirate level, the Department of Transport (DOT) is responsible for all transport-related matters and transport policy and development in Abu Dhabi.[37] In Dubai, transport matters are regulated by Dubai Roads and Transport Authority (land and maritime transport), and the Dubai Civil Aviation Authority (DCAA) and Dubai Airports (air transport).

(b) Air transport and airports

Air transport services

120. The UAE's air transport industry grew continuously during the review period. In 2011, the UAE had a total of six national airports and five national carriers.[38] The UAE plans to become a global transport hub by investing around AED 500 billion (US$136.12 billion) in the aviation industry over the next decade. It intends to capitalize on its transport and communications infrastructure by introducing new aircraft for the five UAE flag carriers, huge investments in new airport capacity throughout the seven emirates, and plans for Abu Dhabi to become a regional centre for aircraft maintenance, manufacturing, and flight training.

---

[37] Previously, responsibility for Abu Dhabi's transport was held by a variety of entities, both the local and Federal, including the General Civil Aviation Authority (GCAA), the Department of Civil Aviation, the Department of Municipal Affairs, and the Sea Ports Authority (SPA).

[38] The five national airports are: Abu Dhabi International Airport, Al Ain airport, Dubai International Airport, Fujairah airport, Ras Al Khaimah airport, and Sharjah International Airport. The five national airlines are: Air Arabia, Emirates Airlines, Etihad Airlines, FlyDubai, and RAK Airways.

121. All activities related to civil aviation in the UAE, at the federal level, are managed by the General Civil Aviation Authority (GCAA). An autonomous body, the GCAA ensures safety and security for the aviation sector through oversight and the development of regulations. It also provides navigation services, registration, and licensing services for the UAE aviation industry. The GCAA proposes general air transport policy guidelines and relevant legislation to the Council of Ministers, and enforces international agreements and conventions. The aviation authorities at emirate level are involved with operational matters at their respective airports. They represent the interests of the stakeholders in each emirate in air services agreements (ASA), through participation in preparatory meetings, work committees, and exchanges of views with the GCAA. For example, Abu Dhabi's DOT secures traffic rights in coordination with the GCAA. Carriers wishing to conduct commercial air transport in the UAE must obtain an Air Operator Certificate from the GCAA.

122. Cabotage operations, of cargo and passengers, are limited to national airlines; in practice, however, no such operations take place. Airports are the property of the different emirates. Foreign companies may provide certain services, including: freighter and charter passenger services; maintenance, repair and overhaul (MRO); aircraft leasing; and parts manufacturing.

123. The UAE has bilateral air services agreements with 144 countries, including 90 open skies agreements. Based on the traffic rights specified in the respective air services agreements, airlines decide their own capacity (frequency and aircraft type), subject to approval by the authorities. In 2009, the UAE joined the IATA air services agreement, along with six other countries, in order to further liberalize its air space by signing the deal under IATA's Multilateral Statement of Policy Principles.[39] Under this non-binding multilateral agreement, airlines may merge across borders, acquire airlines in other countries, or tap into international equity markets or private equity investors.[40]

124. The UAE aims to become a global aviation hub, chiefly by encouraging airlines to commence and maintain operations in the UAE. This policy includes developing several key clusters, such as airport-related activities and services, aircraft leasing and financing, aircraft maintenance and manufacture, as well as other aviation-related activities. In Abu Dhabi, an airport free zone is being established to promote foreign participation in providing aviation logistics. The governments of Abu Dhabi and Dubai recognize the contribution the UAE airline industry makes to the economy; both encourage major foreign carriers to commit to long-term presence and seek to continue to attract new airlines.

Airports

Abu Dhabi

125. Abu Dhabi International Airport is the larger of Abu Dhabi's two airports. It serves as the base and hub airport for Etihad Airways, the Abu Dhabi national airline, and consists of three terminals with a total handling capacity of around 12 million passengers annually. Currently, more than 30 scheduled airlines operate from Abu Dhabi International Airport, serving more than 80 scheduled destinations in 47 countries.

126. Al Ain International Airport, Abu Dhabi's second airport, serves the Eastern region of Abu Dhabi and is used mainly as a cargo hub and as a base for low-cost and regional carriers.

[39] The signatories of IATA's Multilateral Statement of Policy Principles are Chile, Malaysia, Panama, Singapore, Switzerland, and the United States. The agreement has the endorsement of the European Union. In total, signatories represent 60% of global aviation.

[40] Online information. Viewed at: www.agenda-for-freedom.aero.

127. Abu Dhabi Aircraft Technologies (ADTA), formerly known as Gulf Aircraft Maintenance Company (GAMCO), is a major provider of aviation technical services for the commercial and military aviation industries. The company's main facilities and operations are to the south-west of Abu Dhabi International Airport. ADTA is a part of the Mubadala Development Company, wholly owned by the Government of the Emirate of Abu Dhabi.

128. In addition to the Department of Transport, Abu Dhabi Airports Company (ADAC) was created in 2006 through a mandate from the Executive Council of Abu Dhabi, to manage and operate Abu Dhabi International Airport and oversee its multi-billion-dollar expansion plan. ADAC has plans to create a free-trade zone in the vicinity of Abu Dhabi Airport, as part of the airport's development and expansion.

129. As of July 2011, Etihad Airways operated more than 1,000 flights per week in 42 countries. In 2010, it carried 7.5 million passengers, compared with 340,000 in 2004, its first full year of operation. In addition to its core activity of passenger transportation, Etihad earns significant revenue from its cargo operation, Etihad Crystal Cargo, which serves 14 destinations.

130. Abu Dhabi is investing AED 25 billion to improve its airport infrastructure. The second runway of Abu Dhabi International Airport was completed in 2008, and an exclusive Etihad Airways terminal was finished in 2009 (Terminal 3). A mid-field terminal complex (MTC) is currently under construction; upon its completion, the total airport capacity will rise to 42 million passengers annually.

Dubai

131. Dubai International Airport was the fastest growing airport for international passengers in 2009, and is one of the busiest in the world in terms of international passenger and cargo traffic. Dubai International is connected to over 220 destinations across six continents through some 130 scheduled airlines. It comprises three terminals, including Emirates Terminal 3, which opened in October 2008. The new terminal helped boost the airport's operational capacity to 60 million passengers per year.

132. In 2007, the Department of Civil Aviation was restructured, leading to the formation of Dubai Airports, the entity responsible for developing and managing Dubai's airports, and of the Dubai Civil Aviation Authority (DCAA), the local aviation regulatory body. The DCAA oversees the administration and coordination of all matters relating to civilian airport operations, including traffic rights, operating permissions, flight training, duty free shops, and cargo. The DCAA formulates civil aviation policies, signs air agreements on behalf of the Dubai Government, authorizes and provides landing approval for foreign air transportation and aircraft charters, monitors air-crew, and is responsible for licensing travel agencies and restricting the carriage of dangerous goods.

133. Dubai-based Emirates airline maintained its ranking as the world's largest carrier of international traffic in 2010.[41] Dubai is investing heavily in developing the reach of Emirates. Its aim is to develop Dubai's air transportation industry so that passengers from any city can fly directly to Dubai.

---

[41] IATA (2011).

134. In 2008, Dubai International Airport opened Terminal 3, adding 1.5 square kilometres to the airport's structures. A third concourse is being built, and will push capacity to 75 million travellers a year. The focus on boosting capacity at Dubai International Airport is in tandem with a gradual transfer of airlines over the next decade to Al Maktoum International Airport, in Jebel Ali. Completion of the new airport envisages a capacity of up to 160 million travellers a year and five runways, with the aim of making it the largest airport in the world.

Sharjah

135. Sharjah International Airport, the UAE's oldest airport, is an important cargo hub and trans-shipment point in the region, especially for intermodal cargo arriving by sea and air-freighted onwards. Landing fees and basic handling charges are considered competitive compared with regional standards. A major expansion programme is expected to quadruple its capacity. It is run autonomously by the Sharjah Airport Authority. Non-aeronautical activities (e.g. duty-free shops, car rentals, currency exchange) are generally outsourced, as well as certain aeronautical services, such as maintenance operations, and fire and crash rescue.

(c) Maritime transport and ports

136. Due to its strategic location, the UAE has over 30 ports, of which 15 are commercial. These include container-handling facilities, oil terminals, industrial ports, and fishing ports. In 2009, the UAE ranked 23rd in the world in terms of ship owners with 9.3 million dead weight. In 2010, the commercial fleet under UAE flag totalled 1.6 million gross tonnages (GT). The UAE's ports export mainly oil and gas, but also raw materials and finished goods. Imports consist of intermediate and consumer goods, as well as a significant re-export trade within the Gulf regional, East Africa, and the Indian subcontinent.

Maritime transport

137. The NTA's Maritime Transport Sector manages the ship registry and seafarers licensing, issues navigational licences, monitors compliance with international standards, and levies fees. The NTA is also in charge of all security, seaworthiness, and communications aspects of marine navigation, as well as compliance with international standards. The regulation of port and shipping services is shared between the NTA and the respective port authority of each emirate. For purposes of regulation, a distinction is made between foreign flag vessels calling at UAE ports; national flag vessels; and foreign flag vessels operating in UAE territorial waters, mainly in the context of offshore projects (e.g. Dubai Maritime City, Palm Island) as well as pleasure craft. In addition, in Abu Dhabi, the Department of Transport is responsible for regulating all intra-emirate maritime transportation, such as ferry services between and among the Abu Dhabi mainland and islands.

138. At the federal level, maritime transport is governed by UAE Federal Law No. 26 of 1981 as amended in 1988 (known as the UAE Maritime Code). The Code governs and regulates all maritime practices in the UAE. It covers, *inter alia,* vessel registration and ownership; crew issues and maritime insurance; safe operation of vessels; pilotage and towage; and marine accidents salvage. The law is applicable to all the emirates and is based on maritime principles set out in international conventions. In addition to the Maritime Code, several relevant ministerial decrees or local laws regulate registration of vessels, crewing, classification of vessels, restrictions with regard to activities undertaken by foreign flag vessels, and other port activities.

139. The UAE has adhered to the following international treaties and conventions: IMO Amendments 1993; SOLAS Convention 1974; SOLAS Protocol 1978; LOAD LINES Convention 1966; TONNAGE Convention 1969; COLREG Convention 1972; STCW Convention 1978; SAR Convention 1979; INMARSAT Convention 1976; INMARSAT OA 1976; LC Convention 1972; INTERVENTION Convention 1969; CLC Convention 1969; CLC Protocol 1976; CLC Protocol 1992; FUND Convention 1971; FUND Protocol 1992; LLMC Convention 1976; and SALVAGE Convention 1989.

140. To register a vessel in the UAE with a UAE flag, the vessel must be 51% owned by a UAE national or a company with its management based in the UAE. Exceptions to the management rule are allowed in the case of companies based in Arab League countries. Foreign owners may register their vessels in the UAE with a maximum of 49% (foreign) ownership. If a UAE vessel is sold to a foreign entity that is located outside the UAE and owns over 49% of the vessel, the UAE registration must cancelled.

141. The authorities indicated that the restrictions noted above would be phased out through new legislation currently under consideration. In early 2011, the Federal National Council approved major amendments to Federal Law No. 26 of 1981 (Maritime Law). Under the draft law, foreign vessels with 100% ownership would be allowed to register under the UAE flag and benefit from, *inter alia*, zero taxation and easier movement between ports, and be part of the International Maritime Organization's white list as UAE vessels.[42]

142. According to the authorities, the UAE aims to have its maritime sector among the top five in the world. In its strategic plan 2011-2013, the National Transport Authority aims to, *inter alia*, increase the size of the marine fleet registered under the UAE's flag and to increase the rate at which marine vessels are inspected so as to support both the security and environmental aspects of maritime transport.

143. The UAE's fleet comprises all ships registered in the UAE with 100% ownership by UAE nationals or by companies with at least 51% of "national capital". Only ships registered in the UAE may conduct cargo or passenger cabotage operations.

144. Foreign flag vessels may operate in UAE territorial waters, mainly in the context of offshore projects (ex. Dubai Maritime City and Palm Island). Unless they obtain a waiver, at the discretion of the NTA Chairman, foreign flag vessels must have a contract with one of the federal or local governments to operate in UAE waters, and may not carry out cabotage on their own account. Crews working on ships servicing the territorial waters must have residency visas. Foreign companies must obtain approval from the NTA in the form of a licence. All UAE flag ships operating must be classed under one of the recognized organizations of the International Association of Classification Societies (IACS).[43] In addition, foreign ships must not be older than 25 years, and local ships must receive IACS approval issued within five years.

---

[42] The so-called White List of countries comprises IMO members deemed to be giving "full and complete effect" to the revised STCW Convention (International Convention on Standards of Training, Certification and Watchkeeping for Seafarers (STCW 95)).

[43] The classification process requires the periodic evaluation of a vessel to determine its compliance with the applicable rules to ensure the safety of life, property, and the environment. For a vessel to remain 'in class' it must meet the applicable requirements.

145. The United Arab Shipping Company (UASC) is the largest container carrier operating from the Middle East. It was established jointly by the six GCC states; the UAE Federal Government owns 10.96%. A number of other domestic shipping companies are partly or fully owned by the Federal Government or by the governments of the emirates, including: the Abu Dhabi National Tanker Company (ADNATCO), the National Petroleum Construction Company, and the National Marine Dredging Company (all owned by the Federal Government); Etisalat and Delma Cooperative Society (owned by the Abu Dhabi Government); and the Arab Maritime Petroleum Transport Company which is owned by the Abu Dhabi Government, the Dubai Government, and nine other Arab countries.

146. The UAE's shipping agency and freight forwarding market comprises several companies. One of the world's largest shipping agencies, the Gulf Agency Company (GAC), is based in the Jebel Ali Free Zone.

Ports

147. UAE ports are mostly regulated and run by the respective emirate authorities. Most services are provided by the managing company, although outsourcing is also used. Foreign participation remains limited except in free zones, which is one of the reasons why many main ports have an adjacent free zone.

148. DP World's flagship terminal, Jebel Ali, was the world's 9th largest container port in 2010. It has a current capacity of 14 million TEU (twenty-foot equivalent container units) and work is under way to construct a 400 metre quay extension at Jebel Ali Port, increasing capacity at the facility by an additional one million TEU. The expansion, expected to be concluded by the end of 2012, will permit Jebel Ali to handle up to six vessels of 15,000 TEU simultaneously, hence improving efficiency and reducing turn-around times.

149. The port of Fujairah is one of the top three bunkering ports in the world alongside Singapore and Rotterdam. Private tank storage, principally for refined petroleum products, is due to increase from 3 million cubic metres (121 tanks), to 8 million cubic metres (262 tanks) by the end of 2012. There are 2,340 metres of fully-equipped oil berths already operational, with a further 1,000 metres going to tender. Further expansion is planned: to the north of the port, the Abu Dhabi Crude Oil Pipeline (ADCOP) project, which involves the transport of crude oil through a 360-kilometre land pipeline, is expected to cater for 60% of the UAE's total crude oil exports. For the completion of future projects, including a new refinery to complement the ADCOP project, an additional 225 hectare of land has been reclaimed from the sea.

150. Port Zayed is the main gateway for container and general cargo vessels in Abu Dhabi. Other ports in Abu Dhabi, include: Mussafah Port, which services mainly smaller vessels, tugs, barges and service craft; and Khalifa Port and Industrial Zone (KPIZ), which is under construction and expected to be completed by 2013. The Khalifa Port and Industrial Zone will be developed in five phases and will include a container-handling terminal and piers for handling raw and bulk cargos. The KPIZ will replace Abu Dhabi's largest existing port, Port Zayed by 2013. The KPIZ will offer 100% foreign ownership to companies and individuals.

151. Responsibility for the regulation and operation of Abu Dhabi's ports, previously held by the Sea Ports Authority, has been devolved to the Department of Transport (Maritime) and the Abu Dhabi Ports Company (ADPC) respectively. Port terminal operations in Abu Dhabi are the responsibility of Abu Dhabi Terminals, a joint-venture company owned by ADPC and Mubadala of Abu Dhabi. DP World, which has a management agreement with Abu Dhabi Terminals is the de facto operator of Port Zayed.

152. The main ports in Sharjah are Port Khalid, Al Hamariah Port, and Khorfokan, on the east coast. Sharjah's ports are regulated and run by the Sharjah Port Authority (Sharjah's Department of Seaports and Customs). Port operations are governed by the (Sharjah) Port Act of 1977. In 1976, the Authority established the company Gulftainer to manage and operate the container terminals in Port Khalid and Khorfakkan. The port of Ajman, which also services the Ajman Free Zone situated in the port, has eight berths designed to handle both container and general cargoes. The port is regulated and managed by the Ajman Port Authority, which has also set up two dry docks to provide maintenance and repair services. Port Saqr, in Ra's al-Khaimah, specializes in the transportation of cement, marble, and gravel from nearby quarries and factories. In 2004, Ra's al-Khaimah Port Authority awarded the Kuwaiti firm KGL a US$45 million contract to build, operate, and manage its container terminal at Port Saqr for 21 years.

(d) Road and railway transport

153. The UAE land transport sector, including highways and railways is regulated by the National Transport Authority (NTA), formed under Federal Law No. 1 of 2006. The NTA is the Federal Authority in charge of developing land transport regulations and for granting licences to relevant transport bodies, land transport infrastructure companies and operators relating to highways, railways, and all modes of land transport for federal inter-emirates transport and international transport movements. The NTA also issues safety certificates, reviews and accepts safety management systems (SMSs) and develops railway standards for the UAE. Federal Law No. 9 of 2011 was enacted to strengthen the governance of the overall land transport sector. According to the NTA's strategic plan 2011-2013, the Authority aims to raise the efficiency of land and railway transport and guarantee its sustainability by developing federal legislation according to international best practices.

154. The UAE encourages international competition in land transport to achieve cost-effectiveness, use best practices, follow international standards, and promote technology transfer to the UAE. This approach supports the UAE Vision 2021 objective to be one of the best countries in the world by 2021. Under its 2030 plan, Abu Dhabi seeks to transform itself into "Greater Abu Dhabi" by linking the city to the large-scale mixed-use developments currently under construction on the mainland as well as offshore. The Government of Abu Dhabi has earmarked AED 98 billion for infrastructure, tourism, and economic development in the Western Region.

155. Within Abu Dhabi, the Department of Transport is responsible for: regulating the Abu Dhabi public transport systems and infrastructure; the maintenance and construction of the main roads; and the operation of public buses. The Department also has plans to implement rail projects within the emirate. On the basis of the Abu Dhabi 2030 plan, the Department of Transport prepared the Abu Dhabi Surface Transportation Master Plan (STMP) and a strategic transport plan for 2012-2016. This is expected to help Abu Dhabi develop a metro system and on-street light-rail transit for the city. Under the STMP, together with the introduction and expansion of bus services, the role of public transport in Abu Dhabi and Dubai will be substantially enhanced. The investment plans seeks to involve the private sector in the funding, implementation, and operation.

156. The UAE's highway network comprises about 4,000 km of asphalt paved roads. Road and other public transport, including inter-emirate roads are regulated by the NTA and by each emirate transport entity. All road transport companies must be majority-owned by UAE nationals, although they may employ foreign drivers.

157. Federal Law No. 2 of 2009, established the Etihad Rail Company (formerly known as Union Railway Company) with a mandate to manage the development, construction, and operation of the UAE's national railway, with capital of AED 1 billion (US$272m). The railway will link the principal centres of the UAE, covering a network of 1,200 km stretching across all seven emirates. Initially, it will cater to freight transport, with passenger services being added at a later stage.

158. The Dubai metro was launched in September 2009; the cost of the project was US$7.6 billion. The first two lines of the Dubai metro are operational, and expansion of the system is planned. The Abu Dhabi and Dubai metro systems are to be integrated eventually, into a railway network that will link up to a GCC railway system. By 2017, the GCC railway system will help connect the six GCC countries, with a total of 2,117 km of railway, and will be mixed traffic use (freight and passenger) with priority given to freight.

(iv) Tourism

159. For the past decade, tourism has become a cornerstone of the UAE's plan for a diversified economy. In 2009, tourism capital investment was around AED 69 billion. Travel and tourism contributed an estimated 7.4% of GDP in 2009, and 11.7% of UAE non-oil GDP, and employed some 158,262 people, despite the sector being greatly affected by the global financial crisis, with revenues plunging by 16% in 2009.

160. The UAE is an attractive destination for travel and tourism, with good infrastructure. The WEF ranked the UAE first in the Middle East region in terms of tourism receipts, fourth in terms of its air transport infrastructure, and eighth in terms of the Government prioritizing the travel and tourism sector.[44] However, there is room for improvement with respect to market access and policy rules and regulations.

161. Dubai has positioned itself as a regional tourism hub, accounting for around two thirds of total tourism revenue in the UAE, followed by Abu Dhabi (16%) and Sharjah (10%) (Table IV.10). Fujairah and Ras Al Khaimah represent the remainder. Most tourists to the UAE are Europeans, with around one third from GCC countries.

162. Until 2008, the tourism sector in the UAE was regulated at the emirate level only. Currently, it is regulated at both the emirate and federal levels. The UAE National Council for Tourism and Antiquities (NCTA) was established under Federal Law No. 6 of 2008 and became operational as a federal entity in 2009. The Council's main role is to promote the UAE's tourism sector within the country and overseas, and help coordinate the UAE tourism-related policies at the federal level. However, policy-making and issuing tourism licences in the UAE is at emirate level.[45]

---

[44] World Economic Forum (2011).

[45] National Council for Tourism and Antiquities online information. Viewed at: http://www.uaetourism.ae/en/.

163. Planning, supervision, and development of the tourism sector in Dubai is under the Dubai Department of Tourism and Commerce Marketing (DTCM).[46] This includes licensing and classification of hotels, hotel apartments, tour operators, travel agents, and all other tourism services. However, Federal Law No. 6 of 2006 regulates licensing procedures in the tourism sector. There are four types of tourism activities in Dubai, each requiring a licence: general sales agent, travel agent, outbound tour operator and inbound tour operator.

Table IV.10
Hotel indicators, 2000, 2005, and 2010

				Average annual percentage change over the period	
	2000	**2005**	**2010**	**2000-05**	**2005-10**
Number of hotels					
Dubai	265	407	573	54%	41%
Abu Dhabi	49	55	115	135%	109%
Sharjah	23	57	102	148%	79%
Ras Al Khaimah	..	6	42	..	600%
Fujairah	..	..	13	..	..
Ajman	..	..	22	..	..
Hotel revenues (US$ million)					
Dubai	715	2,403	3,613	236%	50%
Abu Dhabi	..	..	1,151	..	..
Sharjah	43.5	88	131	102%	49%
Ras Al Khaimah	..	..	55	..	..
Fujairah	..	..	..	..	..
Ajman	..	..	38	..	..

.. Not available.

Source: Information provided by the authorities.

164. Dubai's traditional niche tourism activities have been in shopping, leisure, and business tourism. More recently, its market has been expanding to include sports, eco, healthcare, and cruise tourism. More than 30 entertainment resorts and theme parks are being developed in Dubai with a projected investment of AED 228 billion; they include the Dubai metro; Dubailand; Dubai Sports City; Burj Dubai; and the World.[47]

165. Abu Dhabi Tourism Authority (ADTA) has been responsible for the development and promotion of Abu Dhabi's tourism industry since 2004.[48] The ADTA's activities include: the regulation and monitoring of the tourism industry; infrastructure upgrade and product development; destination marketing; the issuance of tourism licences; and the setting up of classification standards. Tourism in Abu Dhabi is regulated by Law No. 13 of 2006, which requires tourism business providers to obtain a licence from the ADTA in order to set up any tourist-related business.

[46] Dubai Department of Tourism and Commerce Marketing online information. Viewed at: http://www.dubaitourism.ae/.

[47] For a detailed account of Dubai's resorts and theme parks, see WTO (2006), p. 71. Also see: http://www.definitelydubai.com/.

[48] Abu Dhabi Tourism Authority online information. Viewed at: http://www.visitabudhabi.ae/en/adta.

166. Business tourism remains a vitally important market segment for Abu Dhabi, and the ADTA is engaged in increasing the significance of leisure tourism and establishing Abu Dhabi as a regional culture hub. The emirate's culture focus is centred on Saadiyat Island (the Island of Happiness), an AED 99.3 billion commercial, residential, and leisure project off the coast of Abu Dhabi. The project is developed by the Tourism Development and Investment Company (TDIC), a large developer of major tourism destinations in Abu Dhabi. The project will house the first branch of the Louvre Museum outside Paris, a Guggenheim Museum, and the Sheikh Zayed National museum. The island is expected to attract 1.5 million visitors a year when completed by 2018 and will be home to around 160,000 people.

167. Sharjah, Ras Al Khaimah, Ajman, Um Alquain, and Fujairah have been promoting their tourism sectors with strong campaigning to develop the industry and attract more tourists. The major attractions of these emirates are heritage, architecture, natural landscapes, leisure, sports, and facilities for business conferences and exhibitions.

168. Most tourism advertising campaigns are launched individually by the emirates. The UAE Government has started to raise awareness of the country by promoting the complementary tourist attractions of its emirates through a campaign of "seven emirates, one destination". The main markets for visitors to the UAE continue to cover traditional countries in Western Europe and the GCC, while new markets are being explored in North America, China, and the Asian sub-continent. The UAE aims to expand its tourist base through the development of budget and mid-range hotels as well as luxury hotels.

169. In its GATS commitments, the UAE has bound without limitations, provision of hotel and restaurant services through modes 1 to 3. Commercial presence is permitted with a maximum foreign equity participation of 49%.

(v) Construction services

170. The UAE's private construction sector suffered a major downturn as a result of the 2008-09 global financial crisis.[49] In particular, Dubai's real estate sector suffered a major price correction from the previous real estate bubble and values dropped by 50%.[50] The crisis was exacerbated by the large number of new units on the market, coupled with a slowdown in residential and business demand. In Abu Dhabi, real estate prices have fallen by 40% on average since peaking in June 2008. The tightness of supply of all types of property in Abu Dhabi had resulted in sky-high prices and rents.

171. Prior to the crisis, the UAE has witnessed a proliferation in property development and a construction boom, which helped garner the emergence of conglomerates in this sector. During 2007-08, Dubai had more than 30% of the world's cranes working on its ambitious mega-developments. By the end of 2009, there were more than 750 sky scrapers in Dubai.

---

[49] In the course of this Review, the UAE authorities indicated that federal government construction projects has not been affected by the crisis.

[50] *Financial Times*, "Economy: Recession exposes need for reform", by Simeon Kerr, 20 July 2009. Viewed at: http://www.ft.com/cms/s/0/5bfacef4-7270-11de-ba94-00144feabdc0.html#ixzz1Vqqs7LiE.

172. The UAE boasts some world-renowned buildings and developments, such as: Burj Khalifa, the world's tallest building by EMAAR, the region's largest developer; Palm Jumeirah, the world's largest man-made island by Nakheel; Masdar, the world's first carbon-free city; the Dubai Mall, the world's largest shopping mall; and Ski Dubai, the world's first indoor ski resort. In addition, fully-integrated communities like Jumeirah Lake Towers by Nakheel, Downtown Dubai by EMAAR, Al Raha Gardens by Aldar properties in Abu Dhabi, and Al Hamra Village in Ras Al Khaimah have been created.

173. One of the largest Dubai-based developers, Dubai World (DW)'s subsidiary Nakheel has been hard hit by the financial crisis. The Government of Dubai enacted a special insolvency regime for Nakheel through the Dubai Financial Support Fund (DFSF). Created in July 2009, the DFSF provided Nakheel US$8 billion in new equity and converted the company's existing debt into equity. In order to protect DW's non-real-estate assets, the Government of Dubai currently owns Nakheel directly. More recently, Nakheel announced a comprehensive recapitalization plan of its debt and liabilities. The plan enables Nakheel to offer creditors 100% of agreed amounts owed and to fulfil its obligations to customers through the prompt completion of near-term projects.

174. Established in 2007, the Real Estate Regulatory Authority (RERA) has full legal authority to regulate the real estate sector in Dubai, and is part of Dubai's Land Department. The RERA's main responsibilities include: licensing real estate agents; and regulating and registering rental agreements and owners associations. To boost the UAE's real estate industry, the RERA has embarked on a code of governance for the real estate development industry, to promote transparency and disclosure, investor protection, performance optimization, and risk management practices in the industry. Under the RERA's ambit, the Real Estate Investment Promotion Center encourages investments in Dubai's real estate sector through its Tanmia and Tayseer programmes, which provide investors with financial facilities.[51]

175. As a result of the crisis, the construction sector has been affected by disputes between investors, developers, and contractors. The disputes range from disgruntled retail investors in planned developments that are unlikely to materialize, to contractors complaining of missing payments. According to the Dubai Chamber of Commerce, its arbitration centre handled 280 dispute cases in the first ten months of the 2010. From January until end September 2011, the centre handled 315 dispute cases. Major state-linked developers have reportedly offered only 65% of money owed and no payment was made until 2010.

176. The deflating real-estate bubble continues to restrain prospects for recovery, particularly in Dubai. Nevertheless, construction has been identified as a vertical building block in the Dubai strategic plan for 2015. A series of measures have been put in place to improve the real estate sector in the UAE. In Dubai, for example, the Ruler promulgated Decree No. 22 of 2011 waiving up to AED 300,000 in mortgage repayments for borrowers that repay home loans ahead of their maturity date. However, as a counterpart to this incentive, as of January 2011, Dubai imposes a mandatory 5% housing tax on all residential units. In Abu Dhabi, an allocation of AED 7 billion from the emirate's 2011 budget is to be distributed to citizens in the form of housing loans.[52]

[51] For more information see: http://www.dubailand.gov.ae

[52] Arabian Business, "Home loan fees waived on early settlement", 17 July 2011.

177. While construction remains depressed in Dubai, it has been growing rapidly in Abu Dhabi, where the target is to triple the size and population of the city by 2030. To achieve this goal and accommodate the population increase, real estate projects in excess of US$140 billion are in the pipeline. These include Sowwah Island, which is intended to be Abu Dhabi's new central business district.[53] Other emirates, like Ajman, Ras Al Khaimah and Sharjah, have also undertaken large-scale construction projects.

(vi) Trade in business and professional services

178. In its GATS Schedule of specific commitments, the UAE bound measures affecting the cross-border supply, consumption abroad, and commercial presence (modes 1-3) of: accounting, auditing and book-keeping services; certain taxation services; architectural, engineering, urban planning and landscape services; and veterinary services.

179. The UAE's labour market is generally open to foreigners, and it is estimated that over 90% of the UAE workforce is foreign. However, although the exercise of several professions is allowed provided a licence is obtained, the use of a local service agent is required, which adds to the cost and, to a certain extent, discourages market entry. In this respect, foreign professionals are allowed to practice business services and professions such as auditing, medical services, engineering, legal practice and consultancies, computer consultancies and similar services only by setting up "sole proprietorship" businesses. To obtain a licence applicants require: a valid UAE residence permit; a professional licence from the government of the emirate in which they intend to operate; and a service agency contract with a local services agent that is a UAE national. The agent's duties and obligations towards the foreign professional are limited to facilitating the practice of an activity in the emirate, including assisting in obtaining and renewing work permits issued by the Ministry of Labour, and other government authorities. The local service agent holds no share in the "sole proprietorship" firm and does not participate in its management.

(a) Legal services

180. Legal services are regulated both at the emirate and federal levels. Federal Law No. 23 of 1991, concerning the Lawyers Ordinance and amendments thereof, regulates the law profession in five of the seven emirates. Under this law, lawyers are licensed federally and are free to move within the UAE, except for the emirates of Dubai and Ra's al Khaimah. A local licence is required to practice law in these two emirates. Dubai requires lawyers to have an office in Dubai in order to appear in a Dubai Court.

181. The request for a licence is presented to the Ministry of Justice through a local law firm. If all procedural conditions are met, the Ministry of Justice registers the applicant as a lawyer and allows him to practice, but only as an employee of the local law firm. Licences for both foreign and local lawyers must be renewed annually. In principle, they may be revoked only for professional reasons. The UAE does not have a Bar Association.

182. Establishment of a law firm, which must be 100% owned by UAE nationals, is regulated at the federal level. In the five emirates applying Federal Law No. 23 of 1991, foreign lawyers may offer legal advice on foreign, international, and local law, and may represent clients in a court of appeal for a maximum of four years, and in a court of first instance for a maximum of eight years. To represent a client in court, a foreign lawyer must obtain a permit from the Ministry of Justice, which

[53] *Financial Times*, "Real estate: Congested city hopes for relief in vast construction projects", by James Drummond, 28 October 2009. Viewed at: http://www.ft.com/cms/s/0/8c4dc7c2-c28f-11de-be3a-00144feab49a.html#ixzz1VqAxhlzW.

requires a diploma from a foreign professional body recognized by the Ministry of Education. The foreign lawyer must be registered in the bar of his home country, have 15 years of experience, and meet conditions of good reputation. There is no prior residency requirement. Firms of legal consultants may not represent clients in courts. Foreign lawyers may not appear in the Supreme Federal Court and in courts of cassation.

183. In Abu Dhabi, international law firms are regulated under Decree No. 30 of 2006. International law firms may open a branch in Abu Dhabi subject to several requirements: practicing law for at least 15 years outside the UAE; having at least 50 partners across the board in all its offices; and obtaining approval of the Executive Council of Abu Dhabi. The request for a licence must be filed with the Department of Development and Planning in Abu Dhabi.

(b) Accounting and auditing services

184. Accounting services are regulated at federal level. Federal Law No. 22 of 1995 and the relevant ministerial decisions regulate auditors and certified accountants, firms and individuals. Accountants must be registered in a particular emirate. They may exercise throughout the UAE, but must obtain a professional licence from the relevant authorities of the emirate where they wish to practice. A licence is granted for each activity, rather than for each individual.

185. The Accountants and Auditors Association (AAA), established by Resolution of the Ministry of Labour and Social Affairs No. 227/97, is the professional body for accountants in the UAE. Auditors are not obliged to register with the AAA.

186. Foreign accounting firms have traditionally been able to practice audit and accounting services in the UAE. In 2008 (the latest available information), some 263 foreign individual auditors, 264 local (or GCC) individual auditors, 65 local firms, and 12 foreign firms were operating in the UAE. These firms were established before 1995. No new firms have been established since as a consequence of the introduction of the emiratization policy in 1997, by which foreign ownership in new foreign firms established in the UAE was limited to 75%. This requirement was also made applicable to firms established before 1995, which were given a transition period, until 2010, to find local partners for the remaining 25% participation in the firm.

187. Foreign accounting firms operating in the UAE may do so by opening a branch. Branches established before 1997 were allowed to be 100% foreign-owned, until 2010, and have several sub-branches operating in the various emirates. After 2010, they are obliged to take a local partner and may retain maximum ownership of 75% of property. As noted, foreign firms must have a local services agent.

188. The Register of Auditors includes local, GCC, and other foreign natural persons and firms. There are three categories in the Register: practising auditors; non-practising auditors; and trainees (only for nationals). Registration conditions for foreigners include: a university degree in accounting or an equivalent degree; three years of experience in accounting; five years of registration with an auditing professional body recognized by the Ministry of Economy; and evidence of a partnership with a UAE citizen or company or a certificate of employment.

189. One partner or manager in every auditing firm must be a UAE national, registered as a practicing auditor in the Registry; all other partners must be registered as practicing auditors. If one of the partners is a firm established outside the UAE, that foreign firm must hold a certified licence for practicing as an auditor in its country of registration.

(c) Engineering services

190. The engineering profession is regulated at emirate level. A foreign engineering consultant or contractor may operate in the UAE through a joint-venture with a local firm; a partnership with a local engineering firm; or a foreign branch with a local service agent. In some cases, particularly those concerning large engineering projects, foreign engineering contractors may be invited to tender without having to incorporate locally.

191. Licences of foreign branches are generally limited to the fields of specialization not commonly provided by local engineering firms. The head office of the foreign firm must have existed for not less than 15 years, and carried out a number of projects of large technical and financial value. The firm's manager must be registered in the Engineers Society of the UAE and have no less than 15 years of experience in the practice of the profession. The foreign branch must have technical staff for each of the licensed fields of activity to be practiced; it must be led by an engineer with no less than 15 years in the specialization, assisted by a number of assistant engineers (consistent with the volume of the current works assigned to the firm) with no less than seven-years' experience. The head office must also undertake to appoint the required staff to reside in the emirate granting the licence.

192. All engineers, local and foreign, must be registered with the Engineers Society of the UAE. Typically, a licence for the practice of engineering consultancy requires the applicant: to be a UAE national of good conduct and reputation; to hold a BSc. in engineering from a recognized university in one of the engineering fields; to have at least three years of experience in the specialized field after obtaining the university degree; and to be a member of the engineers' association of the country of study.

REFERENCES

Butt, G. (2001), "Oil and Gas in the UAE", in *United Arab Emirates, A New Perspective.* Eds I. Al bed and P. Hellyer, London.

Central Bank of the United Arab Emirates (2011), *Annual Report 2010.* Viewed at: http://www.centralbank.ae/en/pdf/reports/CBUAEAnnualReport2010_English.pdf.

Dubai Financial Market (2011), *Monthly Bulletin, July 2011.* Viewed at: http://dfm.ae/documents/Publications/e0724b3f-c1f5-4be1-98a6-90d4d1e8348c.pdf.

Dun and Bradstreet (2006), *Exporters' Encyclopaedia*, Harleysville, PA.

Emirates Industrial Bank (2011), *The Bank and its Objectives.* Brochure.

Federal Customs Authority (2010), *Free Zones Trade Bulletin*, December. Viewed at: http://www.customs.ae/mediacenter_en/StatisticalBulletins/Free-Zones-Trade.aspx.

Federal Customs Authority (2011a), *Electronic Statistical Bulletin*, February. Viewed at: http://www.customs.ae/CMSPages/medialibrary_en_rss.aspx.

Federal Customs Authority (2011b), *Free Zones Trade Bulletin*, May. Viewed at: http://www.customs.ae/mediacenter_en/StatisticalBulletins/Free-Zones-Trade.aspx.

Gulf Cooperation Council (undated), *Implementation Procedures for the GCC Customs Union.* Viewed at: http://www.gcc-sg.org/eng/index9038.html? action=Sec-Show&ID=93.

IATA (2011), *World Air Transport Statistics (WATS) 55th Edition.* Viewed at: http://www.iata.org/ps/publications/Pages/wats.aspx.

IMF (2011a), *United Arab Emirates: 2011 Article IV Consultation-Staff Report; Staff Supplement; Public Information Notice on the Executive Board Discussion.* IMF Country Report No. 11/111, May. Viewed at: http://www.imf.org/external/pubs/ft/scr/2011/cr11111.pdf.

IMF (2011b), *United Arab Emirates: Selected Issues and Statistical Appendix,* IMF Country Report No. 11/112. Viewed at: http://www.imf.org/external/pubs/ft/scr/2011/cr11112.pdf.

International Telecommunications Union (2011), *Measuring the Information Society 2010.* Viewed at: http://www.itu.int/ITU-D/ict/publications/idi/2011/Material/MIS_2011_without_annex_5.pdf.

Ministry of Economy (2010), *Annual Economic and Social Report 2009*, Abu Dhabi.

OPEC (2010), *Annual Statistical Bulletin 2010/2011.* Viewed at: http://www.opec.org/opec_web/static_files_project/media/downloads/publications/ASB2010_2011.pdf.

Sturm and Siegfried (2005), *Regional Monetary Integration in the Member States of the Gulf Cooperation Council*, ECB Occasional Paper Series No. 31, June (Frankfurt am Main: European Central Bank).

World Bank and International Finance Corporation (2010), *Doing Business in the Arab World 2011: Making a Difference for Entrepreneurs*. Viewed at: http://www.doingbusiness.org/~/media/FPDKM/Doing%20 Business/Documents/Special-Reports/DB11-ArabWorld.pdf.

World Economic Forum (2011), *Global Information Technology Report, 2010-2011*. Viewed at: http://www3.weforum.org/docs/WEF_GITR_Report_2011.pdf.

World Economic Forum (2011), *The Travel and Tourism Competitiveness Report: 2011*. Viewed at: http://www3.weforum.org/docs/WEF_TravelTourismCompetitiveness_Report_2011.pdf.

WTO (2006) *Trade Policy Review*: *United Arab Emirates*, Geneva.

APPENDIX TABLES

Table AI.1
Structure of exports, including re-exports, 2005-10
(US$ million and %)

	2005	2006	2007	2008	2009	2010
Total	**115,453.0**	**142,505.0**	**156,634.0**	**210,000.0**	**174,725.0**	**198,362.0**
Total primary products	48.5	54.6	54.2	53.8	40.0	40.8
Agriculture	2.2	1.9	2.0	1.8	2.3	2.5
Food	2.0	1.7	1.7	1.7	2.2	2.4
0222 Milk concentrated or sweetened	0.0	0.1	0.0	0.0	0.1	0.1
Agricultural raw material	0.2	0.2	0.2	0.1	0.1	0.1
Mining	46.3	52.7	52.2	52.0	37.8	38.3
Ores and other minerals	0.3	0.7	0.7	0.6	0.5	0.5
2882 Other non-ferrous base metal waste and scrap, n.e.s.	0.1	0.1	0.2	0.1	0.1	0.2
2734 Pebbles, gravel, etc. for concrete aggregates	0.1	0.2	0.3	0.3	0.2	0.1
Non-ferrous metals	1.5	1.1	2.0	2.2	0.3	0.5
Fuels	44.6	50.9	49.6	49.2	36.9	37.3
3330 Crude oils of petroleum and bituminous minerals	35.1	37.9	37.7	38.3	24.9	33.0
Manufactures	19.8	16.4	19.9	19.5	23.0	26.6
Iron and steel	0.4	0.4	0.4	0.4	0.4	0.4
Chemicals	1.4	1.3	1.5	1.5	1.6	1.6
5822 Other plastics, flat shapes, non-cellular and not reinforced, etc.	0.0	0.0	0.1	0.1	0.1	0.2
5531 Perfumes and toilet waters	0.3	0.3	0.3	0.2	0.1	0.1
Other semi-manufactures	4.6	3.3	4.7	5.8	6.8	9.7
6672 Diamonds (excl. industrial, sorted) not mounted/set	2.7	1.3	2.5	3.2	4.4	7.7
6911 Iron or steel structures, tubes and the like, for use in structures	0.1	0.1	0.1	0.1	0.6	0.1
6652 Glassware, of a kind used for table, kitchen or similar purposes	0.2	0.2	0.2	0.1	0.1	0.1
6924 Reservoirs, tanks, vats of iron, steel or aluminium, <= 300 litres	0.0	0.0	0.0	0.1	0.1	0.1
Machinery and transport equipment	9.2	7.8	8.9	7.5	9.5	10.1
Power generating machines	0.2	0.4	0.2	0.4	0.3	0.3
Other non-electrical machinery	1.2	1.3	1.4	1.2	1.7	1.7
Agricultural machinery and tractors	0.0	0.0	0.0	0.0	0.1	0.1
Office machines & telecommunication equipment	4.2	2.6	2.7	1.9	2.3	2.5
7599 Parts and accessories of 751.1, 751.2, 751.9 and 752	0.5	0.4	0.5	0.4	0.4	0.4
Other electrical machines	0.7	0.6	0.7	0.6	0.7	0.7
7781 Batteries and electric accumulators, and parts	0.1	0.1	0.1	0.1	0.1	0.1
Automotive products	2.5	2.5	3.4	2.9	3.2	2.9
7843 Other motor vehicle parts and accessories of 722, 781 to 783	0.9	0.6	0.7	0.6	0.7	0.7
7821 Goods vehicles	0.4	0.3	0.3	0.3	0.4	0.4
Other transport equipment	0.3	0.5	0.5	0.5	1.4	2.1
7935 Special purpose vessels; floating docks	0.0	0.1	0.0	0.0	0.2	0.8
Textiles	1.2	1.0	1.1	0.9	1.0	0.9
6531 Fabrics, woven, of synthetic filament yarn, excl. pile/chemille	0.6	0.5	0.6	0.5	0.6	0.5
Clothing	0.7	0.6	0.5	0.4	0.6	0.6

Table AI.1 (cont'd)

	2005	2006	2007	2008	2009	2010
Other consumer goods	2.4	2.0	2.8	3.0	3.2	3.2
8973 Jewellery of gold, silver or platinum metals (except watches)	0.6	0.5	1.2	1.8	1.7	1.9
8746 Automatic regulating and controlling instruments	0.0	0.0	0.0	0.0	0.0	0.1
Other	31.7	29.0	25.9	26.6	37.0	32.6
Gold	2.5	3.4	3.6	4.3	6.6	6.4
9710 Gold, non-monetary (excl. gold ores and concentrates)	2.5	3.4	3.6	4.3	6.6	6.4

Source: WTO Secretariat estimates, based on UNSD, Comtrade database SITC Rev.3 data.

Table AI.2
Structure of imports, 2005-10
(US$ million and %)

	2005	2006	2007	2008	2009	2010
Total	**80,814.0**	**97,863.6**	**127,022.0**	**175,486.0**	**164,251.0**	**180,726.0**
Total primary products	11.2	11.4	11.6	12.6	9.3	9.9
Agriculture	7.2	6.9	6.5	6.5	6.4	6.5
Food	6.6	6.4	6.0	6.1	6.1	6.2
0741 Tea	0.3	0.3	0.3	0.3	0.2	0.3
0123 Poultry, meat and offal	0.2	0.2	0.3	0.3	0.3	0.3
0222 Milk concentrated or sweetened	0.3	0.3	0.2	0.3	0.3	0.3
Agricultural raw material	0.5	0.5	0.5	0.4	0.3	0.3
Mining	4.0	4.5	5.1	6.1	2.9	3.3
Ores and other minerals	0.9	1.1	1.1	1.0	0.8	1.0
2852 Alumina (aluminium oxide)	0.5	0.5	0.6	0.5	0.4	0.5
Non-ferrous metals	2.5	2.5	3.2	4.1	1.0	1.3
6821 Copper anodes; alloys; unwrought	0.0	0.0	0.0	0.2	0.2	0.4
6842 Aluminium and aluminium alloys, worked	0.3	0.5	0.5	0.5	0.4	0.3
Fuels	0.7	0.8	0.8	1.0	1.1	1.1
Manufactures	64.4	61.6	64.1	66.6	55.6	53.0
Iron and steel	4.4	5.3	5.9	8.7	3.5	3.2
6791 Tubes, pipes, hollow profiles, seamless, iron/steel	0.5	0.8	0.7	0.6	0.6	0.5
Chemicals	5.3	5.3	5.7	5.1	4.6	4.7
5531 Perfumes and toilet waters	0.5	0.4	0.4	0.3	0.3	0.3
5532 Beauty or make-up preparations; manicure or pedicure preparations	0.3	0.2	0.3	0.3	0.3	0.3
Other semi-manufactures	10.7	9.0	10.0	10.3	9.7	11.7
6672 Diamonds (excl. industrial, sorted) not mounted/set	4.6	2.7	3.6	4.2	4.4	7.3
6911 Iron or steel structures, tubes and the like, for use in structures	0.4	0.5	0.6	0.8	0.7	0.3
6997 Articles, n.e.s., of copper/nickel/ aluminium/etc.	0.1	0.1	0.1	0.1	0.2	0.3
Machinery and transport equipment	30.1	29.5	30.0	31.1	27.3	23.2
Power generating machines	1.4	1.8	1.6	1.4	2.2	1.7
Other non-electrical machinery	7.0	8.0	8.2	7.9	7.4	5.5
Agricultural machinery and tractors	0.1	0.2	0.1	0.1	0.2	0.1
Office machines & telecommunication equipment	7.9	5.9	4.9	4.5	3.9	3.7
Other electrical machines	3.1	3.3	3.9	4.4	3.9	2.8
7731 Insulated wire, cable etc.; optical fibre cables	0.5	0.7	1.1	1.6	0.9	0.6
7725 Switches, relays, fuses etc. for a voltage not exceeding 1000 V	0.5	0.4	0.5	0.4	0.4	0.3
Automotive products	8.0	8.0	9.0	9.7	5.3	5.9
7843 Other motor vehicle parts and accessories of 722, 781 to 783	1.3	1.3	1.3	1.2	1.0	1.0
7821 Goods vehicles	0.7	0.8	0.9	0.9	0.4	0.5
Other transport equipment	2.6	2.6	2.4	3.3	4.6	3.6
Textiles	2.7	2.3	2.1	1.6	1.4	1.3
6531 Fabrics, woven, of synthetic filament yarn, excl. pile/chemille	0.9	0.8	0.7	0.6	0.5	0.5

Table AI.2 (cont'd)

	2005	2006	2007	2008	2009	2010
Clothing	1.9	1.9	1.8	1.6	1.5	1.4
Other consumer goods	9.2	8.4	8.7	8.1	7.5	7.4
8973 Jewellery of gold, silver or platinum metals (except watches)	3.9	3.5	3.7	3.5	3.2	3.4
Other	24.5	27.0	24.2	20.9	35.0	37.1
Gold	7.1	7.6	7.2	8.4	9.0	10.1
9710 Gold, non-monetary (excl. gold ores and concentrates)	7.1	7.6	7.2	8.4	9.0	10.1

Source: WTO Secretariat estimates, based on UNSD, Comtrade database SITC Rev.3 data.

Table AI.3
Destinations of exports, including re-exports, 2005-10
(US$ million and %)

	2005	2006	2007	2008	2009	2010
Total (US$ million)	**115,453.0**	**142,505.0**	**156,634.0**	**210,000.0**	**174,725.0**	**198,362.0**
America	0.7	0.6	0.7	0.8	1.1	1.8
United States	0.7	0.5	0.4	0.6	0.5	0.5
Other America	0.1	0.1	0.2	0.3	0.6	1.3
Europe	3.6	3.5	3.3	3.8	3.9	4.7
EU(27)	2.6	2.0	2.0	2.2	1.7	1.9
Belgium	0.5	0.5	0.5	0.6	0.5	0.6
United Kingdom	0.2	0.3	0.3	0.2	0.2	0.4
EFTA	0.9	1.4	1.2	1.3	2.0	2.6
Switzerland	0.9	1.4	1.2	1.3	2.0	2.2
Norway	0.0	0.0	0.0	0.0	0.0	0.4
Other Europe	0.1	0.1	0.2	0.3	0.2	0.2
Commonwealth of Independent States (CIS)	1.0	1.3	1.5	0.8	0.5	0.8
Africa	4.1	3.9	4.2	3.7	4.3	4.1
Other Africa n.e.s.	0.7	0.5	0.5	0.7	0.6	0.9
Middle East	10.3	9.4	10.8	9.4	12.7	12.0
Iran Islamic Rep.	3.5	3.6	4.2	3.2	4.4	4.7
Iraq	1.9	1.6	1.9	1.4	2.4	2.3
Saudi Arabia	0.9	0.9	1.1	0.7	1.4	1.3
Bahrain	1.3	0.4	0.5	0.8	0.7	0.9
Qatar	0.6	0.7	1.0	1.5	1.5	0.9
Kuwait	0.8	1.0	0.8	0.5	0.7	0.7
Oman	0.4	0.5	0.6	0.7	0.8	0.6
Asia	41.8	42.6	45.2	48.2	34.4	49.1
China	0.3	0.3	0.3	0.5	0.2	0.3
Japan	24.2	25.5	25.4	16.4	0.0	0.0
Six East Asian Traders	11.0	12.1	12.2	22.8	1.2	35.6
Chinese Taipei	10.2	11.4	11.3	21.6	0.0	34.3
Hong Kong, China	0.3	0.3	0.5	0.6	0.6	0.7
Other Asia	6.3	4.7	7.2	8.4	32.9	13.2
India	4.6	3.3	6.0	7.3	7.2	11.0
Afghanistan	0.4	0.2	0.2	0.3	0.6	1.1
Pakistan	0.8	0.8	0.5	0.4	0.6	0.5
Other	38.4	38.7	34.4	33.3	43.0	27.5

Source: WTO Secretariat estimates, based on UNSD, Comtrade database SITC Rev.3 data.

Table AI.4
Origins of imports, 2005-10
(US$ million and %)

	2005	2006	2007	2008	2009	2010
Total (US$ million)	**80,814.0**	**97,863.6**	**127,002.0**	**175,486.0**	**164,251.0**	**180,726.0**
America	8.5	8.6	8.7	8.8	8.8	8.1
United States	6.3	6.5	6.6	7.0	6.9	6.2
Other America	2.2	2.1	2.1	1.9	1.9	1.9
Europe	29.0	27.3	26.6	29.9	21.7	19.0
EU(27)	24.8	23.0	21.9	22.2	18.3	15.8
Germany	5.6	6.1	5.7	5.8	5.0	4.5
United Kingdom	5.4	4.1	3.6	4.3	3.1	2.6
Italy	2.9	3.4	3.7	3.4	2.9	2.3
France	3.0	2.5	2.4	2.2	2.3	1.9
Belgium	1.5	1.7	1.5	1.5	1.1	1.0
Netherlands	1.1	1.0	0.9	0.8	0.8	0.7
EFTA	2.4	2.4	2.5	3.4	1.8	1.8
Switzerland	2.3	2.3	2.4	3.2	1.6	1.7
Other Europe	1.8	2.0	2.3	4.3	1.6	1.4
Turkey	1.8	1.9	2.2	4.3	1.6	1.4
Commonwealth of Independent States (CIS)	1.3	1.0	0.9	1.1	0.7	0.7
Africa	2.0	2.4	2.7	3.6	2.7	4.4
Sudan	0.1	0.1	0.1	0.2	0.4	0.7
Middle East	5.2	6.8	5.1	5.2	5.3	5.3
Saudi Arabia	2.6	3.3	2.8	2.5	2.0	1.8
Iraq	0.1	0.1	0.0	0.0	0.5	0.7
Asia	36.8	34.3	38.1	38.3	33.9	34.5
China	8.5	8.7	9.7	9.9	7.9	7.5
Japan	5.8	6.0	6.4	6.6	4.5	4.3
Six East Asian Traders	8.2	7.5	7.9	7.9	7.8	6.6
Korea, Rep. of	2.2	2.1	2.2	2.4	3.0	1.8
Malaysia	1.9	1.8	2.0	2.0	1.7	1.6
Thailand	1.1	1.1	1.4	1.4	1.2	1.2
Singapore	1.5	1.0	0.9	0.7	0.7	0.8
Other Asia	14.3	12.2	14.2	13.9	13.7	16.0
India	10.8	8.7	9.6	9.6	10.2	12.5
Australia	1.2	1.5	2.1	1.9	1.1	1.1
Pakistan	0.6	0.5	0.6	0.8	1.0	1.0
Indonesia	0.9	0.9	1.2	1.0	0.8	0.7
Other	17.3	19.6	17.8	13.1	26.8	27.9

Source: WTO Secretariat estimates, based on UNSD, Comtrade database SITC Rev.3 data.

Table AIII.1
Applied MFN tariff averages by HS2, 2011

Code	Description	No. of lines	Average tariff (%)	Range (%)	Standard deviation	Duty free (%)
	Total	7,101	0-100	4.9	5.7	9.4
01	Live animals	44	0.0	0.0	0.0	93.2
02	Meat and edible meat offal	79	0-5	4.1	1.9	17.7
03	Fish and crustaceans, molluscs and other aquatic invertebrates	142	0-5	3.0	2.5	40.8
04	Dairy produce; birds' eggs; natural honey; edible products of animal origin, not elsewhere specified or included	44	0-5	4.9	0.7	2.3
05	Products of animal origin, not elsewhere specified or included	29	5.0	5.0	0.0	0.0
06	Live trees and other plants; bulbs, roots and the like; cut flowers and ornamental foliage	19	0-5	3.4	2.3	31.6
07	Edible vegetables and certain roots and tubers	74	0-5	2.3	2.5	54.1
08	Edible fruit and nuts; peel of citrus fruit or melons	75	0-5	2.3	2.5	53.3
09	Coffee, tea, maté and spices	35	0-5	3.4	2.3	31.4
10	Cereals	22	0-5	0.5	1.4	90.9
11	Products of the milling industry; malt; starches; inulin; wheat gluten	86	0-5	3.7	2.2	25.6
12	Oil seeds and oleaginous fruits; misc grains, seeds and fruit; industrial or medicinal plants; straw and fodder	66	0-5	2.5	2.4	45.5
13	Lac; gums, resins and other vegetable saps and extracts	28	5.0	5.0	0.0	0.0
14	Vegetable plaiting materials; vegetable products not elsewhere specified or included	9	5.0	5.0	0.0	0.0
15	Animal or vegetable fats and oils and their cleavage products; prepared edible fats; animal or vegetable waxes	60	5.0	5.0	0.0	0.0
16	Preparations of meat, of fish or of crustaceans, molluscs or other aquatic invertebrates	38	5.0	5.0	0.0	0.0
17	Sugars and sugar confectionery	38	0-5	3.6	2.3	28.9
18	Cocoa and cocoa preparations	20	5.0	5.0	0.0	0.0
19	Preparations of cereals, flour, starch or milk; pastry cooks' products	53	0-5	4.7	1.2	5.7
20	Preparations of vegetables, fruit, nuts or other parts of plants	106	5.0	5.0	0.0	0.0
21	Miscellaneous edible preparations	41	0-5	4.9	0.8	2.4
22	Beverages, spirits and vinegar	40	0-50	22.9	22.2	2.5
23	Residues and waste from the food industries; prepared animal fodder	30	0-50	6.3	8.2	3.3
24	Tobacco and manufactured tobacco substitutes	20	100.0	100.0	0.0	0.0
25	Salt; sulphur; earths and stone; plastering materials, lime and cement	97	5.0	5.0	0.0	0.0
26	Ores, slag and ash	37	5.0	5.0	0.0	0.0
27	Mineral fuels, mineral oils and products of their distillation; bituminous substances; mineral waxes	76	5.0	5.0	0.0	0.0
28	Inorganic chemicals; organic or inorganic compounds of precious metals, of rare-earth metals, of radioactive elements or of isotopes	260	0-5	5.0	0.4	0.8
29	Organic chemicals	484	0-5	4.2	1.8	15.7
30	Pharmaceutical products	40	0-5	0.1	0.8	97.5
31	Fertilizers	28	5.0	5.0	0.0	0.0
32	Tanning or dyeing extracts; tannins and their derivatives; dyes, pigments and other colouring matter; paints and varnishes; putty and other mastics; inks	76	5.0	5.0	0.0	0.0
33	Essential oils and resinoids; perfumery, cosmetic or toilet preparations	63	5.0	5.0	0.0	0.0

Table AIII.1 (cont'd)

Code	Description	No. of lines	Average tariff (%)	Range (%)	Standard deviation	Duty free (%)
34	Soap, organic surface-active agents, washing preparations, lubricating preparations, artificial waxes, prepared waxes, polishing or scouring preparations, candles and similar articles, modelling pastes, dental waxes and dental preparations with a basis	48	5.0	5.0	0.0	0.0
35	Albuminoidal substances; modified starches; glues; enzymes	32	5.0	5.0	0.0	0.0
36	Explosives; pyrotechnic products; matches; pyrophoric alloys; certain combustible preparations	10	5.0	5.0	0.0	0.0
37	Photographic or cinematographic goods	40	5.0	5.0	0.0	0.0
38	Miscellaneous chemical products	111	0-5	4.9	0.8	2.7
39	Plastics and articles thereof	153	5.0	5.0	0.0	0.0
40	Rubber and articles thereof	116	5.0	5.0	0.0	0.0
41	Raw hides and skins (other than furskins) and leather	37	5.0	5.0	0.0	0.0
42	Articles of animal gut (other than silk-worm gut)	34	5.0	5.0	0.0	0.0
43	Furskins and artificial fur; manufactures thereof	15	5.0	5.0	0.0	0.0
44	Wood and articles of wood; wood charcoal	151	0-5	4.9	0.7	2.0
45	Cork and articles of cork	18	5.0	5.0	0.0	0.0
46	Manufactures of straw, of esparto or of other plaiting materials; basketware and wickerwork	20	5.0	5.0	0.0	0.0
47	Pulp of wood or of other fibrous cellulosic material; recovered (waste and scrap) paper and paperboard	22	5.0	5.0	0.0	0.0
48	Paper and paperboard; articles of paper pulp, of paper or of paperboard	127	5.0	5.0	0.0	0.0
49	Printed books, newspapers, pictures and other products of the printing industry; manuscripts, typescripts and plans	50	0-5	1.5	2.3	70.0
50	Silk	9	5.0	5.0	0.0	0.0
51	Wool, fine or coarse animal hair; horsehair yarn and woven fabric	50	5.0	5.0	0.0	0.0
52	Cotton	124	5.0	5.0	0.0	0.0
53	Other vegetable textile fibres; paper yarn and woven fabrics of paper yarn	23	5.0	5.0	0.0	0.0
54	Man-made filaments	73	5.0	5.0	0.0	0.0
55	Man-made staple fibres	109	5.0	5.0	0.0	0.0
56	Wadding, felt and nonwovens; special yarns; twine, cordage, ropes and cables and articles thereof	44	5.0	5.0	0.0	0.0
57	Carpets and other textile floor coverings	49	5.0	5.0	0.0	0.0
58	Special woven fabrics; tufted textile fabrics; lace; tapestries; trimmings; embroidery	43	5.0	5.0	0.0	0.0
59	Impregnated, coated, covered or laminated textile fabrics; textile articles of a kind suitable for industrial use	36	5.0	5.0	0.0	0.0
60	Knitted or crocheted fabrics	43	5.0	5.0	0.0	0.0
61	Articles of apparel and clothing accessories, knitted or crocheted	106	5.0	5.0	0.0	0.0
62	Articles of apparel and clothing accessories, not knitted or crocheted	149	5.0	5.0	0.0	0.0
63	Other made up textile articles; sets; worn clothing and worn textile articles; rags	92	5.0	5.0	0.0	0.0
64	Footwear, gaiters and the like; parts of such articles	34	5.0	5.0	0.0	0.0
65	Headgear and parts thereof	24	5.0	5.0	0.0	0.0
66	Umbrellas, sun umbrellas, walking-sticks, seat-sticks, whips, riding-crops and parts thereof	8	5.0	5.0	0.0	0.0
67	Prepared feathers and down and articles made of feathers or of down; artificial flowers; articles of human hair	11	5.0	5.0	0.0	0.0
68	Articles of stone, plaster, cement, asbestos, mica or similar materials	96	5.0	5.0	0.0	0.0

Table AIII.1 (cont'd)

Code	Description	No. of lines	Average tariff (%)	Range (%)	Standard deviation	Duty free (%)
69	Ceramic products	45	5.0	5.0	0.0	0.0
70	Glass and glassware	88	0-5	4.9	0.7	2.3
71	Natural or cultured pearls, precious or semi-precious stones, precious metals, metals clad with precious metal, and articles thereof; imitation jewellery; coin	65	0-5	3.2	2.4	35.4
72	Iron and steel	167	5.0	5.0	0.0	0.0
73	Articles of iron or steel	183	5.0	5.0	0.0	0.0
74	Copper and articles thereof	61	5.0	5.0	0.0	0.0
75	Nickel and articles thereof	23	5.0	5.0	0.0	0.0
76	Aluminium and articles thereof	62	5.0	5.0	0.0	0.0
78	Lead and articles thereof	8	5.0	5.0	0.0	0.0
79	Zinc and articles thereof	23	5.0	5.0	0.0	0.0
80	Tin and articles thereof	9	5.0	5.0	0.0	0.0
81	Other base metals; cermets; articles thereof	52	5.0	5.0	0.0	0.0
82	Tools, implements, cutlery, spoons and forks, of base metal; parts thereof of base metal	75	5.0	5.0	0.0	0.0
83	Miscellaneous articles of base metal	62	5.0	5.0	0.0	0.0
84	Nuclear reactors, boilers, machinery and mechanical appliances; parts thereof	610	0-5	4.6	1.4	8.0
85	Electrical machinery and equipment and parts thereof; sound recorders and reproducers, television image and sound recorders and reproducers, and parts and accessories of such articles	326	0-5	3.7	2.2	25.5
86	Railway or tramway locomotives, rolling-stock and parts thereof; railway or tramway track fixtures and fittings and parts thereof; mechanical (including electro-mechanical) traffic signalling equipment of all kinds	23	5.0	5.0	0.0	0.0
87	Vehicles other than railway or tramway rolling-stock, and parts and accessories thereof	184	0-5	4.9	0.6	1.6
88	Aircraft, spacecraft, and parts thereof	15	0-5	2.7	2.5	46.7
89	Ships, boats and floating structures	23	0-5	1.3	2.2	73.9
90	Optical, photographic, cinematographic, measuring, checking, precision, medical or surgical instruments and apparatus; parts and accessories thereof	209	0-5	4.4	1.7	12.9
91	Clocks and watches and parts thereof	55	5.0	5.0	0.0	0.0
92	Musical instruments; parts and accessories of such articles	26	5.0	5.0	0.0	0.0
93	Arms and ammunition; parts and accessories thereof	25	5.0	5.0	0.0	0.0
94	Furniture; bedding, mattresses, mattress supports, cushions and similar stuffed furnishings; lamps and lighting fittings, not elsewhere specified or included; illuminated signs, illuminated name-plates	102	5.0	5.0	0.0	0.0
95	Toys, games and sports requisites; parts and accessories thereof	36	5.0	5.0	0.0	0.0
96	Miscellaneous manufactured articles	68	5.0	5.0	0.0	0.0
97	Works of art, collectors' pieces and antiques	10	5.0	5.0	0.0	0.0

Source: WTO Secretariat calculations, based on data provided by the Emirates authorities.

PART C

REPORT BY THE UNITED ARAB EMIRATES

CONTENTS

I. ECONOMIC DEVELOPMENT

1. Successive developments in the economy of the United Arab Emirates, and the adoption of free market policies and regulations, have led to impressive growth rates and a trend towards sustainable and diversified development.

2. The UAE Government has successfully pursued a strategy to create an enabling business environment that is conducive to economic growth. This has contributed to the world-renowned status of the UAE as an international centre for trade, finance and services and has attracted reputable global companies. The UAE has always focused on strengthening its stance as a hub for business. Hence, it demonstrates an exemplary model to be emulated in all patterns of economic development and modernization.

3. The United Arab Emirates continues to pay attention to the foreign trade sector, which is perceived as the cornerstone of any economy. In recognition of the importance of this sector to the country's economic development, the UAE created the Ministry of Foreign Trade under law no. 10 of 2008, assigning it the responsibility of developing and implementing the country's trade policy in coordination with other ministries, federal and local bodies. Indeed, the UAE adopts a trade policy marked by openness and harmony with international markets, including the member states of the World Trade Organization. The UAE's economic strategy is centred on building a flexible, diverse, competitive and sustainable economy that makes use of the lessons learnt from the impact of the global financial crisis. The UAE was able to overcome the repercussions of this crisis in record time, which contributed to developing its economy and promoting its forecasted role in the future global economic arena.

4. The Ministry of Economy and the Ministry of Foreign Trade are currently pursuing the Government's progressive economic agenda, focused around economic liberalization, diversification and promotion of the role of the private sector.

(1) ECONOMIC GROWTH

5. Economic growth in the UAE has witnessed a substantial increase over the last few years. Gross Domestic Product at current prices has risen from USD 222.1 billion in 2006, to USD 314.6 billion in 2008 and USD 297.5 billion in 2010. The GDP trend is likely to have accelerated in 2010 due to the increase in the average oil price and the strong expansion in the non-oil economy. Specifically, the fall in the price of oil in 2009 from its peak in mid-2008 reduced hydrocarbon revenues by 32% to USD 69.9 billion, which led to the decline in the UAE's GDP in 2009 compared to 2008. This decline was also aided by the fall in real estate prices and the slowdown in global trade.

6. Despite the economic crisis, which is still casting its shadows on most economies worldwide, the UAE economy has been gradually recovering as reflected in its 2010 growth rate, with a real GDP of 1.4% compared to a negative 1.6% in 2009, i.e., realizing a USD 266 billion real GDP in 2010 compared to USD 262.2 billion in 2009 at constant 2007 prices. This growth has been propelled mainly by higher growth achieved by non-oil sectors, which registered a 5% growth rate in 2010 compared to 2009.

7. The Government emphasizes continued diversification away from dependence on oil and gas to non-oil industries. This is evidenced by the fact that the oil sector contributed around 31.5% of the country's GDP in 2010 (31.4% in real GDP), with the rest accounted for by the non-oil sector,

compared to 37.4% in 2006. The services sector is another policy focus; the growth of services will contribute to increased diversification and broad-based growth.

8. Regarding the relative importance of economic activities, 2010 has not witnessed a considerable change in comparison with the year before. Commodity activities groups witnessed a limited decline in 2010 to 56.3% from 57.5% in 2009. This decline is attributed to the relatively small decline in the oil sector from 33.7% in 2009 to 31.4% in 2010. However, a number of other commodity activities groups, such as construction, manufacturing, electricity, water and gas witnessed an increase in 2010 in their contributions to the GDP, by 11.8%, 9.6%, and 2.6% respectively compared to 11.0%, 11.0% and 2.3% in 2009. For their part, the services activities groups increased their contribution to the GDP in 2010 to 43.7%, up from 42.5% in 2009. Excluding the financial projects, the contributions of other services activities to the GDP grew in 2010 in comparison with 2009, while the share of the Government service sector and the household services activities sector remained the same in terms of their contribution to GDP in 2010 in comparison with 2009.

(2) EXTERNAL TRADE PERFORMANCE AND OUTWARD INVESTMENT

9. The UAE is a trading nation, as witnessed by its high ratio of imports plus exports (of goods and services) to GDP (around 147% in 2010). The UAE is also an important participant in global capital markets through several investment institutions, including, *inter alia,* the Abu Dhabi Investment Authority, the Dubai Ports Authority, Dubai Holding, Dana Gas, and Abu Dhabi's International Petroleum Investment Co. (IPIC).

10. The growth rate of the UAE's non-oil foreign trade has been steady for the last ten years except in 2009 when global trade dropped by 13% due to economic turmoil. However, 2010 saw a strong come-back when the UAE's total foreign trade increased by 14%, from USD 179.8 in 2009 billion to USD 205.42 billion.[1] The continuing growth in foreign trade reflects the country's strong commitment, through its free trade policies, advanced logistics and encouraging innovative projects to preserve its strong standing in the global trade market. The UAE's foreign trade volume increased from 2005 until 2010 with an average growth rate of 19% as a result of an increase in exports (non-oil exports and re-exports). The share of total exports (non-oil exports + re-exports) amounted to 35.7% of the country's total foreign trade in 2010.

11. The country's non-oil exports share has increased from 5% in 2000 to 11% in 2010. This increase is not only attributed to the growth of the exports value but also to the changes that occurred to the other components of foreign trade; imports and re-exports. In 2010, the value of the UAE's exports reached USD 22.6 billion, a 27% increase from its level in 2009, which is still lower than the 30.7% average annual growth rate recorded since 2001. UAE exports penetrated 198 markets around the globe in 2010. However, more than 77% (USD 17.32 billion) of it were concentrated in 12 major markets. These twelve markets have been playing a significant role in the development of UAE exports. In fact, 92% of the growth witnessed in UAE exports in 2010 is attributed to the growth of exports in these markets, of which India and Switzerland are the largest destinations.

12. The re-export sector, the second most important component in the UAE's foreign trade with a share of 25% in 2010, reached a value of USD 50.54 billion during the same year. This steady growth is a result of the Government's ongoing support to this vital sector through a variety of different initiatives. The ease of customs procedures, low administrative import and export costs and the country's advanced seaport and airport infrastructure and facilities, have all reflected the high competitiveness that the UAE enjoys. Today, the UAE is a major global re-export hub, ranking first

[1] The UAE Foreign Trade Analytical Report 2010, Ministry of Foreign Trade.

among Arab countries and the sixth globally. The growth rate of this sector has been fluctuating especially in the last five years, where it grew by 94.5% in 2010 in comparison with 2006.

13. The UAE's imports make up to 64% of the country's total non-oil foreign trade. The high percentage is mainly due to the high demand of an expanding population and to the important role the country plays as a major re-exporter in the region. In 2010, imports increased by 8%, reaching USD 131.9 billion, up from USD 121.5 billion in 2009.

14. 2010 statistical data of major commodities, by value, has revealed that with regards to imports, gold took the lead among all imported commodities with a value of USD 18.0 billion; followed by diamonds at USD 13.1 billion; cars at USD 7.3 billion; ornaments and jewellery at USD 6.1 billion; in addition to telephone sets at USD 2.8 billion. Moreover, gold also took the lead of exported commodities in 2010 at USD 10.4 billion; followed by light-vessels, fire floats, dredgers or ice class barges at USD 1.5 billion; waste and scrap of precious metals or ordinary metals at USD 1.0 billion; sugar cane or sugar beet at USD 0.7 billion and finally Ethylene Polymers in primary forms at USD 0.6 billion. Regarding re-exports, diamonds topped the list of re-exported commodities in 2010 with a total value of USD 15.2 billion, followed by ornaments, jewellery and parts thereof at USD 3.5 billion, motor vehicles USD 3.2 billion and telephone sets USD 2.3 billion.

(3) Inward Investment

15. The UAE strongly believes that the private sector (both local and foreign) is the true engine of growth in the long run. Foreign direct investment (FDI) is regarded as crucial in order to transfer knowledge and expertise in areas that are not yet the country's core competencies, open new market opportunities through the creation of new networks and create employment in knowledge intensive and high value-added sectors.

16. Following the success of the Jebel Ali Free Zone, the UAE currently boasts over 32 Free Zones. Most of these zones are located in Dubai, though the other Emirates are emulating the lead. Some of the zones cater to service sectors (e.g. Dubai Internet City, Dubai Media City, Dubai Health Care City, Knowledge City, Dubai International Financial Center) while others are industrial zones (e.g. ZonesCorp, Hamriyah Free Zone, Ajman Free Zone and Ras Al Khaimah Free Trade Zone).

17. The underlying formula for success in these zones has been; 100% foreign ownership, corporate tax holidays, no personal taxes, freedom to repatriate capital and profits, and no import duties or currency restrictions.

18. Outside the Free Zones, the formula is somewhat similar; corporate tax holidays for most sectors, no personal taxes, freedom to repatriate capital and profits, and no currency restrictions, except for the foreign ownership requirement, which is generally set at a ceiling of 49%, though that is changing with the proposed amendment of the federal law on commercial companies.

(4) Population and Employment

19. The population of the UAE is on the rise. Over the last few years, estimates based on administrative records have revealed that the country's population has risen to approximately 8.26 million in 2010 from 6.22 million in 2006, registering a 0.78% growth rate for that period.

20. In 2010, expatriates constituted the majority of the UAE's population (around 88.5%). Unemployment did not exceed 4.3%. In 2010 almost 65.2% of the population were economically active workers (based on 1995 and 2005 Survey).

(5) FISCAL POLICY

21. The Fiscal policy of the UAE at both the federal and Emirates level remains prudent. Substantial progress has been made in implementing fiscal management reform. The UAE economy started to recover in 2010 benefiting from higher oil prices and a strong demand from traditional trading partners.

22. Total public revenue has increased from USD 68.1 billion in 2009 to USD 85.7 billion in 2010 and is estimated to be USD 121.8 billion in 2011. This is primarily due to the increase in oil and gas earnings.

23. While public earning has increased in 2009, public expenditure and grants have decreased from USD 102.2 billion in 2009 to USD 89.6 billion in 2010. It is estimated to be around USD 99.5 billion in 2011. As a result of the prudent management of public revenue, the public deficit has declined from 12.9% of the GDP in 2009 to about 1.3% of the GDP in 2010.

(6) MONETARY POLICY

24. In light of state-driven efforts for a stable and a better investment climate, encouraging investment-attractive environments, the investment flow witnessed a significant increase as it moved up from USD 70.2 billion in 2009 to USD 76.3 billion in 2010, with a growth rate 8.8%.[2]

25. Given the fixed peg of the AED against the U.S. dollar and the full and free flow of capital, the effectiveness of monetary policy in the UAE is limited. Local interest rates follow the interest rates on the dollar. Therefore, the Central Bank offered banks the opportunity to better manage their liquidity through investment in the Central Bank's Certificates of Deposits, which reached USD 19.6 billion at the end of 2009, USD 25.6 billion at the end of 2010 and USD 21.8 billion at the end of October 2011.

II. TRADE POLICY DEVELOPMENTS

26. The UAE believes that free trade is a necessary condition for increased competitiveness and productivity in the long run. Protectionism, in the form of high tariff barriers and technical barriers to trade, would only result in a stagnant and inefficient private sector. It is in this spirit that the UAE has signed several free trade agreements with some Arab Countries and embarked on negotiations, under the GCC umbrella, to establish free trade agreements with the main trade partners of the GCC.

(1) BILATERAL AGREEMENTS

27. The UAE has signed bilateral preferential agreements with some Arab Countries (Syria, Jordan, Lebanon, Morocco and Iraq). According to these agreements, the UAE and its partners accord each other preferential access for a specified list of goods. As of the end of May 2011, the UAE had signed 39 bilateral investment agreements and 58 treaties on avoidance of double taxation. The UAE is a member of the Multilateral Investment Guarantee Agency (MIGA). The UAE has bilateral economic agreements with 50 countries.

---

[2] Annual Economic Report 2011, Ministry of Economy.

(2) Regional Agreements

(i) Gulf Cooperation Council (GCC)

28. The UAE was a founding member of the GCC on the 25th of May, 1981, alongside Bahrain, Kuwait, Oman, Qatar, and Saudi Arabia.

29. The Unified Economic Agreement (UEA), signed on the 11th of November 1981 under the Gulf Cooperation Council (GCC) created a Free Trade Area between the GCC states compatible with Article XXIV of GATT Agreement 1994. The free-trade area had eliminated duties and other restrictive regulations of commerce on all trade between the members of the GCC in the products originating in the member states, and work was proceeding to further harmonize trade and commercial policies.

30. In December 2001, the GCC Economic Agreement was signed to provide for a GCC Customs Union, and the harmonization of economic, financial, and monetary policies, with a view to achieve more economic integration through the establishment of the Gulf Common Market (GCM), which went into effect on January 2008.

31. The GCC Customs Union was established and has been operative since the beginning of January 2003. GCC member states have been applying the GCC common tariff ever since. The rates for more than 89.1% of the common tariff lines were 5%, while 10.4% of the tariff lines had a common tariff of 0%. Moreover, 0.2% of the tariff lines had a rate of 50%, while the remaining 0.3% of the tariff lines had a rate of 100%.

32. On the liberalization of services within the GCC, the Council had liberalized trade in services for roughly 100 sub-sectors of services, including professional services, most business services, telecommunication services, banking and other financial services, distribution services, education services, environmental services, health and related social services and tourism services. The GCC members had agreed to progressively liberalize other services sectors and sub-sectors.

33. The UAE is currently participating in the ongoing negotiations between the GCC and its main trade partners. These negotiations have led to signing Free Trade Agreements between the GCC members and Singapore, the EFTA States, and an initial signing of a draft Agreement with New Zealand. The negotiations to conclude a Free Trade Agreement between the GCC and the European Union (EU), Turkey, Japan, South Korea, China, India, Pakistan, Australia, and the Southern Common Market (MERCOSUR) are still open. The scope of these negotiations covers market access for goods and services, intellectual property, and in some cases, government procurement, investment and competition.

(ii) Greater Arab Free Trade Area (GAFTA)

34. The UAE is a member of The Greater Arab Free Trade Area (GAFTA), which was signed on the 19th of February 1997 and was entered into force on the 1st of January 1998. This agreement has eliminated all tariffs among its members on the 1st of January 2005. The Agreement covers trade in goods only, however, members have been engaged for the past few years in negotiations to create an agreement in trade in services.

(3) UAE PRIORITIES IN THE DOHA DEVELOPMENT AGENDA (DDA)

35. The UAE is a strong believer and advocate of the Multilateral Trading System. It is playing an active role in the current round of multilateral trade negotiations. Its main interests in the Doha Development Agenda (DDA) include greater non-agricultural market access (NAMA) and further liberalization of trade in services.

36. In NAMA, the UAE proposed the inclusion of an additional sector under the sectoral tariff elimination initiative.[3] The UAE has called on Members to eliminate all tariffs on raw materials, in particular on primary aluminium, a vital and strategic input for its manufacturing sector.

37. The UAE also submitted its initial offer in services, which is basically in line with the policy objectives set by the Government and its reform process that is currently underway.[4]

38. The UAE also recognizes the importance of an effective and rational "differential and special treatment" that enables domestic sectors to benefit from transitional periods of adjustments in order to take necessary steps to consolidate competitiveness. It is crucial for the survival of those sensitive activities.

39. The UAE also supports the strengthening of technical assistance programs for developing and least-developed countries in the following areas: Information on the Multilateral Trading System, Implementation of the WTO Agreements, and Capacity Building. The specific needs and priorities for the UAE are related to the following issues: Competition Law, SPS & TBT, customs procedures and trade facilitation, classification of some services sectors like energy services and maritime transport, evaluation of trade in services, notifications procedures related to all WTO agreements, and regionalism/bilateralism and the multilateral trading system.

III. SECTORAL DEVELOPMENTS

40. Diversification away from oil and into industry and services has been high on the government's agenda for the last couple of decades. The UAE's investment in new economic components, such as in renewable and nuclear energy, is adding more value to the country's overall economic components. Below are a few developments in some economic sectors.

(1) MANUFACTURING

41. Manufacturing is one of the largest non-oil economic sectors in the country, contributing around 9.7% of the GDP in 2010 and around 14.2% of the entire non-oil economy. This sector includes cement and blocks, ceramics, textiles and clothing, pharmaceuticals, gold and jewellery, aluminium, plastics, steel and other subsectors. Growth in manufacturing was a result of both increasing demand (due to a rapidly rising population) and increased national and foreign investments.

42. The manufacturing industry continues to play an increasingly important role in the UAE's economy, as it is strengthened by the availability of basic infrastructure and communications within the country, buyers of final products (e.g. EU and Arab countries), liquidity and the geographic proximity of the UAE to suppliers of raw materials (e.g. India and China).

[3] WTO document TN/MA/W/37, 37Add.1 & Add.2.

[4] WTO document TN/S/O/ARE.

43. The number of industrial establishments operating in the UAE as of the 31st of December 2010 was about 4960 with a combined investment volume of around USD 27.6 billion, registering an increase of 316 facilities from 2009. In comparison, the number of industrial establishments in 2006 was 3567 with an investment volume of USD 17.1 billion.

(2) TELECOMMUNICATION

44. The telecommunication sector in the UAE is one of the most advanced in the world. In the past few years, the sector has witnessed rapid growth in mobile penetration, which in August 2011 reached 193.6%. In addition, internet penetration (Broadband + dial-up) reached 23.1% with an internet users penetration of 57.6%. Moreover, broadband internet penetration has reached 14.4%, one of the highest rates in the Middle East. Various initiatives to accelerate the advancement of the telecom sector have been taken by the UAE Government. Since the Telecommunications Regulatory Authority (TRA) was established by Federal law (Decree No. 3 of 2003) and its Executive Order, which initiated the telecom liberalization process, it has been vested with powers to regulate a competitively sustainable telecom sector. In February 2006, Du (Emirates Integrated Telecommunications Company) was awarded a comprehensive licence to become the UAE's second telecom services operator.

45. The UAE was the first country in the region to offer fourth generation (4G) mobile data services. To help maintain the country's leading position, the TRA has established an ICT Fund, financed by licensed telecom operators, which will foster research and development in the UAE telecom sector.

(3) TOURISM

46. Tourism is a growing sector in the UAE. The sector was regulated at the Emirate level until the creation of the UAE National Council for Tourism and Antiquities (NCTA) on the 14th of December, 2008, when its regulation shifted to the federal level while maintaining a level of cooperation with each emirate's local authorities.

47. Over the past decade, tourism has become a cornerstone of the UAE's plan for a diversified economy. The subsector is an important source of foreign exchange. The full economic impact of tourism, including tourism capital investment and indirect impacts, tallied USD 18.8 billion in 2009. Tourism contributed 7.4% of the UAE's GDP and 11.7% of the country's non-oil GDP in 2009. Dubai holds a 66% share of the UAE tourism economy, Abu Dhabi 16%, and Sharjah 10%.

48. The UAE has been ranked the 30th among 139 countries and the 1st in the Middle East in the "Travel '&' Tourism Competitiveness Report 2011", issued by the World Economic Forum under the theme "Moving beyond the Downturn".

49. The UAE has attracted visitors for a multitude of business and leisure purposes. Cultural/recreational attractions, shopping and relaxation are popular activities for visitors. An important focus of tourism development from a marketing and product development perspective has been the creation of an impressive range of sporting, cultural and lifestyle events.

50. The Abu Dhabi Tourism Authority (ADTA), which was established in 2004 has set itself a target of increasing annual visitor numbers to over 3 million by 2015. To achieve that, the Emirate plans to invest substantially in the development of major tourism and cultural infrastructure over the coming twenty years. ADTA statistics show that the number of hotel guests and hotel apartment stays in Abu Dhabi has risen by 10% during the first four months of 2011, compared to the same period in

2010. This was accompanied by an increase of 26% in the number of hotel nights and an increase in occupancy levels, revenue and average periods of stay.

51. In addition to being the commercial hub of the UAE Dubai invested heavily in tourism to become the main tourist attraction in the Middle-East. It has the world's tallest building, the Burj Khalifa, the world's biggest mall, the Dubai Mall -which also houses the largest indoor seawater aquarium, and the world's largest collection of man-made islands, and the world's longest fully-automated metro. Dubai hotels recorded a growth of 14% in the number of visitors in the first quarter of 2011, compared to the same period in 2010, and achieved an occupancy rate of 81%.

52. Sharjah, has made huge milestones in developing culture related ecotourism. Sharjah has 17 museums and cultural centers. The museums are dedicated towards showcasing the different aspects of the country's past, such as literature, archaeology, natural history and the pearl trade tradition.

53. The emirate of Ras Al Khaimah has an interesting heritage. The emirate also has a national museum, ancient buildings, archaeological sites and an ancient sun-worshippers temple. Although these sites are not yet tourist-ready, the government of Ras Al Khaimah is seeking serious partnerships to restore these sites and turn them into tourist destination.

54. Ajman, Umm Al-Quwain and Fujairah have been rapidly growing their tourism sectors with strong campaigning to develop the industry and attract more tourists. The major attractions of these emirates are heritage, architecture, natural landscapes, leisure, sports, and facilities for business conferences and exhibitions.

(4) BANKING AND INSURANCE

55. Commercial banks operating in the UAE witnessed a highly volatile growth during the recent years. Double digit growth rates continued until 2008 when customer deposits increased by 27.4%, bank loans by 47.5% and bank assets by 20.4%. A slowdown followed with the outbreak of the international financial crisis. The immediate pressure was felt on capital adequacy and the profitability of banks, following a pull down of deposits from banks, which created a substantial mismatch and a liquidity constraint. This necessitated certain liquidity and capital support from the Central Bank and the Federal Government. In 2010, bank deposits increased by 6.8%, bank loans by 1.4% and bank assets by 5.8%.

56. In 2011, the UAE had 23 national Banks of which 8 are licensed as Islamic banks and the remaining 15 as conventional banks, in addition to 28 foreign banks. Local conventional banks' share in total net assets declined from 63.6% at the end of 2007 to 62.8% at end of June 2011, while the Islamic banks' share has increased from 14.2% to 16.5%. However, the share of Islamic banks in capital and net profits recorded a decline, during this period, due to larger provision for a higher level of non-performing advances.

57. The insurance sector has also grown; a large portion services the hydrocarbon and construction industries – sectors that have significantly developed, over the last few years, and are expected to continue to grow. This asserts the significance of this sector and its substantial role in the national economy due to the considerable funds invested therein. The total volume of underwritten insurance premiums in the UAE reached USD 6.0 billion in 2010, a 10%increase in comparison with 2009, while the total value of invested funds in the sector rose to USD 7.5 billion, with 48.2% of this amount in the form of shares and bonds followed by 32.5 % as bank deposits. Given the UAE's fast population growth, the sector's outlook is very good. The insurance sector in the UAE is regulated by

Federal Law No. (6) for the year 2007 concerning the creation of the Insurance Authority, which was enforced as of the 28th of August 2007.

(5) AIR AND MARITIME TRANSPORTATION

58. Passenger and cargo transportation has risen in importance over the last few years. UAE airline companies (Emirates Airlines, Etihad Airlines, Air Arabia Airlines Fly Dubai Airlines and RAK Airways) are updating their fleets and are pursuing a forceful strategy to capitalize on the increased passenger demand by pursuing several strategies, including the adoption of transportation options that focus on superior passenger experiences as well as options that emphasize affordability.

59. The UAE's air industry has been continuously growing. In 2011, the UAE had a total of five national airports (Abu Dhabi International Airport, Al Ain Airport, Dubai International Airport, Fujairah Airport, Ras Al Khaimah Airport and Sharjah International Airport). The UAE has plans to become a global transport hub by investing around USD 136.1 billion in the aviation industry over the next decade. The UAE intends to capitalize on its transport and communications infrastructure by introducing new aircrafts for the five flag carriers in the UAE, huge investments for new airport capacity throughout the seven emirates, and plans for Abu Dhabi to become a regional centre for aircraft maintenance, manufacturing and flight training.

60. In addition, the UAE has developed as a regional hub for maritime transportation and logistics. UAE ports handle a large volume to and from the region, and ship and boat building are emerging as strategic competencies.

(6) PETROCHEMICALS AND FERTILIZERS

61. Most of the UAE's oil reserves are located in Abu Dhabi, which is home to several major chemical, petrochemical and fertilizer industrial complexes.

62. Borouge, a joint venture between Abu Dhabi National Oil Company(ADNOC) and Austria based Borealis, has a current manufacturing capacity of 2 million tons per year. In mid-2011, the second phase of its massive petrochemicals complex at Ruwais industrial zone has enabled it to reach full operational capacity. The company is also planning to increase its capacity to reach 2.5 m tons per annum by 2013 to meet the increasing local and international demand. ADNOC has also established Ruwais Fertilizer Industries (FERTIL) with a capacity of 1,000 tons of ammonia and 1,500 tons of urea per day. It signed a USD 1.2 billion contract with Samsung Engineering to construct a new fertilizer complex, increasing its urea capacity to 3,500 tons per day. Both companies are located in Al Ruwais Industrial Zone and are looking forward to expand their production capacity by installing more plants, increasing utilization, and depending on new advanced technologies. Borouge and FERTIL's expansion plans have been attracting local and international investors who are been actively participating in the construction of chemical plants, storages, processing and treating units, and other related projects like cooling systems.

63. Abu Dhabi's petrochemicals' strategy has been shifting from the basic products to end-user products. It has been establishing itself as one of the major petrochemicals producers in the world. Strategic International and local investors have been invited to join the development convoy in petrochemicals.

64. In November 2008, Abu Dhabi National Chemicals Company "Chemaweyaat" was established to enhance the involvement of Abu Dhabi's chemicals industry production's holdings. Its plants are planned to be operating by 2015 with a total capacity of 1.5 million tons per year.

65. As Abu Dhabi enters its second phase of modernization guided by vision 2030, developing a globally-competitive petrochemicals industry based is one of the main economic pillars to achieve the desired position. Not only dose Abu Dhabi invests heavily in creating petrochemicals conglomerate but also it opens its door and provides the necessary business infrastructure and environment for international investors to establish ventures at all levels of the industry value chain. Abu Dhabi Basic Industries Company's (ADBIC) polymer's park project is a clear example of the emirate's strong commitment to attract international players. Abu Dhabi Polymer Park will span 4.1 million m2 with up to 1 million tons/yr conversion capacity of a wide range of resins.

(7) NUCLEAR AND RENEWABLE ENERGY

66. The UAE's investment in new economic components, such as in renewable and nuclear energy, adds more added-value to the country's overall economic components and aids it in reaching the goals it set for itself in "UAE Vision 2021", to "be among the best countries in the world by 2021".

67. The Emirate of Abu Dhabi has put in place a comprehensive energy strategy till the year 2030. The strategy aims at diversifying and developing the Emirates' sources of energy to include more renewable ones and to secure a healthy environment that is in line with the country's goals. The strategy will reduce the country's reliance on gas to produce electricity from around 99% presently, to 70%. It also aims at producing 30% of the required energy from clean coal, nuclear and renewable energy sources. Moreover, there is currently a joint project with the United Nations to reduce carbon emissions through the Dubai Carbon Center. The vast "Mohammed Bin Rashid" solar park is also being constructed in Dubai. The UAE has ratified the Global Climate Treaty, joined the Modified Kyoto Protocol, hosted the International Renewable Energy Agency (IRENA), and carried out a number of projects and initiatives that are related to climate preservation. It has introduced the use of solar power – albeit still limited – in government buildings, and worked on substantially increasing the country's vegetation cover.

68. The UAE has adopted an ambitious plan that aims at increasing the contribution of renewable energy so that it would supply 7% of the country's energy needs by the year 2020. The Government has also launched the MASDAR initiative, which aims at advancing alternative energy solutions, commercial production and applications. MASDAR city is set to become the first Zero carbon and waste emitting city in the world. Masdar is also considering the ambitious plan of constructing the world's largest solar power tower in Abu Dhabi, which is expected to generate 150-200 Megawatts.

69. The United Arab Emirates has launched a peaceful nuclear energy program. The program includes the construction of 4 electrical nuclear power plants in cooperation with a South Korean Company. Investments in this program are worth around USD 20.4 billion. Work is set to commence on the construction of the first nuclear power plant in 2012, with a production capacity of 1400 megawatts for every station. The first plant is expected to start supplying the national grid with electricity in 2017. All four plants are set to be completed by the year 2020.

IV. FUTURE DIRECTION

70. The UAE has made significant strides in economic development over the last few years. This was primarily due to the UAE government's provision of an enabling regulatory environment. It is expected that services will play a larger role in the UAE economy over the medium to long run, with rapid increases in niche sectors such as air and maritime transportation, logistics, medical tourism, pharmaceuticals and IT.

71. The vision of the Government of the UAE is to transform the country into a global hub for entrepreneurship in several industrial and service spheres. To achieve that vision, the Government is committed to maintaining *laissez faire* policies and an effective public-private partnership.

72. It is important to shed light on some of the challenges that have faced the country and the government's steps to address them.

(1) Reform of the Investment Framework

73. Currently, discussions are underway in the UAE to re-examine the Federal Law on Commercial companies that limits foreigners to hold a minority equity in companies incorporated in the UAE (the historical cap of 49%). A Federal Unified Foreign Investment Law is in the legislative level which reflects government policies towards foreign investments. This new Law is expected to increase the foreign ownership in some sectors to more than 49%. Furthermore, there are several business laws that which will enhance the investment environment in the country such as the new Arbitration law that is to be developed in line with the UNCITRAL Arbitration Law.

74. To some extent, the minimum national ownership requirement affected the flow of FDI. However, two parameters should be taken into consideration to understand this situation. First of all, the demographic structure of the UAE is such that nationals constitute the minority *vis-à-vis* foreigners. Second of all, the UAE is a major capital exporter. Those factors explain the philosophy of the current regime i.e. preserving and protecting the economic interests of the nationals and guaranteeing them a share in their own market.

75. However, after reaching a certain maturity, and taking into account UAE obligations under international trade negotiations, the Government is developing a comprehensive strategy to deal with this new juncture. The main objective is to further diversify the economy. The reform of the current investment framework (through amendments to the Company Law) is perceived as one of the most important ways to materialize this objective and attract more FDI to support this endeavour.

(2) Knowledge Economy

76. Being in its way to achieve the goals of federation strategy and its vision for 2021 as well as changing the economic structure. The UAE has taken several positive wide steps regarding the transformation of its economy from the traditional economy to knowledge economy. Some of these steps are consolidating the legislative and regulatory structure in the field of technology and communications, building up human and institutional capacities concerning information and communication technology, consolidating information and communication infrastructure, and state orientation towards knowledge economy.

(3) Competition

77. In order to protect consumers from unjustified price increases, a draft Competition Law was drafted after evidence surfaced of possible anticompetitive practices and it is now being reviewed by the Federal National Council. This is in line with the strategy of the UAE government to create an enabling business environment that is conducive to economic growth.

78. The UAE has already set up a consumer protection authority.

79. The UAE established the Emirates Competitiveness Council (ECC), which is comprised of 18 representatives from the seven emirates at the federal and local levels of government as well as the private sector. The council works together in partnership with public and private entities. The council enacts policies and undertakes actions that will drive the UAE's competitiveness agenda and unite the country towards achieving the nation's vision for sustainable growth and prosperity.

(4) E-GOVERNMENT

80. The UAE is ranked the 49th in the UN eGovernment survey issued in early 2010. Since then, great efforts have been made by the Emirates eGovernment and various government entities to further enhance the eGovernment profile and enrich the value delivered to both the public and business sectors.

81. The national portal of the country (government.ae) has been revamped recently to reflect the country's shift towards Government 2.0. The portal leverages social media tools to promote the adoption of key new concepts and practices such as citizen online participation and Open Data.

82. The portal also offers a single point of entry to more than 500 government services provided by the federal and local government entities. These services target citizens, residents, businesses and tourists and can be browsed and searched in different methods.

83. All these new developments have extended to cover the websites of key government entities such as the Ministries of Economy, Finance, Foreign Trade, Education, Social Affairs, Labour and Environment and Water. These developments are being implemented in alignment with "UAE Vision 2021" and the United Nations Millennium Development Goals.

84. As a result, (government.ae) has been honoured with the Best Strategic Website Award by the Arab League and the Best National Portal award at the 2nd GCC eGovernment conference. Moreover, continuous efforts are being made to foster cross-government integration to ease business initiation and management for local and foreign investors.

(5) LABOUR MARKET AND EMIRATIZATION POLICY

85. The UAE is, perhaps, the only country in the world where foreigners dominate the private sector, both as employers and employees. In almost all countries that allow immigration, the rule is that foreigners are only allowed to take up jobs when suitably-qualified nationals are not available.

86. This situation is in need of serious thinking and careful policy-making that sets targets with a long-term vision. One of the mechanisms to improve the situation is to adopt a more flexible mobility policy. The Government has adopted a more flexible labour mobility approach within the local market with the aim of maximizing the utilization of the available foreigner labour supply and granting opportunities for skilled and professional expatriates to choose the most suitable job where they can maximise return for themselves and for their employers. This policy is expected to have a positive impact on the sources of labour. This means that demand for labour will be satisfied more from the internal labour supply and less from outside. This will also improve wage levels and will thus have a positive impact on Emiratization.

87. It is largely recognized that expatriate workers will continue to play a vital role in the country's economy. Nevertheless, the authorities feel that the growth of the private sector and the employment of non-nationals cannot be left unregulated. Hence, they propose the establishment of a quota system for nationals in certain sectors.

88. It is also recognized that in order for nationals to become active participants in the private sector, efforts need to be exerted by both parties. This requires fundamental changes in attitudes, conditions and environment within the private sector as well as among UAE nationals seeking employment.

89. The authorities will continue to support the current labour market strategy in order to increase employment opportunities for U.A.E. nationals. This strategy should continue to rely on a qualitative approach consisting of raising the skills of nationals through better education and training programs geared towards private sector labour demand.

(6) WATER

90. Water consumption in the UAE increased, this increase is related to the increase in population and change in lifestyle. The Government is giving this issue a priority. Therefore; the UAE is now increasing the number of studies and researches. It also started to create plans and find solutions to preserve this paramount source for future generations. The UAE has around 583 km^3 of ground water which includes 20km^3 of pure water.

(7) BETTER SYNERGY BETWEEN MULTILATERALISM AND BILATERALISM

91. Currently, the UAE is involved in a vast programme of trade liberalization at the regional level. The UAE policy is not the only example of such trends. A growing number of economies are also seeking to liberalize their trade swiftly and on the basis of sound disciplines, even in services and investment. In doing so, their preferred instrument has been agreements concluded outside the WTO, the reason being that negotiations in the WTO are slow and their ambition is not always set as high as the level that can be achieved in bilateral agreements. The UAE, nevertheless, believes that it is essential to strengthen the current system within the framework of the principles and rules of international trade.

92. Consequently, the UAE Government is committed to pursuing trade liberalization globally, regionally, and individually with some leading partners. However, it still believes that the international economic system will prosper most if the regional and bilateral agreements fit within a global framework of rules (i.e. within the WTO framework).

ANNEX: THE UAE'S NEEDS IN TRADE-RELATED TECHNICAL ASSISTANCE

(1) INFORMATION ON THE MULTILATERAL TRADING SYSTEM

- Exploring the possibility of setting up a cooperation program between the WTO and a selected UAE University to create a University Degree on WTO issues in the Department of Law or Economics.
- Building on the success of previous experiences, continuing to organize regional seminars, workshops, and conference on WTO-related issues in the UAE.
- Organizing seminars for the Business Community and Academics with targeted messages on the advantages and rights as well as the constraints and obligations emanating from membership to the WTO.

(2) IMPLEMENTATION OF THE WTO AGREEMENTS

- Organizing national seminars and workshops, either by the WTO secretariat or in cooperation with other international organizations, on:

    - Trade Facilitation.
    - SPS & TBT.
    - Trade in Services: Classification of some service sectors e.g. energy services and maritime transport; evaluation of trade in services.
    - IPR: the familiarization of the Judicial and Customs authorities with the protection of IPR, legal and institutional impacts of the adherence to new international agreements on IPR (other than those required by TRIPS).
    - Notifications procedures related to all WTO agreements.
    - Regionalism/bilateralism and the Multilateral Trading System.
    - Trade and environment.

- The Adaptation of domestic legislations regarding contingency trade remedies and professional services.

(3) CAPACITY BUILDING

- Strengthening negotiation skills and capacity building.
- Allowing UAE candidates to benefit from training courses in the WTO Secretariat.
- Export promotion technical and institutional support.
- Trade capacity building and competitiveness enhancement, awareness, and networking.
- Technical assistance and capacity building in improving UAE's e-commerce environment.